NOT PEACE BUT A SWORD

☆

VINCENT SHEEAN

NOT PEACE
BUT
A SWORD

Doubleday, Doran & Company, Inc.
New York
1939

PRINTED AT THE *Country Life Press*, GARDEN CITY, N. Y., U. S. A.

Surely thou hast greatly deceived this people and Jerusalem, saying, Ye shall have peace; whereas the sword reacheth unto the soul.

JEREMIAH IV, 10

Think not that I am come to send peace on earth: I came not to send peace, but a sword.

For I am come to set a man at variance against his father, and the daughter against her mother, and the daughter in law against her mother in law.

And a man's foes shall be they of his own household.

MATTHEW X, 34–36

Contents

[*vii*]

CONTENTS

NOT PEACE BUT A SWORD

☆

CHAPTER I

The Thirteen Bus

THE DISTRICT of Maida Vale, according to the English novels of twenty or more years ago, was inhabited by light ladies, aspiring playwrights and gentlemen who were likely at any moment to be arrested by the police. If this was ever so (and you can't always tell about English novels) it is no longer so. The region exposes an innocent face to whatever sun it can get in a London December: its wide streets and blank brick houses, sometimes with gardens and oftener without, appear to harbor a population of blameless citizens. But then we Americans are always being taken in by English literature: it is what they call our heritage. Millions of us who have never seen London feel the cold thrust of mystery down our necks at the mention of Baker Street; we hear the roll of the printing press when one street is named, the chink of coin when we read of another. If Maida Vale is, after all, no odder than any prosperous district in New York or Chicago, and gives shelter and leg room to an equal number of merchants, bankers, film stars and legislators, we are wrong to be disappointed.

The fault lies partly in our gullible selves and partly with those English novels of the days before and just after the war of 1914–18, which purported to tell us what life in London was like and misled us so badly that we are always craning our necks from the top of the bus to exclaim "So *that* is the Strand! So *that* is Pall Mall!" In years of casual visits to London I had never beheld Maida Vale: when I did it reminded me of Chicago. I might have written a letter of discovery to *The Times,* but didn't, for my only practical interest in Maida Vale was that somewhere near there was where you got the Thirteen Bus.

I heard about the Thirteen Bus from a sound authority.

"When I have relatives up from the provinces," the sound authority said, "I always take them for a nice ride on the Thirteen Bus. You go right through London and can do all your sight-seeing without getting off. It starts at Golders Green or Hendon or some such place, but you get on in the Abbey Road. I've tried them all, and the Thirteen Bus is best."

Well, I have tried it now, too, and am prepared to give a report. I can hardly do so without paying a fervent tribute to the London General Omnibus Company (and to the Traffic Combine of which it forms a part) for the solidity of its rolling stock; for the unfailing courtesy of its hired hands; and for the extreme latitude permitted in such matters as smoking and lolling about on the top deck. No General Omnibus Company in the world—indeed, no Traffic Combine—can do you better for fivepence.

2

Maida Vale is respectable upper-middle-class, with the wintry sun trickling down on well-fed people who are not in a great hurry to get anywhere. It blossoms, after a bit, into St John's Wood, which is more elegant: there are some huge houses here, with walled gardens, and steps down which people come at night, they say, in garments white and glistering. The bus careens along; not many people seem to need it in these parts; it takes its corners with a kind of fleet, self-confident dignity, its balance ever sure, until we come to a stop to let an old lady with a dog descend. Regent's Park. That is where they have all the monkeys and elephants and Professor Julian Huxley (God bless 'im!). If you belong to the London Zoological Society you can go to the Zoo on Sunday, which is a private day; you can even do this if you know a man who knows a man who is a member, and it doesn't make the slightest difference to the animals, except that perhaps the ordinary days, being less crowded, are more restful. It is a very fine zoo, although they have spent a lot of their money on fish and snakes, creatures with which I at least do not commune easily. I once saw a python devour a live chicken there, in the Serpent House, while an avid crowd watched. It was a loathsome sight, I thought, and had the effect of causing my throat to distend so that I burst my collar and had to go home.

Baker Street. Now this is a really curious phenomenon: a street so huge, so crowded, so lined with shops and humming with the purposeful din of a lot of people going after what they want, suggests to most Americans one thing only, and that is Sherlock Holmes. For all I knew, it might have been a cavernous hollow place deserted of all living, the haunt of bats by night, a forgotten corner between yesterday and the day before: the place where Sherlock Holmes and Dr Watson had "rooms". In that far-off period when I read and reread the chronicles of the great detective, I probably thought of it as a permanently darkened street. Such very peculiar things used to happen there, things that had no place in the ordinary light of day. Every ring at the door meant that somebody had been done to death in a mysterious manner; the postman brought nothing but clues; there were jewels in the gutter. And there it lies before us, straight, bright and noisy, for all the world like lower Fifth Avenue, a street which has forgotten its ghost. Along its cluttered pavement the posters of the newspapers blare out in red or black letters eight inches high:

TUNIS:
FRANCE SENDS
MORE TROOPS

But I don't really believe that anybody in this street cares much what happens to Tunis, no matter how many more troops France sends there. That woman in the red hat, for instance, making tracks into the hairdresser's: what does she care? She is going to get a permanent wave (which she probably calls a "perm") and perhaps to get her nails done, so that she can keep her appointment at lunch with a feeling that she is looking her best and that forty-two isn't really so old, after all, if a woman takes care of herself. I don't see anybody buying the newspapers, in spite of the poster which the boy waves lackadaisically, now and again, to attract any interested eye. That man in a bowler hat with the envelopes under his arm: what does he care about Tunis? He knows that if he doesn't deliver such-and-such to so-and-so in the Marylebone Road by eleven o'clock he will lose his job, or at least get a sharp reprimand from Mr 'Iggins. They don't any of them care about Tunis because they don't know where it is. They don't know that it is here, in London, in Baker Street, and that practically every place is the same place now. That is the extraordinary and almost unbelievable truth which will shake them out of the frame of their lives when it does come. Unfortunately it probably won't reach them at all until it dawns in red tracer bullets across the dingy sky, and then it may be just a little late to do them any good.

ROME:
ANTI–FRENCH
SCUFFLE

There you are, another one, and with no different results in the sale of newspapers, so far as I can see. Everybody is doing something of supreme interest to himself, of immediate, exact, practical interest, catching the bus, buying the book, hailing the cab, keeping the appointment, running the errand: the whole street is alive with the needle points of concentrated selves, so many selves in purposive immediate activity that they are unaware of each other and of the desperate speed with which they approach their end.

Never mind. Here's another poster.

WEST END
THRU'
A KEYHOLE

That's better. I did actually see somebody buy that paper. It was a weekly paper the name of which I couldn't quite read from the top of the bus, but it must be a very fine paper. It must be rather like a number of our papers in America, which attempt with some success to describe the private lives of the rich. I know enough about London newspapers to understand that the term "West End" is only used of the rich, the titled, or the notorious. No doubt that good housewife who bought the paper is going to have

herself a nice hot cup of tea at the Corner House and rest
her feet while she reads about how Lady Mary Fiddlesticks
is not really going to do this or that because she is already
doing something else. It is amazing how the Anglo-Saxons
will eat up that kind of stuff. You get hardly any of it in
France or elsewhere in Europe; but the English and the
Americans like it very much. Vast fortunes are built on it
by clever newspaper proprietors. It seems to me that there
is a difference—slight, but true—between the Americans and
the English in respect of this appetite for scandal about the
rich. The Americans in these matters are much farther advanced into the dream world than the English: such
stories are not very real to them. They devour scandal
about all sorts of people without thinking of them as
people at all, but as mere characters in a drama contrived
for the general amusement. Your taxicab driver in New
York will discuss the persons in a celebrated divorce case
with you, whether you like it or not; it is all part of a show
at which you and he are equally spectators. There is no
cruelty in this: there is a deficient sense of reality, a kind
of fantastication of life which is created by the films, radio
and newspapers. In that region of half-belief it is as easy
to accept an invasion from Mars as it is to accept any of the
other stories that are poured out in an immense and inconceivable stream of tittle-tattle. The Englishman who buys a
paper because its poster says "West End thru' a Keyhole"
is probably a little furtive about it; he loves to know all he
possibly can about Lady Mary Fiddlesticks, and will repeat
it at the earliest opportunity, but if he ever met the lady,
or any of her friends, he would pretend that he had never
heard of her. The English are still aware that these persons
described in the papers are real; that is all. Otherwise there
isn't much difference: on both sides of the ocean the press

that reaches the largest number of people is the press that deals most in this line of goods.

Meanwhile Tunis and the French troops and the anti-French scuffle in Rome don't stand much of a chance. Not with this crowd in Baker Street.

3

The Thirteen Bus turns from Baker Street (which has un-accountably called itself Orchard Street for the last small stretch) into Oxford Street, at a corner massively held down by Selfridge's Stores. You can, as is well known, buy anything there, and a very large number of people seem to be doing so at the present moment. With Oxford Street we reach a higher point in the crescendo of noise and confusion in which the Thirteen Bus thunders on to its terminus. Here it is no longer possible to watch any single person for more than a few steps: these are the merest glimpses, not even of a whole person at a time, a leg, an arm, an eye, a hat; the parts extrude from the mass and enter it again; there is a sale on at Selfridge's. The Thirteen Bus, adding its bulk to what was already there, jams in the thick of it and stops: the traffic is blocked. Taxis, bicycles, buses, and even the resplendent closed car with the superb old lady in it can move no more. The people down in the street, as if aware of the temporary superiority of their legs, walk with increased decorum. They are detached again, each complete in himself, pursuing a definite aim with speed but dignity. What would happen, I wonder, if I got off the bus now and went over to that white-haired woman who is looking into the shopwindow and said to her: "Madam, do you know anything about the Ebro?"

She would probably call the police. If by any chance

she did not, and took the question for what it was, she would no doubt say: "The Ebro? The Ebro? It's a river, isn't it? Somewhere in India, or is that the Ganges? No, I've got it. It's a river in Spain. Is that right?"

If I told her it was a river flowing down Oxford Street she would be sure I was a lunatic. ("The most astonishing thing happened to me today, my dear. I was standing looking into Selfridge's window when a man came up to me and said the river Ebro was flowing down Oxford Street. Fancy!")

But if she said what was really in her mind, instead of trying to guess where the river Ebro was, her reply would probably be something like this:

"I told Ellen yesterday that I wouldn't put up with those wretched cretonne curtains any longer, and I won't. Three-and-six a yard. That seems very expensive. I wonder if I went in and looked about—— But they always persuade one to buy something. Now if I could find something at about one-and-nine the yard, that would be the thing. I wonder if I should go in and get it over with?"

There she stands, protected by the Ebro, an isle in the Ebro, no less, while the guns thunder on all sides of her and the upper air is filled with the moaning of shells. She is very tidily dressed in gray, with brown shoes and a fur, and there is the wing of a brown bird on her hat. Presently she will go in and look at cretonne curtains and buy none, but on further thought may go up to the third floor and poke about among the toys to see if she can't find something for Sarah's little boy, who will be five in a week or two. He is fond of all sorts of mechanical gadgets, particularly airplanes.

4

"This is the national program. . . ."

From Oxford Circus (which we reach through successive congelations and degelations of traffic) there is a moment when passengers on the top of the Thirteen Bus may, if they look sharp, get a view of the British Broadcasting Company's building. It lies up there to your left, beyond the Queen's Hall, and you can see its square white stone growing dirty in the London smoke. It is a tremendous building, a tremendous company, a tremendous transaction going on all the time between the whole world and the minds of the people living in these islands. Its organization is something of a curiosity: it is a corporation not for profit, a monopoly not directly of the state, supported by the licenses paid to the state by the owners of radio sets. The autonomous corporation invented to deal with the new invention grew so rich on the licensing fees that it has been able to spend more and more money on programs and equipment; to build this vast building; and to contribute part of its annual surplus to various suitable enterprises. It has its own orchestra or orchestras, its own companies of actors, singers, and even (for television) dancers; it has its press, too. No advertising is permitted on programs of the British Broadcasting Company. But these advantages, formidable as they are, are outweighed by the one tremendous disadvantage: it is a semigovernmental monopoly. The air in England is not free.

How often have we heard the pale voices of the B.B.C. young men reciting their nightly translation of the events that change the world!—heard them, and cursed. This was once when we lived for a while in a village on the south coast and listened to the news at six forty-five and nine and ten and sometimes at eleven-fifty. There was one young man in particular who had the knack of making the most incontrovertible events sound like hypotheses emitted with caution at a sewing bee.

"According to reports from the Franco-Spanish frontier," he would say, "the Nationalists are approaching San-tan-daire."

This was a long time ago—two whole years. Last summer he used to say:

"Republican sawces assert that the Republican offensive across the river Ebro has been a complete success, maw than seven thousand prisoners having been taken in three days. Nationalist sawces deny this, and say that the Republican attack has been repulsed all along the line."

Two years ago he had a lot of trouble over the word Gijon. He wanted to pronounce it very Spanish, so that it came out of the radio like the click of castanets, but it didn't quite work, and until you got the hang of it you didn't know what he was talking about.

The voices don't matter so much; it is what they say. The low temperature, the pallor, the desuetude. There were certain plain facts in late August and early September: facts which only had to be stated. Hitler's maneuvers had the quality of direct menace. His intentions were clear. He was going to dismember Czechoslovakia. The B.B.C. continued in righteous unawareness of this fact during the time when I was hearing it in England—and is, perhaps, still unaware. I had no secret source of information, but I knew in August what was going to happen in September, and made my plans accordingly. Facts plain enough to be seen by an American journalist ought to have been plain enough to be seen by the B.B.C. and by the government which whispers in its ear. If they had been seen, clearly and in time, there would have been no "crisis" of surprised horror and confusion: there would have been a course decided upon with the full knowledge and approval of the people, and adhered to thereafter. In the political disaster of 1938, the worst of modern times, the British Broadcasting Company did its bit.

So far as I know the air is not free in any country. In most countries of Europe, broadcasting is a monopoly of the state. In America there is not only a Federal Commission which exercises some degree of control, but there are innumerable small censorships created by the advertisers' fear of antagonizing groups of listeners. These are evils; but the B.B.C. has its own variety of evil, which derives from the ambiguity of its constitution and even more from the general ambiguity of the life around it. It is of the state and not of the state at the same time. It has a mighty instrument and is afraid to use it. When the world as we have known it lies all in ruins, those pale voices will still be murmuring into the void their careful alternatives, yes and no and yes and no, she loves me, she loves me not.

How could that woman in front of Selfridge's be expected to know where the Ebro is? She only hears about it from the B.B.C., and they make it sound very far away indeed—far away, and of no positive account, since nothing that happens there can be stated as a fact.

5

Once upon a time Regent Street curved grandly down to Piccadilly Circus between buildings of the Regency period; these are gone now, and what you see from the top of the bus is much the same as what you might see in Milwaukee. The crowds show the same urgency in getting in and out of shops, time presses, the road is long; they are all in a hurry. Even more do they press and churn in the great pit of Piccadilly Circus, where the lighted signs burn all day and the old woman with the stubby fingers sells apples in front of the Criterion. Piccadilly to the right there, broad and proud: that way to the hotels, gentlemen, to the Ritz, to the Berkeley, to the Park, to Mayfair: scented ladies, pâté de foie gras, next year's strawberries. The West End thru' a Keyhole. But the Thirteen Bus does not go that way; it wheels round firmly through the gyratory traffic and—with a glimpse of the bawds and gauds of Leicester Square—turns its beam to the West End and heads down the Haymarket.

This is the place where Tree built his wonderful theater —His Majesty's Theatre, it is called—and I never see it without thinking of the funniest theatrical criticism I ever read. It was by G. Bernard Shaw, and gave an account of the opening of His Majesty's Theatre. Among other things (after a long discussion of the building of a theater, and of the disadvantages of plush and velvet) Mr Shaw said:

"The first night was exceedingly glorious. Our unique English loyalty—consisting in a cool, resolute determination to get the last inch of advertisement out of the Royal Family —has seldom been better pushed. Not a man in the house but felt that the Jubilee was good for trade. Mr Tree told us that he would never disgrace the name the theatre bore; and his air as he spoke was that of a man who, on the brink of forgery, arson and bigamy, was saved by the feeling that the owner of Her Majesty's Theatre must not do such things. Mr Alfred Austin contributed as straightforward and businesslike a piece of sycophancy in rhyme as ever a Poet Laureate penned; and Mrs Tree recited it with an absence of conviction that was only emphasized by her evident desire to please us all. Miss Clara Butt shewed what a Royal College of Music can make of a magnificent voice in singing God Save the Queen at full length (with a new verse thrown in) alternately with the Queen's Hall choir, the whole audience standing up determinedly meanwhile, with the Prince of Wales representing Royalty at one corner, Mr Labouchere representing Republicanism at the other, and the British Public representing Good Taste (formerly known as Hypocrisy) in the middle. The contents of the pay-boxes, it was announced, amid the enthusiasm of those who, like myself, had not paid for their seats, are to be handed over to the Prince of Wales' Ratepayers' Relief Fund. The proceedings terminated with a play, in which Mr and Mrs Tree . . . and about a dozen other artists had the honor of appearing."

This was written on April 28, 1897, and as Tree did not assassinate Shaw for it, both His Majesty's Theatre and the author of the criticism continue to flourish at the present moment. The theater is dark and empty now, but it has had forty profitable years and more to come, so that Shaw was quite right when he rudely said that the theater would be on Tree's credit side and his *Falstaff* on the debit.

Except, perhaps, that there is nothing much to put in a London theater nowadays. The funny plays come from America or France, and there are to all intents and purposes no serious ones. Unless a manager is to run his theater on Shakespeare, Sheridan and Shaw—a thought which would drive any proper London manager to suicide—he has to take what comes, and mostly it is pretty bad. The last thing I saw in His Majesty's Theatre was an exceedingly pretentious production of an ornate and fancy play, Flecker's *Hassan*, many years ago. Since then it has not harbored anything that called for my money. Across the street, there,

[*13*]

is the Haymarket Theatre. The last thing I saw there was *Ten Minute Alibi*. Well, that, anyhow, was a good thriller.

6

Pall Mall, to the right, is where the clubs are. (Not all of them, we say hastily, not all.) We don't see much of them from the top of the bus; in fact we are rapidly turning our backs to them as we wheel into Cockspur Street for Trafalgar Square. But we can hardly catch even a glimpse of those solemn gray exteriors, all Regency or early Victorian, without thinking of the extraordinary form of life they sequestrate and fertilize. The club would not be possible, I suppose, without the university; it is the university which trains Englishmen of the upper classes to believe that they must shelter themselves from their womenfolk in order to read a newspaper. Hence these huge, comfortable monasteries where you can eat a very bad lunch and drink magnificent wine with it, in the best English tradition, and sit over your coffee afterwards in a lounge where everybody talks in a discreet undertone, and all the papers published in London, daily and weekly, are to be seen if somebody else hasn't got what you want first. These are the political clubs, the clubs which date from the nineteenth century; the purely aristocratic clubs are further away, in St James's, and do not come within the purview of the Thirteen Bus. There is an exception even to this rule: for that club up the way (next to the Athenaeum) is aristocratic enough, and nonpolitical, having been founded "for gentlemen who have made the Grand Tour".

The Grand Tour . . .

Well, at that, the men in those clubs do have some idea of what is going on. They know exactly where Tunis is, and the Ebro, and Slovakia, and the Ukraine. They have at times an absolutely terrifying plenitude of information, combined with a set of opinions fully worked out and not susceptible of modification. Their information is of the sort you get in a *Times* supplement, import and export, balance of trade, alignment of political parties, architectural monuments, etc., etc. They don't actually know how the people feel about anything, but they don't want to. Their interest in the people is of a purely electoral or philanthropic nature; they want them to vote this way or that, and they are quite willing to contribute to funds to keep them from starving to death outright. They also support the "voluntary" hospital system of England, which, although very bad, is regarded with the utmost pride by a class which appreciates its own virtue before everything else. They take an unflagging interest in all public affairs, which to them are mere shoptalk; for they are the governing class of England.

Americans often do not know what the governing class of England is. Sometimes they think it is the aristocracy; sometimes they think it is the democracy (although not often); sometimes they think it is the rich. Such clues as I have been able to obtain lead me to think that the English governing class is recruited from the public schools and the universities, which is a purely economic selection only slightly mitigated by the system of university scholarships offered to promising students of the ordinary schools. But this economic selection (which is basic) is supplemented by an intricate machinery of social selection as well. A man may come of the most respectable family, pass all his examinations handsomely at Oxford or Cambridge, and still not get into the Foreign Office if he has the bad luck to offend in any one of a number of ways. He may be forced into the Treasury; or, if the Treasury will not have him, into the Colonial Office or the India Office or the Admiralty or the Home Office. When you see what did get into the Foreign Office, you marvel that anybody could ever have been refused for it; but they say people are refused all the time. One man I know had his eye on the Treasury all through Cambridge, and then landed in the Colonial Office, to his bitter disappointment. Some day he will no doubt be exercising the powers of empire over some godforsaken tribe of blacks which never will be able to understand why, at times, his eyes grow misty and his arm of justice falters; for how can the Senegambian know about Pall Mall and Whitehall?

It does seem a foolish way to govern, but it worked remarkably well during the great imperial period of which the present time is the dregs. The men who made the empire were, of course, seldom from the governing class: they were the traders, merchants and adventurers who came from all classes and expressed in their way the bursting vitality of a people too big for their island. The governing class came along afterwards and wielded the scepter. H. G. Wells once said that they had all been brought up by governesses and consequently had the minds of governesses, which may indeed be true; I never knew a governess. But it seems to me that their chief limitations come rather from this lifelong habit of secluding themselves in quiet rooms with deep carpets among other men exactly like themselves. It starts in school (without the quiet or the deep carpets), is fixed by the university, and continues throughout the lives of hundreds of men who might otherwise—in spite of the economic and social prejudices of their class—achieve a fairly comprehensive view of the material which is, after all, what they deal with, the existence of the population.

They can tell you almost anything in the way of statistical, political, geographical, historical or ethnological information, but they don't seem to realize why it matters. To expect any collection of such men to solve a problem involving the passions of a people would be idiotic, you might say; and yet the Runciman mission was sent to Czechoslovakia.

All the English governing class is not in Pall Mall clubs, of course; nor does everybody in the clubs belong to the governing class. But all those men from the Foreign Office and the Home Office and the rest of it, with their parliamentary cousins, their womenfolk and their friends—the people who have the habit of their company—make up what can be called, fairly accurately, the governing class. It is a thing distinct from the aristocracy, although members of the aristocracy often belong to it; and it is certainly distinct from "society", an institution which exists in England (as elsewhere) for enjoyment or display. I think it has no exact counterpart in any other country, for it does not fit into an exact economic or social category. Like the B.B.C., it is and it is not an organ of the state. This ambiguity and lack of definition characterize so much of the structure here that foreigners are sometimes (like the bewildered French writer) inclined to put it all on to climate, and say that England as a whole lives in a fog.

But even if it were true, it is a fog from which all those gentlemen in the clubs in Pall Mall have emerged at some time or other. They have surveyed the foreigner in his habitat; they have made the Grand Tour.

7

Cockspur Street is a brief interlude of shipping offices, with posters inviting the passer-by to visit India, Egypt,

Ceylon, the South Seas; the bus makes no stop here, but plunges up the slight incline that leads to Trafalgar Square. Here, alongside the early-Victorian-neo-Grecian hideosity of the National Gallery, it comes to a determined stop, behind a line of other buses similarly at rest. The big square is in its ordinary bustling mood today, with ordinary traffic proceeding as usual, and the policemen in the observation post near the tube station have nothing much to observe. Sometimes, at least on Sundays, there are rousing political demonstrations here, and vigorous speeches are made to the reward of loud cheers. The crowd then, on occasion, takes its foot in its hand and goes to Downing Street—just below there, off Whitehall—and "demonstrates" in front of the Prime Minister's house, or the Foreign Office across from it, or even simply at the entrance to that little blind alley about which so much has been heard. The demonstrations usually consist of a few cheers, hisses and boos, a little noise, a little jostling. Nobody pays much attention to them. It is well understood in all ranks of society that only cranks, crackpots, people slightly off in the head, will take part in such assertions of disagreement with the governing class.

The big square is dominated by the statue of Nelson on its column one hundred and eighty-four feet and ten inches (184 ft. 10 in.) high. Now there was a man. He had a fine command of language, and although his political intelligence was rudimentary, he could say a plain thing or two when it was his will. It would be interesting to hear his opinion of the present British government. He was not much given to criticizing his betters—being only their hired hand, after all —but when he did, it was something. That time when Emma was going to ask the Prince of Wales to dinner (the Prince of Wales who now, as George IV, stands just over there beneath the shadow of Nelson) the little Admiral wrote a number of letters filled with the choicest abuse. The Prince ("that damned fellow") was a "villain" and he had "not a spark of honour". Those were some of the words. He was more respectful to Castlereagh, but earlier on in his career he had his moments of sharp rebellion against the cautious tergiversations of his superiors. Nelson's genius as a leader of men and a designer of naval attack has so obscured everything else about him that a few words of sense on the subject are always taken amiss; the national saint must be that and nothing else, supreme on his column in the middle of London. Bernard Shaw told me a story about this once. He said that some scheme of physical and moral tests for officers of the navy had been proposed, and he had written a letter to *The Times* inquiring where the British navy would be now were it not for a "one-armed little adulterer". This candid, innocent question aroused the fury of all the bishops, generals and admirals in England, who wrote with sputtering pens to *The Times* in consequence. Shaw's curiosity was pricked by such a show of anger; he investigated the matter. He asked if it was denied that Nelson was one-armed, and the answer was no. He asked if it was denied that he was an adulterer, and the answer was again (reluctantly) no. He then inquired if the trouble arose over the harmless word "little", and the answer was yes. The bishops, generals and admirals were willing to admit that Nelson was short, but they did not like anybody to describe him as "little".

But little he was, and sickly, with characteristics of astonishing personal vanity, jealousy and pettiness, with a mind so limited in every direction that it scarcely classified as an intelligence, with passions so near the surface that they were seldom completely under control. He had hardly any external characteristic of what is called "an English gentleman". I remember once describing to a friend the unbridled anger of a mutual acquaintance over some triviality in a shop. The friend's son, a schoolboy, was in the room, and promptly inquired: "But he wasn't an Englishman, was he?" I said yes. The boy said, "I didn't know Englishmen ever behaved like that." What that boy would have said if he had ever seen Nelson in a rage I don't know. But Nelson's rages we have, in a mass of letters, diaries and papers of the time, and we can see him strut, the one-armed little adulterer, with his head in the wind.

The only thing is, the man was an authentic blazing hero. In that, the instinct of the English people has somehow driven through the fog and found a truth. He was brave, tender and honest, with a gift of inspiring devotion and with a genius for naval battle; but most of all he had the special thing, the single mind, the passion and fire of the antique hero, the thing Napoleon never possessed. It is a pity he is dead.

8

There are a lot of notables in the neighborhood. Not all of them would have been acceptable to Nelson in life. We know what he thought of George IV, who now sits a horse in the northeast corner beneath the column. But what would he have made of General Gordon, who is just behind him now, between the two fountains? Gordon, that psalm-singing maniac who made the "Ever-Victorious Army" in China, in the Taiping days, and came back to die at Khartoum? Nelson's eccentricities were not Gordon's—were, in fact, so different that it is difficult to imagine the slightest communication between them. But least of all is it possible to imagine him having any truck with Miss Edith Cavell, whose monument stands across the way in St Martin's

Place. A woman capable of saying such a shocking thing as "Patriotism is not enough" was not for Nelson. He thought patriotism was not only enough, but that it was everything; and when he did fall in love—once and once only—he merged his love and his patriotism so completely into one that he came to think of Emma, lovely fat Emma, as being practically the same thing as England. Miss Cavell's virtues were of a different kind.

The bus is off; we are for Charing Cross and the Strand now. Below us on the right is the broad straight street called Whitehall, lined with aging buildings in Portland stone, some of them good (at least one is). That, and mark it well, is the seat of administration of the British Empire. The Admiralty, the War Office, the Foreign Office, Scotland Yard—there they all are, and the little alley called Downing Street, alongside the Foreign Office, and God knows what else besides. These are the immense and none-theless crowded offices in which all the men who lunch at the clubs in Pall Mall do their work, along with other men who don't belong to clubs, and others who are too grand to go to them. Cabinet ministers are two-a-penny down there, and the crowd which is so eager to watch almost any curiosity scarcely notices them as they come and go. Somehow, by means of an incalculable amount of writing on paper (some of it still done with pen and ink), the British Empire gets governed. A young man who has lunched too well at his club may possibly mislay a dispatch, as a result of which ten sentences of execution in India cannot be commuted in time and cause popular disorders which in turn cost many lives, but these are the accidents of the trade and can't be helped. Somewhere down there is also a vast Victorian Gothic building which shelters that cele-brated debating society, governed by party caucus, called the House of Commons. The Thirteen Bus, showing un-impeachable judgment, passes up all that and, pausing for the necessities of traffic at the Charing Cross railroad station, dives recklessly into the Strand.

This, again, is not all that the novels and stories of some years ago might have led us to expect. The Strand was (or so they told us) something like New York's Broadway, lined with theaters and bright with lights. But time has changed all that. The theaters are mostly scattered about in side streets of the West End now, and there are not enough of them in the Strand to give it a special character. Small shops and nondescript nineteenth-century buildings with an infinity of tenants line the street; we read twenty different signs on the windows of one floor; there is a multiplication of business here, like the multiplication of traffic in the road. The Strand is so crowded because it is the main thoroughfare between the West End and the City of London: for centuries no other straight road was built between the two, which is one explanation of their extraordinary separateness. Downtown New York is separate from uptown New York, but it is neither unknown nor inaccessible; whereas there are millions of people who live for years in the West End of London without ever seeing the City. The Strand is choked with people going between the two, but the City remains a different world.

HITLER'S
THREAT TO
CATHOLICS

That is what the posters say here, in glaring red, but nobody seems to mind. Perhaps there are no Catholics in the Strand. Off there to the right there used to be the buildings called the Adelphi, a region all built by the four Adam brothers; on Adelphi Terrace there were flats overlooking the river, and some very distinguished literary gentlemen, among others, inhabited them. Shaw and Barrie lived there. The region is still vaguely called the Adelphi, but the Terrace is occupied now by a big new block of flats. Beyond it, the Savoy—the theater, the courtyard, the hotel: Gilbert and Sullivan, the Savoy Grill.

I have a great deal more to say for the Savoy Grill than for Gilbert and Sullivan; but since it is regarded as a high crime in all English-speaking countries to criticize these citizens of another era, I will be brief. Their operas were mostly produced at the Savoy Theatre, and constitute, to the present moment, the favorite humorous works of the gentlemen who eat lunch in Pall Mall and work in Whitehall. The ruling ideas of Gilbert and Sullivan—that everything is very funny, especially in foreign countries, and that everything will be all right if you laugh at it—have made an indelible impression upon the minds of the British governing class. They can all make jingles in the style of Gilbert, and do; they can quote him by the yard; they are even willing to endure the music (if you call Sir Arthur Sullivan's compositions music) so long as it is dominated by the arch and skittish rhymes of the master. These productions, as intensely English as a game of cricket, form an important part of the culture of an English gentleman. They form him, as the school and the university form him, and as Shakespeare never succeeded in forming him. It is in great part because of Gilbert and Sullivan that they worship "the sense of humor", which is such a peculiar invention that each one of them is free to suppose that each other one of them lacks it. It is chiefly to Gilbert that they owe their capacity for laughing at every human passion the moment it takes visible form or causes a deviation from their visible standards.

The best thing I know about W. S. Gilbert is that a man named Jim Lardner, while marching with the 15th Brigade to the Ebro, composed a ribald song to the rhythm of "Tit-willow".

The bus, meanwhile, has whisked us along through the Strand, past Somerset House (where you find out about births, deaths, marriages and wills) to the place where the street divides in the middle for the churches: St Mary-le-Strand, St Clement Danes. Like other old London churches, these have tablets and windows and such to inform you of the great men who worshiped there in the past. I think there will be few such mementos left of our day. Dr Johnson, for example, worshiped at St Clement Danes, and St Clement Danes does not mean to let you forget it. There is a brass tablet, there is a window, there is a statue, all to the greater glory of that pompous, disagreeable old man who differs from other forgotten and unread writers in that his biographer was a genius. Dr Johnson, too, is an intensely English phenomenon, and his rolling thunderous style of talk, as recorded by Boswell, may have had some effect upon the more oratorical moments of English statesmen before the war. At present there is nothing of the kind to be detected. Some things, at least, we have been spared.

Gladstone—there he is, opposite the west front of St Clement Danes, in full regalia as Chancellor of the Exchequer, a National Memorial—had a Johnsonian roll to his speech when he wanted to employ it. We have Disraeli's word for that. He was "inebriated with the exuberance of his own verbosity". Besides, he was inebriated with the desire to solve all the world's problems in a largely liberal sense without taking any decisive steps about them or in any way risking England's goods. He did take steps, and he did risk, again and again, but always after an infinity of side steps and with an infinity of caution. The Irish got him in the end; the banshees put a curse on him. But throughout the greater part of his political life Gladstone certainly exhibited the cautious and honorable hesitation in good courses which is one of the traditions of English government. That particular tradition is to hesitate until it is no longer possible to do the right thing, until nothing but the wrong thing can be done. Thus it was with Gladstone and Parnell; he hummed and hawed, he didn't want to do it, but he did. And how is anybody to explain Gladstone's behavior during the American Civil War? Henry Adams confessed that it had puzzled him all his life long. To say one thing in public and another in private is nothing out of the way among politicians, but for a politician whose whole life was devoted to the most sanctimonious principles of liberalism Gladstone's course in those years was indeed mysterious. Even more mysterious was his course with regard to that queer fish, Chinese Gordon, whom we saw in Trafalgar Square; he put Gordon in an impossible place and left him to die. If these hesitations are characteristic of liberalism, then Gladstone and liberalism have triumphed under another name, and can be eminently pleased with their successors.

The Law Courts, another of these immense Victorian buildings in Gothic style, catches our eye (indeed) as we trundle on out of the Strand. The law—in England above all places—inspires us with a respect for its mysteries and a desire never to investigate them. It may be that there have been abuses, irregularities, monstrous inadaptabilities and archaisms, but we are content to accept the current belief that English law is the most equitable in the world, and the best administered, and the least unjust. If we had the desire to question it, the bus would allow us no time, for it parts the traffic like a boat on the water and swings us along to Temple Bar. Here, where a gateway once stood—a gateway where they exhibited the heads of criminals stuck on pikes, you remember; and where they had a pillory which was once occupied by poor old Daniel Defoe—the City of London begins. The City of London, the abode of the burghers in the old days, the home of finance, commerce and the press now, still with an immense and complicated system of privilege, retains all sorts of quaint practices to show its traditional autonomy. One of them is that here, at Temple Bar, the reigning sovereign on his state visits to the City must pause to be received by the Lord Mayor, and to receive from him (for the duration of the visit) the sword of the City of London. I have not inquired, but it seems probable that it is a sword made of cardboard.

And here, as the bus, ignoring such medievalism, pushes along, we enter Fleet Street.

9

Every newspaper in the world has some kind of representation in Fleet Street, even if it is only through the press associations of the various countries. The great London daily papers have their presses on the side streets between here and the river; the principal ones (except *The Times*) are in or near Fleet Street itself. None of them, except the black-and-clear-glass palace of the *Daily Express*, strikes us as particularly noticeable architecturally. It is a street of higgledy-piggledy late nineteenth-century buildings, mostly, some high and some low, some imposing and some shabby, all dirty, all busy at nearly every hour of the day.

The life of the place goes on in the street, in the pubs, in the eating places as much as in the offices themselves. Nearly every kind of human being is to be found hereabouts engaged somehow in the production or distribution of newspapers. There are elegant ladies and gentlemen of high degree employed to collect gossip about their friends and relations; there are millionaires who like to own newspapers because of the power it gives them, and there are millionaires who made their money out of the papers; there are innumerable varieties of journalists and editors, special writers and tipsters and hangers-on; there are the printers themselves, and there are thousands of workers in distribution.

But what is it that they write, print and distribute?

The inquiry could occupy us far longer than it will take for the Thirteen Bus to pass through the street and climb Ludgate Hill. They write, print and distribute newspapers of a wider range than can be found anywhere else in the world except New York. The worst American press is probably worse than the worst English; but the best American press is, I think, better than the best English. That is, our best newspapers will suppress nothing and garble nothing in a moment of great crisis, so long as they are not directly subjected to an official censorship. By reason of its ownership or its relations with the government, the English press has no such independence. This has been shown very clearly in two recent crises which profoundly disturbed the whole country: the first was the abdication of Edward VIII, the second the triumph of Hitler in September, 1938. In the first of these instances the English press, having been silent as the grave about the whole business, suddenly began (on whose signal?) to thunder at the King because of his intention to marry, and by means of a crisis of the most sudden and trumped-up nature, forced an abdication. In that whole affair the press acted simply as an organ of the government of the day. Again in September, when very much graver matters were being decided, the press as a whole, seized by the panic fear of war, followed the lines of policy decided upon (or stumbled into) by the government of the day, and actually saluted Neville Chamberlain as the savior of the world's peace when he returned from Munich. Generations which will have to bear the frightful consequences of that unnecessary surrender may never understand, as they pore over the press of the months just past, how such things could be written, printed and read.

Along there on the left side of the street, as we whisked by, I caught sight of a white shaft let into the wall of the church of St Dunstan-in-the-West. It was surmounted by a marble head, and the inscription beneath it said that it was a memorial to Northcliffe.

That, perhaps, would supply a clue to the relations of the press and government in England: a serious study, which should someday be possible, of the life of Alfred Harmsworth, Lord Northcliffe. H. G. Wells has given us some very illuminating pages on the subject in his autobiography. He taught some of the Harmsworth children (not Alfred) in school, and had seen, in those far-off days, the first copies of the school newspaper, written and printed by Alfred a year or so before. Decades later Wells came again into relations with Alfred Harmsworth when the *Daily Mail* had become a market for a writer's work, and through an association of some years he was able to get an idea not only of the tangle of publications over which Harmsworth was lord, but also of the curious unbalanced man, irresponsible, uninformed, violent and despotic, who wielded that immense power. Northcliffe was, of course, a journalistic genius, in that he was always thinking of some new trick or gadget for catching the public's fancy and making money out of increased circulation and advertising; but that sort of genius can scarcely compensate for an ignorant and irresponsible use of colossal power. Wells tells us that the wartime cabinet, to keep Northcliffe and his younger rival, Beaverbrook, quiet, invented ministries for them; and there is a funny scene in the book, where Northcliffe, seated solemnly in a drawing room at Crewe House as minister of propaganda, says to Wells (in effect): "You are a believer in social revolution. We two are here. Isn't that social revolution enough for you?"

The government is quick to grant peerages to the owners of newspapers, quick to give them any sort of honor, distinction or privilege they may fancy, and to see that they have no cause to complain of the social or political system. Alfred Harmsworth at a smart London dinner party, surrounded by a gaggle of duchesses, could hardly have been expected to retain his independence of judgment, even if he had possessed the powers of intelligence or the education to make a sound judgment on any serious question. He was not, apparently, much taken in by the purely social aspects of his bewildering success, but its ramifications in political power were too much for him; he governed his realm by whim, by fantasy, held everything else of no account, and came to grief in the end because his mind could not stand the strain.

SHIPPING MAGNATE
FALLS TO
DEATH

That is what the new poster says, flourished by the boy down on the corner of Fleet Street and Ludgate Circus; it is just out, with the ink still wet, and covers over the anti-

French scuffle in Rome and the new French troops in Tunis. The shipping magnate (if I bought the newspaper I might find out that he was a bookkeeper in a shipping firm) had apparently fallen or been pushed from a window, and it is possible to imagine fifty reasons why this event should have taken place, but not one of them fully explains why the event is more interesting than the anti-French scuffle in Rome or the new French troops in Tunis.

That is what they are interested in, there is no doubt: that is why most people buy most newspapers, to find out about the shipping magnate who falls to death, to see the West End thru' a Keyhole. The sober journals of opinion (so called) do not circulate widely, and the more unsober the journal the more people it finds to share its insobriety. Northcliffe was among the first to discover the depth and width of this phenomenon, and his monument is not *The Times* (which he did, indeed, own for a while toward the end, out of sheer vainglory) but the popular press of London. That, and a queer legend of Fleet Street, and a shaft of white stone at St Dunstan-in-the-West.

10

We have passed the Temple without a word, for its gates are so lost in the turmoil of Fleet Street that they give no hint of the conventual precincts beyond. If we got off the bus and went in through the gate we might find ourselves transported right out of modern London into a mustier, quieter world, the Inner Temple and the Middle Temple, old buildings with courtyards and fountains, libraries and churches, a sort of university enclave in the midst of the City, where barristers are supposed to have "chambers". Many besides barristers have "chambers" there; for the ubiquitous Dr Johnson lived there, too, and Charles and Mary Lamb, and Goldsmith, poor Noll; and at the present day one of the most celebrated of the B.B.C.'s oracles dwells in a rookery over the gardens. I am glad to know that Blackstone had chambers just beneath poor Noll, and complained of the noise made by his "revelling neighbour"; and that a dozen signers of the American Declaration of Independence had once been members of the Middle Temple. The place was for people to live and work in, and still is, more or less; it is another expression of the Englishman's love of cloisters, but is saved from smugness (the curse of Pall Mall) by this primary fact.

Up Ludgate Hill to St Paul's, with its wonderful Dome that cannot be seen for the crowding buildings on every side: inside here are many architectural curiosities, Wren's own combination of Gothic and classical as modified by the taste of the court ladies and sycophants. There are also an excessive number of monuments to national idols of various kinds, Kitchener, Lord Leighton, Gordon, Wellington, Roberts, Sir Joshua Reynolds, Lord St Vincent, Sir Arthur Sullivan, Dr Johnson, Nelson (this is by Flaxman), Sir John Moore, Florence Nightingale and so on. Nelson was buried under the Dome of St. Paul's in a black marble sarcophagus originally ordered by Cardinal Wolsey for himself. All these facts we can verify if we get off the bus and go in; we can admire nave, aisle and dome, immense and beautiful, or we can count prebendaries and minor canons, depending on our frame of mind. In the present instance, time presses, for our main object of inquiry is the course of the Thirteen Bus, and we pursue it with hardly a pause for the cathedral, on into Cannon Street and the heart of the City of London.

The whole look of the people in the streets has changed now. They are mostly men and they are dressed in two varieties of uniform. One is young men in gray flannel trousers and tweed coats, the other is older men in black suits with bowler hats. I suspect a social and economic difference between the two as well, but I do not know what it is. The black uniform, the "City suit", is predominant here, and you see more bowler hats in five minutes than you would see in the West End of London in five years. They rush in and out of dirty nineteenth-century buildings where the names of a thousand businesses stare at you from grimy windows. The bus pokes its way hardily down the long slanting street, stops briefly at the railway station, and concludes its first exploration of Cannon Street by a halt at the corner of corners.

This is a place where Cannon Street crosses Queen Victoria Street, and it is the stop for the Bank of England. A few steps to the left, there, is a junction of streets: Cheapside, Cornhill, Lombard Street, Threadneedle Street, Princes Street and Queen Victoria Street. It is a very important corner, dominated by the huge new building of the Bank of England, by the Royal Exchange, the National Provincial Bank, and the Liverpool and London and Globe Assurance Company. The newsboy in front of the Liverpool and London and Globe Assurance Company is flourishing a poster which looks like an old friend:

HITLER'S
THREAT TO
CATHOLICS

Poland, Ukrainia, the Ebro? These people have far better fish to fry. The Bank of England is the agent of the government in everything connected with the national debt. (Ten thousand million pounds, twelve thousand million pounds, fourteen thousand million pounds—it rises and must rise, and there are many transactions.) The reserve of every bank in England consists of its account with the Bank of England. The Bank of England receives and registers transfers of stock. The Bank of England is the only bank in England which can issue paper money. It is thus guaranteed in exclusivity the control of the whole banking system, the fiduciary circulation (under the Treasury) and the operations of finance capital. Its Governor, Deputy Governor and twenty-four directors are more powerful than any other group of financial bigwigs in the world. Some consciousness of the immensity of this power and of its importance to all now living, dwellers in the Florida swamps or the plains of the Argentine, the Chinese coolie and the miner in Wales, animates the neat, anxious faces beneath the bowler hats as their owners post from one street to another in the rabbit warren of the City. The whole structure, the system, is centered here; this is the mainspring; no one of the thousands who work here and hereabout can fail to know that the life of the whole world is profoundly influenced by the decisions taken in that great stone edifice across the way. That the decisions taken there are calculated to sustain and fortify at any price the system of which the Bank is the center, that such decisions will be ruthlessly enforced, and that in crucial matters no power alive can stand against the Bank, must be self-evident truths. Self-preservation is still the first law of nature, however often it may be misunderstood by the mood of alarm. The Bank must wield its unique power and all its complicated influences, tangible and intangible, for the preservation (and if possible the extension) of British capital imperialism, with increasing attention to the preservation of kindred capital systems in other countries even when their political structures are profoundly alien. This is the Vatican of capitalism, fully conscious of its mission, and all who bring gold are welcome. Just off the street there is a suggestively placed sign:

INCOME TAX CONSULTANTS

Over there (we can't see it) behind Threadneedle Street is another institution, the Stock Exchange, which plays its own part in the control of events, but (unlike the Bank) most often half consciously or unconsciously. It is a speculative assembly not a deliberative one, governed simply by the motive of profit. Its four or five thousand members are generally not aware of doing anything to influence the world; indeed their most frequent complaint is that the world, by undue agitation, influences their Stock Exchange. To complain of this surface symptom is as far as they get. Many of them are men of merit who support the symphony orchestras, vote Conservative and play golf on Sunday. The church of St Mary Woolnoth, at hand here, has a poster alongside its gloomy entrance advertising a performance of the "Deutsches Requiem" (known in England simply as "Brahms' Requiem"). There will be many City men, Bank and Exchange people who care enough about it to go and listen even on a Sunday. Some of them collect pictures, and all—so my acquaintance with them suggests—eat very well.

The corner is indeed a momentous one, for down on the right, off Queen Victoria Street, is *The Times* newspaper, an institution unique in its sensitiveness to the mood of the governing class. It is scarcely a newpaper at all; it is rather a mirror in which the governing class, and indeed, to make it more specific, the governing clique, can admire themselves. It is an eminently satisfactory mirror because the picture it presents is always flattering under any circumstances. It also has the magic property of leading its devotees onward—few mirrors can predict and make their predictions come true and thereafter cause the accomplished fact to be gazed upon with ecstatic admiration. Yet this is what *The Times* newspaper accomplished in the autumn of 1938. It was *The Times* newspaper that first tipped us off to the impending vivisection of Czechoslovakia, in a leading article of unexampled slyness and perfidy (September 6, 1938). The governing class was not altogether pleased with that, and there was quite a row for a while, but as event followed event, and Mr Neville Chamberlain took airplane after airplane, *The Times* newspaper upheld and carried him like a full Wagnerian orchestra under a shaky soprano, until the goal was reached at last, Hitler had been temporarily appeased by the offering of the flesh and blood of others, and *The Times* could proclaim, as it did on October 1, 1938, "A New Dawn", to the universal satisfaction of its readers.

And let it be clear: if you want to know how those people's minds work you must read *The Times* every day for a long while. It is absolutely indispensable. You must read it all, the dramatic criticisms, the reviews of books, the news from America, the news from India and the colonies, the news of Spain, China and the whole continent of Europe, the correspondence columns. Not even the smallest letter from a clergyman in the country who has heard the first cuckoo should be disregarded. The transaction between *The Times* and the mind of the British upper class is so continuous, intimate and hereditary that it is almost impossible to tell, under ordinary circumstances, which originates and which replies in the flow of communication between them. Yet at important periods, such as this last autumn, you can feel the slight tug of discreet leadership, in which *The Times* reveals (without at all displaying) its conscious direction. Once a crisis is past, *The Times* and its readers subside into their normal state of exchange, in which the editorial comment tells the reader exactly what he already thinks in words which seem to him exactly what he would have used if he could have thought of them; the correspondence columns are filled with the usual debates over dates, places or quotations; conscience funds are started for the victims of the last crisis; and the upper class is enabled again to contemplate its own virtue in the mirror which *The Times* faithfully presents every morning at breakfast.

11

Beyond that tremendous corner Cannon Street slopes to the river. The preoccupied throngs in the street look the same as back there; they wear the same City uniform; but we know as we draw near the river, by the signs on the windows, that the nature of the businesses has changed. We are getting into a region of maritime insurance, shipping, import and export, all the things that have to do with the sea and all the things that come out of it. The distance is small and the pace is swift; we are in King William Street now; the Thirteen Bus is nearing the end of its journey. On the right there already rises the square gray monument of Fishmongers' Hall with its bold inscription: "All Worship Be to God." And here, with a shock of surprise, we leave all the dirty buildings and the curious gloom of the City: we are on London Bridge. There is air here; also space, a wintry, shifting, pearly light, and the immense sweep of the Thames.

The river seems very big. It looks as if it emptied directly there, below Tower Bridge, into the limitless ocean. Ocean-going steamers can come up as far as London Bridge, through the Tower Bridge; there is a steamer moored there now at the wharf, with a name in strange lettering on its prow. It is called the Sibir, and comes from Leningrad. The bus sweeps across London Bridge, through the region of light and air, and plunges into the labyrinth on the other side very briefly, for its terminus is the London Bridge Station.

Here I got off the bus and walked back to London Bridge. The journey was over, and I had half an hour. I was trying to assemble the bits of what I had seen from the Thirteen Bus. What had I omitted to note? There was Portman Square, for instance, which we had passed through long ago, coming down Baker Street. I had taken no note, and yet its trim iron railings, its protected verdure and proprietary grass had struck me as we passed. The Wallace Collection, the National Gallery: works of art. I had no note of them. But it didn't matter much, with the Pool of London lying silver gray below there, the boat from Leningrad moored in it, and Billingsgate just over the way. The Port of London begins here, I was thinking: and this is the real origin of the whole business. Without the sea-borne traffic this city of egoism and indifference could never have filled its streets with millions of people and its pockets with gold. Was it all egoism and indifference?

Such accusations are no easier to make of the English (or even of the Londoners) than of any other collection of people. What it is possible to do is to observe the behavior of a nation in its institutions as they develop, in the men it elects to office or submits to be governed by, in the influences it permits to flow unchecked over its mind, in the high acts of its life. The behavior of England in 1938 (as the culmination of a process which has been going on at least since 1933 if not before) seems to me to indicate a mixture of bewildered weakness and courageous perfidy in the

[37]

dominant characters of the state. The same might have been said of the years 1861–63, or of a number of other periods in which pressure from abroad was felt in England to an uncomfortable degree. Canning's day was a day of little light, and the parallel has occurred to many; Mr Neville Chamberlain himself, in a correspondence in *The Times*, accepted the comparison with gratitude. But will it ever be possible now to call the New World in to redress the balance of the Old?

The river that flows beneath this bridge contains the water of the Ebro, and there is blood in it (some of it English blood). Austria, Czechoslovakia, China, Ethiopia, Spain: they are all around, as near as Billingsgate, as inexorable as the river's movement toward the sea. In the air over our heads you can hear the last breath of the dying, and the tread of the refugees sounds from London Bridge. So many betrayals have no precedent and no explanation. Hypocrisy, perfidy, egoism, all those accusing nouns of an individual flavor do not serve, since they attach themselves to single persons and do not reach to the mass phenomenon underneath. There must be some element of vital decay here—a governing class unsure of its tenure, a nation weary of acting as a nation, an economy and society shaken to their base. The mines and the cotton trade are dead and there is a blight over whole areas in the north. You can drive there through towns which gape empty to the moon. In the vacant valleys of the north (in a place like Todmorden, for instance) you can feel with dismal certainty that life has departed from at least some members of the English body, and that it will never come back again under the system of things as they are. This has gone on for twenty years, and there is a whole new generation in some areas that has never found employment at all. The solvent part of the population never ceases complaining of the necessity of feeding (not well, but feeding) the part that cannot work. In such a state, what preoccupations can there be other than the desire to make money, and more money, and to keep it; to risk nothing; to scurry from task to immediate task, intent and troubled, with no thought for the world that crowds steadily in upon this would-be tight little island; to reach happiness in such economic security that, in the end, one's children may go to the public schools and the universities and eat their lunches in Pall Mall and work in Whitehall? From the top of the Thirteen Bus it looks like a whole population in blinkers. We know that there are millions who do not wear blinkers, who are aware of the interdependence of all peoples in the contemporary world, and who realize to the full that the frontiers of England and of the enduring ideas of England are still in foreign lands. These are to be found even in high places, among Tories of the tradition, among cabinet ministers and former cabinet ministers. Few men in public life can ever have spoken more courageously than Mr Winston Churchill throughout the era of betrayals and surrenders. But it is not courage that is wanted here; it is not clear sight and plain speech; it is something to hide under, a cloud of words, a phrase that will do, anything at all to shut away the terrible reality for a little while longer. The word "appeasement" served as the wing for the ostrich; it made the dominant millions content with their animal comfort that cost half the world. Ethiopia, China, Czechoslovakia, Austria, Spain: to them will be added others before long: the time will come when even the New World cannot redress the balance of the Old, since England will not stir.

And indeed, why should it try? Why should the New World care, I ask, looking down at the crowded Port of London in the pearly winter light, for the freedom of the Old World's inhabitants, since those who have been its guardians for centuries are sunk in coma and decay? With France wavering into timorous reaction, half Fascism and half sheer cowardice, and with England thus covered and drugged by a single word, what is there worth saving in the Eastern Hemisphere?

There is still something: there is the mass of human life that speaks in our blood from ages past, there is the whole treasure of poetry and tradition, liberty and law, which we have taken from here, and there is the surviving life of the millions of ordinary people who are our brothers. These may not even be worth saving if their active possessors make no effort to save them; and yet when the time comes it will be very hard for us in the New World to look at the inevitable struggle with indifference, going busily about our immediate individual affairs as these people in the streets of London now do. Interest and emotion alike will propel us into action, and in all probability we shall save them again, as we did in 1918, even though we know very well that they have deserved their fate to the fullest. The dying empire will die just the same, but not, at least, under the heel of the foreigner. In its peaceful disintegration whole classes of the depressed, the comatose, will come to life again with the realization that the order of things on earth is not changeless. The crusts and layers will be broken and the fences taken down; the English may become a people again, as they were in the nineteenth century.

Now that, I say, leaning on the bridge, is looking very far ahead. At the moment what I can see is Billingsgate, the Pool of London, Tower Bridge, with the tidal river beyond broadening to the sea. The Ebro and Prague are far away; nobody has thought of them in these crowded streets; and here the bus has come along to take me back again.

When I left London Bridge I gave it a good test with both feet. It still seemed solid.

CHAPTER II

The Ebro

THE NIGHT was warm enough when we started out, just after dinner—a spring night without moon or stars, so that the streets of Barcelona seemed even darker than usual, and the car made its stops with caution. We had several stops to make before we turned down the Diagonal and headed out the road to Tarragona. There were, I think, five of us in the car—Al Cohen and Jim Bourne from the Lincoln Battalion, myself, and two Canadians from the Mackenzie-Papineau Battalion.

It was Al Cohen who took me along. I had been cooling my heels in Barcelona for almost a week, unable to obtain either a pass for the front or a car to get there in. These were the last days of Prieto's regime at the Ministry of Defense, and he always insisted on signing every front pass himself—which delayed them indefinitely. That day I had at last obtained my pass, but still had no chance of moving unless I could cadge a lift from somebody. Cars were precious in Barcelona. I was complaining of this circumstance somewhere in the Majestic Hotel, as usual, when Al

Cohen came to the rescue. He said he had a car to deliver to the Estado Mayor of the 15th Brigade, and would take me out in it if I wanted to go.

Nobody talked much in the car. I was in the back with the Canadians; Al was driving. I didn't know the road then at all, so that such landmarks as there were in the darkness meant nothing to me. I got to know that road fairly well afterwards. Jim Bourne had some cigarettes to deliver to the battalion, I think, and there was a lively discussion about how many cigarettes had arrived from America and how soon they could be cleared and brought to the front. There was some talk about the war, but not much—mostly stories that had reached Barcelona about individual episodes of the days just past, when the army in Aragon had been cut to pieces by the Fascists. They all knew that the disaster in Aragon had been a bad one, but I don't think they knew how bad. They were too close to it; they had been in Spain a long time; they knew that this week's defeat may be next week's victory. They were men who had been on leave, or on special duty, or in hospital, during the events of the preceding week or two, and they were on their way back to a remnant of the battalions they had left. Their chief interest was not in the mass movements of the army, or where the lines were if there were any lines, but in the fate of the men in their battalions. Who had survived? Who had crossed the river before the bridge was blown up at Mora? Who had swum the river? Who was still lost on the other side? They showed their hold on life by their language. They said things like this: "No news of Merriman yet? Maybe he got back today." Merriman, of course, was dead.

They kept an active ear for airplanes, all of them, for this Barcelona–Tarragona road had been machine-gunned often during the preceding week. Once we stopped to listen attentively, but the sound we heard was made by one of the Valencia–Barcelona freight trains struggling up the coast road. It was getting colder. We in the back seat fell asleep, and an hour or two passed in the cold and the dark while the car turned off the Tarragona road and headed for Reus. At Reus we stopped to take gasoline, somewhere in the middle of the town, and encountered a truck from the 15th Brigade there. In the blaze of light from their headlights and ours the men met and talked. The dusty gray walls of the houses were just visible on the edge of the light. It was very cold now, and the men from the truck were beating their hands together and stamping their feet to get warm. The conversation consisted of the exchange of news. Where are you going, where do you come from, what do they say there? Any news of Merriman? No. Has Doran come back? No, he's not back yet.

We all got back into the car and started out again. But it was late now, past midnight, and there was not much sense in going all the way to the Ebro when we did not know what we would find there. Some miles beyond Reus (at a place which I afterwards learned was called Rio de Cols) there was a 35th Division base hospital established. Al turned the car in at the gate here and parked it in the driveway. We went up the graveled walk of what seemed in the dark to be a big place and pushed the door open. There was a sentry there (there had been two at the gate) who did not bother us. Al, at least, was in uniform.

Inside the door of the hospital we saw a tiled hall into which a little light came from another room beyond, by the stairs. We could just make out some men sleeping on the floor, rolled in their blankets. Al went over to the room where the light was, and an Englishwoman's voice floated out to us over his shoulder: "Of course you can sleep here!

Of course! But I'm afraid there's only the floor. Wouldn't you like some coffee? I can make some hot for you."

There was a rumble of assent from the darkness. She came out into the hall with a lighted candle in her hand. She was the night nurse: a rounded, innocent face, an eager, busy look. She had been a trained hospital nurse in England, and I think she looked like a nurse.

"Come into the kitchen, boys," she said in a voice extraordinarily like her face, rounded and innocent but brisk. "There's plenty of coffee, and it 'll be hot in a minute."

We went into the kitchen and stood about there drinking coffee out of tin cans while she exchanged her bits of news for such as we had brought. Although this hospital was fairly near the front, she knew even less than we had heard in Barcelona.

"I know Merriman and Doran are not back yet," she said, "but I can't tell you about anybody else. They're turning up here, you know. A lot of them have come in here, I don't know why. They probably got across the river lower down. We've had a lot today. Americans, English, Canadians, French, everything. Don't you want some more coffee? Have you got your blankets? I'm afraid there are no beds free, but you're welcome to the floor."

After we had drunk our fill of the hot coffee (it was hardly coffee, but it was hot) we went out into the dark hall and found ourselves places near the end opposite the entrance. Al Cohen and Jim Bourne elected to go out and sleep in the car. The rest of us went to sleep on the tiles. Sometime in the middle of the night I heard the droning noise of airplanes, but when I awoke it turned out to be the Canadian next to me, snoring.

We got up early and had some more coffee. There were plenty of people who got up with the daylight in this place

—men who had arrived the day before, looking for their units; men who were slightly wounded, waiting for a doctor; nurses rubbing the sleep from their eyes and looking for something to do. The tiled hall of the house, when it filled with light from the glass doors at the garden end, was like what you might have expected—rather crowded, not very clean, with unshaven men in rags sitting against the wall on the floor and waiting. "We have only been here two days," the little English nurse explained. "We're not arranged properly yet. By the time we've got it fixed properly we shall probably get orders to move again. That's the way it always is." She seemed cheerful about it.

We went out and got into the car. The driveway now was filled with men who stood about, talked when they found somebody to talk to, and waited. Many had been sleeping in the garden under the bushes; many had come in during the night from their wanderings; some had been hanging about the base hospital for a day or two, trying to find out where to go. These were shreds of the remnants of an army. They all wanted news, and we had nothing much of the kind to give them. Al backed the car around through the crowd, got through the gate and turned to the left on the road to Falset and Mora.

There was not much more level ground. After the village of Rio de Cols, a little further along, the rise began; before long we were climbing the stiff unfertile hills where the brown rock and yellow clay stuck out bare between occasional black-green scrub. It reminded me of New Mexico, and I wondered again (for the hundredth time) why the places Spaniards went to in the New World tended to be so much like parts of Spain—how they could have fallen upon just those places, that is, when they had no means of knowing beforehand. There were trucks moving up along this road, mostly with ammunition and guns, and there were occasional stragglers.

Above all there were refugees, whom I had never seen before out on the roads. It had been too dark for them to travel last night. Now we passed whole caravans of them, moving with all their household goods in toward Barcelona and away from the guns. These were no doubt the inhabitants of Mora de Ebro and other villages recently taken by the Fascists. They moved in wagons or carts drawn by horses, donkeys or (once in a while) oxen. The father of the family, if there was one, usually walked alongside; the women sat impassively on top of their piled-up bedding and goods in the wagons. They had weather-beaten faces, inured to suffering, and there was seldom a sign of emotion as they moved slowly onward from everything they had known in life to the uncertainties of a refugee camp in wartime. They were of all ages, and only the very young or the very old seemed to be shaken out of composure by the tragedy that had befallen them. The very old were sometimes seen to be weeping; the young children, unaware of the reasons for their trek, were often laughing and playing games. It was strangely moving to see them laugh and salute us with the clenched fist as we passed. Afterwards I was to see many such migrations, both in the north and in the south, but they never ceased to arrest my attention so that I could see nothing else for a while after our paths had crossed.

At a place near the summit of this sierra we stopped to get some water: a fountain was built there against the mountainside and the spring poured out abundantly, very cold and pure. There was a detachment from the English battalion camped in the hollow beyond the fountain—medical service, I think. As usual, their camp of three or four tents, being a fixed point, had attracted a number of the stragglers who did not yet know where to go. They wore a strange assortment of clothing, for they had all lost their uniforms at some time or other and had been dressed (generally after swimming the Ebro) by the Spanish peasants out of whatever rags happened to be at hand.

The road beyond the fountain climbed sharply for another half-hour or so, twisting its way to and fro over the mountainsides and through the gray town of Falset, crowded with military trucks. This, too, had been bombed. We heard airplanes two or three times, and saw them in the distance, but they did not come over us. At last we passed what appeared to be the last summit of the sierra and ran along a plateau where there were planted fields and olive groves and a few almond trees in blossom. A smaller road crossed ours somewhere toward the middle of the flat high land; here Al stopped the car and we all got out. The 15th Brigade was somewhere here, in the fields and ravines of the plateau, although there were no visible signs of an army. A Spanish soldier came down the side road and gave us directions: we were to go straight ahead and look for the Estado Mayor on the right.

We walked down the road toward the Ebro, which we could not yet see. The sun had been getting warmer; it was now near ten o'clock, we were peeling off our sweaters, and the cold of the night before was hard to remember. There was a moderately active artillery duel (if a thing so one-sided can be called a duel) going on in the neighborhood, and the shells could be heard whistling mightily along the river valley and between the walls of the sierra, but none were coming in our direction. At the right of the road, after a few minutes, we saw heads popping up out of the ditch; two or three men scrambled out and came toward us, hailing Al and Jim and the rest of them with the usual request for news. The Estado Mayor was in this ditch, we learned. The Canadians and Jim Bourne vanished, having learned where they were supposed to go; Al led the way down the ditch to the Estado Mayor.

The deep ditch along the roadside had been made still deeper and equipped with a field telephone. Such a ditch in such country reminded me strongly of the lines held by Abd-el-Krim in another war thirteen years ago, across the straits in Morocco. There were men going up and down the ditch, standing in groups talking, or perched in any hollow in its side. Further down we came on three uniformed officers around the field telephone and Al introduced me to them. There was Vladimir Copic, the commander of the 15th Brigade, and there were two Englishmen: Wattis, with gray hair and a look of indignation, and Malcolm Dunbar.

Copic was a man of forty-two or forty-three, I suppose, and he and Wattis were the only ones I can remember in the 15th Brigade who appeared to have reached such an advanced age. Malcolm Dunbar, who was standing there with them, looked his full twenty-two, and so uncommonly trim and tidy that I was startled. His uniform seemed to have been freshly pressed, and he had unquestionably shaved that morning. He looked, in fact, like one of the officers in that play *Journey's End* which aroused so many profitable patriotic sentiments in the theater business a few years ago. When he spoke, even if it was only a word, the accent of the university snapped in the air. Here was one member of the British upper class, I reflected, who would probably not end in Whitehall.

Copic sat down on a heap of dirt, pulled out his map and began to tell me what had happened to his brigade. He spoke Spanish at first, mixed with English, but we finally settled upon German as a compromise. He had been an opera singer at home in Yugoslavia, I believe, and still gratified the brigade from time to time by bursting into song on special occasions. He was very grave and intent this morning, with perhaps a shade of self-justification in his account of the events that had taken place in the past few days—a self-justification which was wholly unnecessary, as Napoleon himself could never have extricated the brigade from the positions they had been in beyond the Ebro. The lines had broken badly in many places, and parts of the brigade had been cut off; the British, Americans and Canadians, with their Spanish comrades, had paid heavily; of the six hundred and fifty Americans who had been in the Lincoln Battalion at Batella, less than a hundred were present to be counted this morning. Copic went into all this in detail, showing me on his Michelin map just where the battalions had been and what had happened to them. I followed the general line of his story, but it came to life for me much more after about half an hour, when I left him to his work and wandered down the ditch talking to various survivors of the retreat.

They were all young, all more or less in rags, and all very glad to be on this side of the Ebro. Every one I spoke to had a tale to tell, but it wasn't always easy to get the tale started; they all wanted to hear news much more than they wanted to talk. There were Americans, Canadians, British and Spanish in the 15th Brigade, and some representatives of each nationality were to be found wandering up and down the ditch. They had been in a desperate losing battle that had lasted three weeks (from March 10 to April 3) and during the last few days of the struggle, after the general collapse of the army, they had been in headlong flight. Some had crossed the Ebro at Mora with the detachment commanded by Copic and had then blown up the bridge; others had been with other detachments, cut off in the hills, and had made their way in small groups or alone through the Fascist lines at night until they reached the river and swam it. There were some who could not swim and had wandered down all the way to Tortosa to cross on the bridge there. There were some who had swum the river while the Fascists were firing on them from the other bank, and had seen their friends killed in the river.

The brigade had been at Belchite when the Fascist offensive began on March 10. The army to the north collapsed almost immediately, Belchite was outflanked and overpowered by bombing, shelling and machine-gunning from the air; the retreat started under conditions which were bound to turn it into a rout in time. The whole countryside was unfortified; a company was asked to take a position which was supposed to be ready for them and which (if they ever found it) would turn out to be a shallow line scooped out of the ground. Again and again this happened, and they stood in positions where there were neither cover nor places for the guns. To make such a position ready would have taken them a day's digging, and in an hour or two the Fascists were upon them again with aviation and artillery. The Fascists were using Italian and German aviation in great force (four or five hundred of them must have been employed in pressing the retreat) and their effect was paralyzing upon a body of infantry with no cover and hardly any support from artillery or airplanes. At Caspe and Alcaniz the brigade had held again for a while, but again they were outflanked by the collapse of other units further along. And when they broke this time, it was final; Gandesa was hardly defended: they were shattered into groups which fled across the hills to the Ebro. Many lost their bearings in the night and were to be heard of (if at all) months later as prisoners of the Fascists; many were killed; not one out of six had come back, by this morning, just two days later.

It was almost incredible, when you thought of it, that these boys (they were all very young) could have gone through such an experience and come out of it still eager to know what Neville Chamberlain was doing, what Léon Blum or Chautemps would do, or what had happened in Austria. And yet that was the way their minds worked. They asked a very large number of questions which I could not answer because I had been too much interested in their own fate for the past week to read the newspapers on other subjects. And they had theories, too—large theories about what France and England would be obliged to do in the event this happened or the other thing happened. They retained at that time a touching faith in the possibility of France and England doing anything. Some of these lads were capable of elaborating on their political and diplomatic theories at indefinite length unless headed off—and all I wanted to know was their stories of escape to this side of the river.

They were amazing stories, too, when I did get them. At Villalba, above Gandesa, a fairly big group of Americans had passed through German troops without being challenged; in another place a group had been challenged by Fascist patrols and had replied with the name of a Spanish unit on the Fascist side; others had come through the Fascist lines singly in the darkness. It sounded to me as if the Fascists themselves, with their mixture of Italians, Germans, Moors and Navarrese, must have been in considerable disorder by this time, uncertain of their lines and of which units held which places; they had been advancing very fast in unfamiliar country, and had done a great many flanking movements, so that they hardly knew where they were or who were supposed to be their neighbors. The survivors of the 15th Brigade, by luck, courage and endurance, arrived on the banks of the Ebro, and were still arriving that day and for days afterwards. Most of them had passed through an enemy army to get here, and some of them were hardly aware of it; none seemed to realize, just then, what an astounding thing it was. They would break off their stories in the middle—out of sheer boredom, no doubt—to ask with eagerness: "What is Chamberlain going to do?" It would have taken more brass than I possessed to tell them at that moment, in that ditch, that Chamberlain was preparing to make a compact with Mussolini.

2

After an hour or two of this I went out by myself to have a look at the Ebro. The flat land was above Mora la Nueva, and by walking across it to the edge of the olive grove I could get a view of the river valley and of the hills opposite, now occupied by the Fascists. I wandered about there for some time, trying to imagine what the stories I had just heard were actually like when they happened two days or three days before. The valley looked peaceful enough in the warm spring sun. There were even a few peasants working in the fields around here, apparently without a thought for the shells which continued to whistle along the valley at fairly frequent intervals. You could hear the shell fired, and then hear its trajectory in a whistling moan, and then the detonation when it landed. None of them appeared to be coming this way: they were all aimed further north. The river was in flood, of course: then, as six months later, the Fascists had opened the floodgates higher up, near Saragossa, so that the current would rise and sweep away all but the strongest bridges and make a natural frontier. That yellow flood down there—glittering silver and gold now, in the sun—was what these men in the brigade swam through, often under fire, as they made their miraculous escape to this place. Many men had died in the river; some had been drowned.

You were not supposed to make yourself visible here, as it was in plain view of the Fascist lines on the other side of the river; so I stuck close to the olive trees. After a while I heard Al Cohen shout for me and went back to the road.

"Come on down to the battalion," he said, "and we'll eat."

The battalion was the Lincoln-Washington, made up of the remains of the two American battalions named after Lincoln and Washington; it was itself only a remnant now. It had been quartered in an area off the smaller road which crossed the main Mora–Falset–Reus highway at this point. Al led me down the side road through planted fields (onions, carrots, cabbages, potatoes, unfortunately none of them far enough along to be eaten). Here, at a place indicated to us by a lazily grinning Spanish sentry, we turned down a path that sloped through the fields. After twenty yards or so the fields broke up into ravines of clay and rock. These ravines were the present quarters of the Americans. One such ditch, a large one which opened from our path on the left with a space as formal as a door, was the particular hole in the ground occupied by the Estado Mayor of the battalion—i.e., its ranking officers and commissars.

Al was greeted with shouts of welcome here, where eight or ten men sat on the ground. The hole was a natural shelter, with steep clay and rock sides where mountain scrub grew. It opened at the side, with the doorlike space through which we had entered, and at the end where it sloped downhill to other ravines and open fields. The man in charge of things appeared to be Johnny Gates, who was to be made political commissar of the whole 15th Brigade a day or so later. He was a small, compact young fellow in a sweater and a stocking cap, with a quiet voice and an air of good sense. Another was George Watt, who had swum the Ebro the day before: very tall, thin and fair, dressed in one of the strangest collections of rags a man has ever been able to pick up in a hurry. There was a long Tennesseean there whose name I have never been able to remember; his clothing was made entirely of patches. Even the patches had dragged apart and were connected only by a kind of openwork design of thread through which his lean shanks gaped. He, too, had swum the river the day before, and his patchwork covering was the gift of a peasant on this side.

We joined the assembled company on the ground. It was warm and pleasant here in the sun. We had a few cigarettes, and everybody smoked (except Gates, who never did). They had not had a cigarette in ten days or so, and made an occasion of it. Comrade Archer, the battalion's cook—a burly American Negro who had the knack of making food out of nothing—came in for a serious consultation with Gates about the organization of the kitchen. Archer had only been back a day, but was ready and anxious to organize. I think this was my first acquaintance with the slightly special flavor of the word "organize" as used in Spain, where it takes the place of half a dozen other verbs both in Spanish and in the languages of the internationals.

The food came along—not cooked by Archer today—and proved to be a kind of stew with beans in it. There was no water, but Gates fished a bottle of champagne cider out of a hole in the ground and we drank that. We had finished the stew and were about to eat some chestnuts when the hum of airplanes was heard.

"Take it easy, fellows," Gates advised. "Just see where they are."

Somebody stuck his head over the edge of the ditch and reported that they were coming our way. The first bombs began to thunder somewhere on the riverbank, or so it sounded to me.

"Scatter and take cover," Gates said in his quiet voice. "Take it easy, take it easy."

Cover was not available, except that by getting as close as possible to the bits of mountain scrub around the ravine we might hope to be invisible from the air. We each grabbed a bush and hung on to it. We were scattered enough so that all would not have been killed even if a bomb had landed in the ditch. The bombs were raining down now, somewhere near, in a close series of reverberating explosions. In a minute or two the planes came directly over us, flying very high—a large number of Savoia-Marchetti bombers, their distinctive white-and-silver bodies flashing beautifully in the sun. We tried to count them and came to no agreement. On their left a swarm of black devils that looked like Junkers were sweeping along to keep them company. They passed over, the thunder of their bombs still sounding, and we breathed a little more freely. There was no antiaircraft to be heard, but in a minute or two there was the bitter crackle of machine-gunning in the air.

"They're coming back," somebody reported, having crawled to the edge of the ditch to have a look.

We got back to our bits of mountain scrub again and made ourselves as unnoticeable as we could. The planes

[56]

swept over us again, white-and-silver and black ones separated, as before. This time I was fairly sure of my count, and it was more than fifty. I saw no Republican airplanes, and yet the machine-gunning was constant. The bombs continued for another two or three minutes, dying away down along the riverbank to the south. We gathered again in the middle of the ravine and proceeded to eat our chestnuts, washed down by the remains of the champagne cider.

The episode (once it was over) meant nothing to the men in the ravine. It was another bombing from the air. They had been through hundreds of them. But except for one bad bombing in Morocco thirteen years before, with five planes operating, I had never been directly underneath a raid of bombers before. Our raids in Barcelona during the preceding week had been noisy but remote affairs, and the airplanes had not actually come over us in the middle of the city. This was therefore the first time that I had been beneath so many bombers, and very nearly (or so it felt) the first time I had been in an air raid. It was curious, the feeling of relief when the planes could be heard no more. Even more curious was the way in which the men in the ravine took it all as a matter of course. They were relieved too, naturally, but the experience was an old one to them.

"When I start to make laws," Al said, "I'm going to make a law abolishing all airplanes. Anybody who makes an airplane or sells one or flies one will be put in jail."

This plan received the approbation of the assembled company, and stories of bombings began to come out. Ever since March 10 at Belchite these boys had been subjected to the constant attentions of the German and Italian airplanes, with hardly ever a Republican plane to oppose them. I asked what had happened in our raid. Differences of opinion at once began to appear. It was agreed that the machine-gunning probably meant a "dogfight" (i.e., that Republican chasers had gone up to meet the invaders and driven them back) but nobody had actually seen a Republican plane. My suggestion that the machine-gunning might have been from the Fascist planes attacking a ground concentration was not well received. The hypothesis of the "big dogfight" was accepted, and for the next two or three days I was to hear about the "big dogfight" all up and down the line, although I never met anybody who had actually seen it. You don't get a very good view from a ditch. The long Tennesseean in the patchwork garments was cynical about the whole matter.

"All airplanes," he drawled, "are Fascist airplanes until you know different."

3

We met and talked to various men of the battalion later. They were all quartered in the ditches of the neighborhood; all were unshaven, lousy and in rags; all wanted to know if anything had been heard of Merriman (brigade chief of staff) or Doran (brigade commissar), and all wanted to know what Chamberlain was going to do. Alvah Bessie, an American writer who had once worked on the Paris *Times*, of which I was also an alumnus, was among these; he had been through the whole retreat from Belchite, and was one of ninety men who started the flight from beyond Villalba to the Ebro together. Of the ninety only four had reached this side of the river. I remember thinking that if Alvah Bessie survived this campaign he would have something outside the usual line of writers' goods to write about. At the moment he was chiefly interested in the food brought up by the soup truck, which was late and not very appetizing.

Chances to go back down the road to the base hospital were not numerous, and Al and I cadged a lift in the Canadians' soup truck, which was returning to their kitchen back of the lines. I wanted to go back to Barcelona and get a lot of cigarettes (mine were all gone now) and some food if any could be found. The Canadians took us on their truck, which rocked crazily down the mountain road at what seemed a frantic speed; in front of the first autopark of the 15th Brigade, three or four miles down the road, it slowed up a little to let us off.

The autopark was operating under difficulties. Many trucks had been lost in the retreat—bombed, machine-gunned or abandoned. There was a shortage of every kind of transport, and such cars and trucks as were available were old rattletraps held together with safety pins and string. The demands for transport that came in to the autopark were impossible to satisfy, and it required the temperament of a philosopher to keep the place going at all. Louis Secundy, who was in charge there, appeared to possess what was needed; he would chew a piece of grass and grin when excited demands arrived for transport that did not exist. I stayed at the autopark for an hour or so, waiting for a lift down toward Reus. Secundy gratified us with a few succinct remarks about the difficulties of working in transport under the conditions of the retreat; he wanted to get back into the infantry. A Jewish boy who looked about seventeen or eighteen was working on the motor of a truck which had broken down. At one point he straightened up from his work and said thoughtfully: "I promised my mother I would be home for Passover, but I guess I won't get there now."

Presently one of the trucks was stuck together again and pronounced ready to take the road. Louis gave me a place

in this with the driver, a youth who hailed from my own
university (Chicago). All the way down the mountain road,
as we twisted and turned noisily, the whole truck threatening to disintegrate at each bump, this young man lectured
me about the meaning of international events, the policy
of England and France, the necessity of fighting Fascism on
all fronts, and the dangers that a Fascist victory in Spain
would represent for the so-called democracies. He was
fluent, well informed and intelligent, but I had trouble
during the discourse; there was something funny about his
fierce earnestness and his capacity for forgetting every immediate detail (his flight to the Ebro; the breakdown of
transport; the precariousness of this very truck, not to speak
of hunger, danger and fatigue) in the high preoccupations
of *Weltpolitik*. He was about twenty years old and had been
in Spain for nearly a year. He took me all the way back to
the base hospital at Rio de Cols and let me off there; he
was going on to Reus.

The gardens and house at the base hospital were crowded
now. It was late afternoon and stragglers had been coming
in all day long asking for their units. Some were wounded
and needed treatment. I found doctors and nurses who were
not busy just then and told them what I wanted: a lift to
Barcelona. They looked dubious. Bill Pyke said he didn't
think anything would be going to Barcelona that evening,
but if I would wait until the morning . . . And anyhow
Comrade Anny, who was in charge of the house arrangements, could find me a bed. Comrade Anny frowned at
me fiercely when she heard this, but she did find me a bed in
the hall upstairs, and produced a blanket to go with it, talking vigorously all the while in Austrian-English about the
war and the revolution.

The house had been the country place of a rich Catalan

painter before the war, and some of his handiwork still
ornamented the great tiled hall. The gardens, although
neglected, had plenty of roses that would be in bloom in another month. There were gravel walks, a pool in a grove,
and some trees on the other side to shut off the fields. The
driveway was choked with battered ambulances now, and
there were hundreds of men, it seemed, swarming over the
place, washing in the pool, repairing their shoes, cooking,
eating, sitting, talking. When it got dark the scene inside the
house, by very sparse candlelight, was vivid: unshaven men,
many of them in rags, very tired and very hungry, crowding up for food from the kitchen. There was bread for
everybody, and there was meat cooked in olive oil. In the
half-darkness, as we stood about eating, American nurses
appeared: Fanny and Gracie. An English voice that
sounded like a Bloomsbury intellectual: another nurse,
Phyllis. Phyllis had been a nurse in the 15th Brigade long
enough to learn some of the American language that had
penetrated all the battalions, and she referred to all males as
"guys". It sounded funny in her Cambridge-and-Blooms-
bury voice.

After the meal was over there was a meeting. One of the
chief political commissars of the 35th Division spoke in
Spanish for half an hour, analyzing the reasons for the
Aragon defeat and saying that if the right steps were taken
it could not happen again. Like most other people at the
front, he seemed inclined to blame everything on Indalecio
Prieto, the minister of defense, although he did not actually
pronounce that name. The men stood or sat in the dimly
lighted hall, on the dark stairs, in the doorways that led to
the wards. You could occasionally hear the moaning of
wounded men from in there. Speechmaking was apparently
a favorite pastime in this superserious and ultrapolitical

[61]

army, for the men listened with attention and applauded whenever the speaker made a point. When he had finished Dr Freedman, the chief of the American surgeons in the division, translated into English. This happened with two more speakers, and by that time I was ready to creep upstairs in the dark and get into my fine bed with the blanket. As I was going to sleep I could hear the oratory still rolling out, broken by hearty applause.

4

In the morning there was an ambulance going in to Barcelona to pick up supplies. Dr Freedman, two nurses, a Spanish officer, the driver and Bill Pyke and I made a good load for it. It was a ramshackle ambulance, in thick green-and-yellow camouflage, with bullet holes in the side and not a piece of glass left, but it served. The ambulances on the whole were in a bad state; many had been lost across the Ebro; some of the best drivers had been killed; the field hospital had been machine-gunned out of existence. There was one spanking new ambulance in the yard of the hospital which had not been in the campaign across the Ebro. It was marked as the gift of the workers of Barre and Montpelier, in Vermont.

It took about three hours to reach Barcelona in our battered vehicle. As we were coming back the same day, this gave us little enough time there. I wanted chiefly cigarettes and knew where I could get them. I went to Jim Lardner's room in the hotel and told him none of the Americans out at Mora had any cigarettes. He had brought in a good many, and handed over about half his supply at once. I had time for a bath and a meal before Freedman appeared again with the ambulance and we started back.

On the way out again he told me the story of the bombing of the hospital at Hijar. I had already heard something about it and questioned him. The hospital there was set up in a tent just behind the lines. Freedman—he was a surgeon from Hackensack, New Jersey—was amputating a leg when the Fascist airplanes came over the hospital and began to bomb. Instructions were that everybody in such a case should lie flat on the floor. Freedman was in the midst of the amputation and wanted to resume it as soon as possible. He ordered all the others in the tent to lie down on the floor; he knelt beside the patient on the operating table, keeping his hands lifted so as to preserve the asepsis. The bombs rained down all around the tent and there was one direct hit in a corner. A Spanish *sanitario* was killed, one American nurse (Helen Freeman) was severely wounded in the head and arm, and the table next to the one used for the operation was riddled with shrapnel; but both Freedman and his patient were untouched. Freedman got up when the raid was over and completed the amputation with success.

The base hospital was not so overrun when we reached it again that evening. Most of the men who had crowded the driveway in the morning had found out where to go and had gone there. It was now Thursday, April 7, and the terrible confusion of four days before was rapidly being overcome. We heard when we got into the hospital that Wolff and Lamb, the ranking officers of the Lincoln Battalion, who had been missing since the disaster, had come back. The nurse who told us this—it was Fanny, the American girl—announced it like a victory. Here we also heard for the first time of the epic escape of Freddy Keller, the battalion commissar, who had been taken prisoner and escaped by killing a guard and then swam the Ebro three times—the first time to show the other escaped prisoners

that it could be done; then back and over again with them
—receiving sharp punishment in the form of rifle wounds on
the third trip.

There was no means of getting up to the front that evening, and Comrade Anny (still unwilling) had to find another bed for me. In the morning, by a combination of lifts
—an ambulance to the autopark and the British soup truck
from there—I reached the crossroads above Mora de Ebro
again and made my way down to the ravines belonging to
the Lincoln Battalion. All the difficulties of transport under
the hitchhike system made it seem at least a month since I
had been here, and evidences of "organization" in the
meantime were soon apparent. For one thing, there was a
sign stuck in the field where the path turned off the road,
saying in plain if inelegant letters: "Lincoln Battalion."
Then, when I came to the ravine where I had been the
other day, it had changed too. At one end straw had been
strewn thickly over the ground, and above this a roof had
been made of pine branches. In the sumptuous apartment
thus created were my friends of the other day, but shaved
and reclothed now in approximately uniform manner. There
were George Watt, Alvah Bessie and some others, and they
were about to eat. They told me their news: there had been
clothing issued, the food was better, Malcolm Dunbar was
going to be the brigade's chief of staff and Johnny Gates
was the new brigade commissar, so long as Merriman and
Doran continued missing; Wolff had come back to command the battalion again, although nobody had seen him
yet, and the Canadians had received some cigarettes.

The food arrived, and, at the same time, from another
direction, so did Milt Wolff. We heard a shout down
beyond the end of our ravine; more shouts; a Spanish voice
yelling "El Lobo!" and just as I was about to find out from

[64]

somebody the reason for the riot, Wolff appeared, loping angularly up from the fields down there, shaking hands right and left as he came and making a quick job of it. He had to bend nearly double to get into our shelter at the end of the ravine.

"You built this thing plenty low," he said. "I guess you guys didn't think I was coming back."

I don't know whether they thought he was coming back or not, but there was no doubt of his welcome. Nobody said anything in particular, but it was obvious that they all felt about forty times better than they had a few minutes before. Wolff folded his immense length into a corner on the straw and demanded food. The food was there—it had come almost unnoticed—and it was good: beans cooked in American fashion, remote from olive oil. There was also plenty of bread and some French chocolate. But before Wolff had made much headway with the beans a Spanish runner appeared, wild with excitement, yelling "El Lobo!" and grasped his hand as if he would never let it go. The occasion for this demonstration was some American mail which had just arrived, and the Spaniard had been elected to deliver Wolff's batch. Good as it was, the food had difficulty competing with the letters after that.

Milt Wolff was twenty-three years old; he had been in the battalion for over a year then, had been in every campaign since Brunete, and had never been wounded. They told many stories in the battalion about him. One was that when he got his first promotion he tried to refuse it because he did not want to leave his gun (he was a machine gunner then). He took command of the battalion after the third or fourth day at Belchite; and in the rout on that terrible night when the brigade was smashed, he had been cut off behind the Fascist lines. For four days and nights nobody in the battalion had seen him; he had been wandering alone in the hills on the other side of the river, getting through the Fascists when he could, hidden by the peasants in their lofts when he couldn't. He had swum the river the day before, lower down, and had been finding the battalion since then. Now he sat doubled up over his beans and his letters, his gaunt young face frowning with concentration. I think he knew how glad they all were to see him, and wanted to ignore it as much as possible. He commanded the battalion from that day until the end.

5

I spent that night in the medical post up at the cross-roads. I had been trying, with no success, to cadge a lift down to the base hospital, but there was no movement of transport after dark, and somebody told me to take shelter (as I had no blanket) inside the farmhouse there.

The ground floor of this establishment was chiefly stable, and rich with odors; but upstairs in the loft there was a clean-swept floor, candlelight and a bottle of red wine. The staff at the medical post consisted of four men: a very young doctor from Philadelphia, assisted by an ex-actor from Los Angeles, an ex-miner from Illinois, and a Spaniard who had worked in California for seventeen years and had become an American. They gave me a fine sanitary stretcher to sleep on (the advantage being that lice and other insects did not crawl up the steel supports) and some hours of talk before we went to sleep. In the morning we were all blown out of our beds by the new antiaircraft gun which had been installed just across the road. We saw no airplanes, but the gunners apparently did. My friend the doctor went out and parleyed for me with a truck that was going down the line; with that, and another truck, and the aid of Louis Secundy for another truck or two, I eventually reached the base hospital at Rio de Cols.

Here it appeared that I might remain for almost any number of days, as no transport appeared to be moving at all. In the warm sunlight the nurses sat on the graveled driveway and rolled bandages. I went into the wards and talked to some of the wounded Americans, each of whom had his story. There was a little flurry of excitement when some airplanes came over, but no bombs fell. Late in the afternoon there was another alarm. We heard some bombs in the distance, and some Fascist planes came directly over the hospital without bombing it. This alarm had the effect of driving a motorcar in off the road—an old Barcelona taxicab which looked like the most splendid limousine alongside the battered trucks and ambulances which stood in the driveway. The car had an American flag on it, and contained Colonel Fuqua, the American military attaché, with Bob Okin of the Associated Press and Leigh White (then of Reuter's). They took me back to Barcelona.

I saw the Americans of the 15th Brigade on a number of occasions after that, but those not very remarkable meetings in the first week made the most lasting impression on me. I suppose the existence of the internationals—of all the International Brigades then contained in the 35th and 45th divisions of the 5th Corps of the Spanish army—was suddenly proved to me with startling reality. I knew their story, roughly. The first of them (mostly Germans) had appeared at Madrid in November, 1936, and many had died there in Madrid's defense. The French had been next in time and number; the anti-Fascist Italians, the Yugoslavs and other southeastern Europeans (including a good many Czechs) and the British, Americans and Canadians had appeared first during the first dreadful winter. The American battalions (there were two to start with) had fought in the campaigns of Jarama and Brunete (for Madrid), in the Quinto campaign (for Aragon), at Teruel and now in this second and disastrous Aragon campaign. But knowing their story, on paper or by hearsay, was not at all the same thing as seeing them there as they returned from the catastrophe, after three weeks of the most ghastly punishment that overwhelming superiority of aviation and artillery could inflict upon them. They had seen their friends butchered; they had been in such acute danger that it is a wonder any of them got across the Ebro again; they had been hungry and cold for a long time, and their clothes were in tatters. A certain number of them had been, of course, dispirited by such a succession of calamities, and there was plenty of grumbling to be heard here and there, as well as some evidences of shell shock and demoralization. There had been (or so I heard) some desertions. But most of the ones I saw—and I wandered about among them pretty freely—startled me by their indomitable spirit, their refusal to recognize even implicitly that this defeat might affect the outcome of the war, their easy, cheerful and implacable resolution. I had been in Pennsylvania only a few weeks before, and had visited Valley Forge on a day of thick white snow when it was easy to imagine what the state of the Continental army must have been in the winter of 1777–78. These boys made me think of Washington's words inscribed on the national arch at Valley Forge: "Naked and starving as they are, we cannot enough admire the incomparable patience and fidelity of the soldiery." They owed this particular strength to their political convictions. The whole Spanish army was political; the system of commissars was instituted partly because the army was of political origin—not a professional soldiery—and partly to make it even more political, since it was clear from the beginning that the professional soldiers, in an enormous proportion, were partisans of the military chieftains who had revolted against the Republic in the service of Fascism, and that the strength of the Republic, if it was ever to have a formidable armed strength, must come from the convictions of its men. In the poverty of materials to which the sinister farce of "nonintervention" had condemned the Republic, the strength of the anti-Fascist cause had to come first of all (and sometimes only) from the willingness of its men to die for it.

In this matter the internationals had already passed through an apprenticeship by enlisting at all. It was difficult for them to get to Spain. All their own governments discouraged it. Their passports were not valid for Spain; the French were busily attempting to keep them from crossing the border; they were promised nothing but hardship and death when they got there. And yet they had come, from all the ends of the earth, from China, Mexico, California, Devonshire, Illinois, Texas and Croatia, in disobedience to their own civil authorities, to cross the Pyrenees on foot in the snow and fight for the Republic. In so doing they expressed their conviction that the struggle of the Spanish Republic against its rebellious generals and their German and Italian masters was in fact the struggle of common humanity against the black forces that everywhere threatened to overwhelm it. This conviction had been sometimes formalized into membership in the Communist party, as the most militant body at hand; a large proportion of the Americans, for example, were Communists. But they were by no means all Communist; there was every form of liberal idealism among them; and the vital thrust of their effort was magnificent.

The cause for which they fought in Spain was not Communism, but the right of the Spanish Republic to find its own peaceful solutions to its internal problems—that, and the necessity of raising a shield in time to defend ordinary mankind against the deadly reaction called Fascism. They had international minds, most of them ("What is Chamberlain going to do?"). They knew that Spain today is certainly no farther from London than Sevenoaks was in 1800. They were nearly all young, products of the age of communication, aware of the whole world as much as of their particular segment of it; they were young enough to do what they had to do in high spirits and (whenever possible) with a laugh. In the darkest moments of the whole dark year of 1938—even in Prague in September—I could think of the International Brigades in Spain and be sure that courage and generosity still existed somewhere on this planet. In such as these is the hope of the world; I think the only hope.

6

It was the next Friday—April 15, Good Friday—when I saw the Ebro again. I had been immobilized by the lack of a car, except for one day when a colleague (Okin of the Associated Press) took me along on a tour of the Segre front. For Friday I was promised a place in one of the cars belonging to the press and propaganda section of the Ministry of Foreign Affairs. It came to the Majestic Hotel at seven in the morning, but there was the usual difficulty in assembling all the passengers, and we started out the Tarragona road at eight. There were four of us, five with the driver: Joe North of the *Daily Worker*, Kell of the *Basler Nazionalzeitung*, Johnny Little and myself. The driver was one of those gems of character to be found sometimes in civilian offices in wartime, a firm devotee of peace, convinced that going to the front was a nonsensical foreign whim which ought to be discouraged. We had hardly left Barcelona before he began to find excuses for turning back; one of our chief difficulties throughout the day was that of promoting locomotion.

The news from the south was very bad, but as lacking in definition as most bad news is in war. We knew that Tortosa had been bombed every day from the air, that the action south of Tortosa had been very severe, and that the four regular Italian divisions were held off by Lister's division at Cherta in a combat which had lasted for some days. The news from San Mateo, further south, was not good. What we did not know was that General Garcia Valino's Navarrese—one of the best armies in the Fascist command, made up of fanatical Catholics who were told every day that the Republic was the enemy of their religion—were operating there in full strength.

The road to Tarragona showed nothing beyond the usual movements of troops and supplies, with an occasional caravan of refugees trekking slowly toward Barcelona. We got to the hill above Tortosa at about eleven and I had my first view of those desolate ruins. The Italians had been bombing Tortosa from the air for the past three weeks. It was very easy for them: they could dart in from the sea, rain bombs and disappear again before any Republican planes could have risen to meet them—even, that is, if there had been Republican planes available. The city was a rubbish heap with walls, parts of floors, sometimes a whole building, standing dusty and surprised amid the wreckage. We drove through it with care, for it was not always easy for the soldiers to keep a clear passageway for cars when every bombing threw down new masses of broken wood and stone, dust and paper and household goods shattered into bits. Here I saw two of the sights which impress everybody most after a bombing: the first was a house intact, on the edge of the city, its women and children still busy about the place. The second was a house which had been cut in two by a bomb, with the bed and chairs and table and mirror in a second-floor room still untouched, although the whole wall had gone. These are common sights in the tortured Republic, as I knew from the villages up on the Segre, and as I was to observe often thereafter; but there is something in both phenomena which so flings ordinary life into your face in the midst of death that your imagination jumps at it with wonder.

The Ebro was wide and deep here, its swift yellow flood broadening beyond Tortosa to Amposta, the delta and the sea. There were three bridges: the main bridge over which we drove; an older, narrower and less stable secondary bridge, no longer used; and the railroad bridge for the main line from Barcelona to Valencia. On the southern side of the Ebro there was a little more of the wrecked town (most of which was on the other bank). After that the motor highway opened out, straight and smooth, all the way to Valencia.

We crossed the bridge a little after eleven o'clock in the morning, and had a few minutes of peaceful progress before we were stopped by waving arms and warning shouts. Two trucks had stopped in the road, and their crews were giving us notice that there were airplanes. We stopped the car and took to the ditch alongside the road. The airplanes were there, circling about, not far away from us—perhaps observing or photographing Tortosa. At any rate they dropped no bombs, but vanished after a few minutes, and we resumed our journey.

THE EBRO

The road had been fairly crowded toward Tortosa, but it was noticeable that there were fewer trucks lower down. This made no impression on me—in fact, the events of that day dawned on me so slowly that it was over before I realized the extent of their meaning. We continued on our way without stopping to ask questions of the occasional military posts we passed. We had set out that morning to go to Vinaroz, and knew no reason why we should not proceed.

At some distance down the road (perhaps fifteen minutes from Tortosa) we passed an olive grove where a group of correspondents from Barcelona were gathered, eating sandwiches. These were Martha Gellhorn (*Collier's*), Tom Delmer (the *Daily Express*, London), Herbert Matthews (the New York *Times*) and Ernest Hemingway (the North American Newspaper Alliance). We stopped to talk to them, and discovered that we, too, had developed appetites. We sat down in the olive grove and had lunch. The quartet of colleagues who were already there were on their way back to Barcelona, having spent the morning further south; and although they were a little reticent about their findings, as is the way of correspondents before they have written their day's stint, we did gather that there was bad trouble lower down. In fact, Hemingway said we ought not to go beyond the crossroads at Santa Barbara, as there was a possibility or probability that the Fascists were advancing on both roads, and we might be caught in a trap.

But such warnings went out of our heads a few minutes later, for a phalanx of Savoia-Marchettis appeared from nowhere, directly over our heads, making for Tortosa. Their white-and-silver bodies were never so beautiful as in large numbers, and there were plenty of them now. They reached Tortosa; and as we stood there gaping, there began the

most concentrated bombing I ever saw. The planes un-
loaded as rapidly as possible, circling over the ruined city
and making way for others as soon as they could; the ruins
rose in the air in a great dark cloud, and the white puffs of
the antiaircraft shells exploding made a line above it—but
beneath, far beneath, the beautiful white-and-silver creatures that were showering destruction. Even though we
knew that they must be bombing the bridge, and that
among so many bombs one at least would surely reach its
target, we could hardly look at that spectacle without some
mixture of awe and excitement. There was one certainty:
the town was empty except for a handful of soldiers who
would take to the refuges, and there would be no dead or
wounded. But the bridge—well, the bridge would be gone,
and we might have to swim the Ebro, which in my case
would have been an enterprise as nearly impossible as
anything could be.

We were all counting the airplanes, and, as usual, arriving
at different results. Herbert Matthews made his count forty-
eight, which was probably right, as he was greatly experienced in such matters. My own count was about ten
less than that. Whatever the number, it was enough. They
went away, and we sat down again to consider; but not for
long. They came back again and again—six times in all,
during about one hour—and at the end it would have been
sheer miracle if the bridge had been untouched. We had
witnessed (in perfect safety—which is rare) one of the
most decisive of all bombings, one of the few in which
aviation alone has accomplished a strategic operation of the
first importance.

Hemingway tried to impress upon us again that we ought
not to go farther than Santa Barbara, but I suppose what he
said did not travel much beyond my ears. His was in some

respects a military mind; at any rate he had the faculty of seeing a whole military position at once (as good commanders have). I was, as usual, going along in the dark—never more so than on this day—and unable to realize anything which I did not actually see with my own eyes. Consequently I was all for continuing as far as we could go on this road, and the four of us, in agreement on that point, left the other four and set out again for Vinaroz.

At Santa Barbara, just the same, we stopped to inquire of the officers in charge at the crossroads. They said the Fascists were attacking on both the road from the west and the road from the south. They advised us to go no further, but made no move to stop us when we continued on our way.

Below Santa Barbara the road, the fields and the whole countryside were suddenly empty. There were no trucks, no straggling soldiers, no refugees; there was not even a peasant working in the fields as far as the horizon; there was nothing. I think this gave us some notion of what Hemingway was talking about. We agreed to stop at Ulldecona and make further inquiries.

Ulldecona had been badly and freshly bombed. It was empty, its wreckage surrounding intact houses where there was no sign of life. It looked like the villages that I had seen a few days earlier along the Segre, deserted and half in ruins. We were now about five miles from Vinaroz, and out of sheer obstinacy we intended to go on there if the military command would permit us to do so. We had some trouble finding the military command, but a lone soldier standing near a battered tank told us it was just beyond the town. We proceeded until we had left the last houses behind and came, abruptly, on a trench.

It was a shallow trench dug at right angles to the road,

sparsely manned by young fellows with rifles and machine guns. We stopped the car and got out. I counted about thirty men in the trench: it did not look like a formidable force, and yet the conviction was being slowly borne in upon me that this was the front line of the Republican army. The dark sierra directly in front of us was decorated with puffs of smoke, and there were perhaps two batteries up there, firing at—and being fired upon by—the Fascists. If there was another line it must be somewhere up there. Seven pursuit planes (they were Fiats, we were told) circled above the sierra and went away again.

We had a talk with the commander here. He seemed calm, even cheerful, and his boys in the trench saluted us with the clenched fist and broad grins, yet in what he told us there was not much cause for satisfaction. He said that the Fascists had broken through the Republican lines two days before, at San Mateo and Chert, by moving across the sierras and attacking the road from both sides. On the next day they had moved on to Calig, and this morning they had occupied San Jorge—two villages about three miles from Vinaroz, or a little less. The commander indicated the sierra in front of us and said that it was now held by tanks and artillery. (I believe there may have been a few tanks and two small batteries.) When we asked him about Vinaroz he shrugged his shoulders and said that he had heard nothing from there since noon.

All this combination of circumstances would have been as plain as a printed sign to Hemingway, for instance, but the civilian mind is infinitely slow to seize the truth of any military situation. As a matter of fact, at the very moment when we stood there in the trench at Ulldecona, General Garcia Valino and his Navarrese were entering Vinaroz. The Fascists had reached the sea. They had cut the Re-

public in two. They had achieved the main objective of
their great Aragon offensive. I was to read all about it a
week or so later, in the florid and interminable descriptions
sent to the Italian press by their special correspondents with
the Fascist army. Those accounts even described the "joy
and acclamations of the population" (*Popolo d'Italia*, April
16, 1938), although actually the population of Vinaroz, as
of Ulldecona and all these villages, had been evacuated the
day before. According to the accounts in the Fascist press,
General Garcia Valino entered Vinaroz at two o'clock in
the afternoon of April 15, and the place had been evacuated
by the Republicans during the preceding night. It was two
o'clock when we were in the trench at Ulldecona.

When we got into the car again and headed back toward
the Ebro I began to realize what the whole thing was—a
really tremendous event in the history of this war, perhaps
its turning point. All the instincts of the newspaper reporter awoke and became painful. I wanted to get to a telephone or a telegraph office at once and tell the story. It had
been nine years since I had done even the most occasional
work for a newspaper, and I had almost forgotten the
curious manias of the craft, but they revived now as furi-
ously as ever. Joe North tried to throw a little good-natured
cold water on this fever: the story of such an immense defeat was really of little use to him, since his paper (the *Daily
Worker*) contrived to make every military action in Spain
appear to be a Republican victory. I suppose he was a little
puzzled as to how he could write about it at all, and consequently was in no great rush to get to Barcelona. Moreover,
a delay of half an hour was caused by our Swiss colleague,
Kell, who wanted to find Modesto (commanding the 5th
Army) and get his account of the events of the day. We
scoured the road between Santa Barbara and Tortosa and

never did find Modesto's headquarters. Kell was one of the best of the military correspondents, and knew exactly what had happened, but his native caution made him want to have a general's word for it. We gave that up as a bad job, at last, and made for Tortosa, and none too soon: for I was in that state of journalistic impatience (a very discreditable disease) in which every minute seems an hour. I think Joe North was quietly enjoying the spectacle, which must have seemed to him an occupational derangement characteristic of the capitalist press; and no doubt he was right. I am unable to think of any reason, at this moment, why it mattered whether the American newspapers were informed of the capture of Vinaroz then or a day later or two days later. The event was of such magnitude, and so pregnant with consequences, that the details of how or when it was reported signified little; and in any case Matthews and Hemingway had been there before us and were no doubt reporting it already. But this particular journalistic instinct—the desire to tell the story as quickly as possible—is the least reasonable of them all, and I am afraid that if our twenty horsepower, or ten or five, had been real instead of figurative, they would have been cruelly driven all the way to Barcelona.

We reached Tortosa at three. Here, as we had expected, the main bridge was gone, but the old secondary bridge was being rapidly put into condition with planks and turf so as to stand heavy traffic. Trucks were not yet permitted to pass, but the officer in charge let us go across. One third of the span of the main bridge lay in the yellow water of the river. In spite of that terrific bombing we had watched in the hot noon sun, the dust had all settled now, and the town looked no more ruined than it had in the morning. (It couldn't.)

I think my journalistic fever lasted (as is usual in this

trade) until my story of the day had at last been written, and censored, and telephoned to Paris. There were endless difficulties at the censorship, for a cabinet meeting had been called and had decided to keep the news of the cut through to the sea a secret in Spain until Easter Sunday night. Instructions had been sent down not to permit foreign correspondents to mention either the bombing of the bridge at Tortosa or the capture of Vinaroz. My story was decorated with many bars of bright red pencil. This made such hash of the whole business that I decided, in self-defense (and also in the natural hatred of all newspapermen for censorships), to say the word "censored" over the telephone when I came to any important part that had been cut out. The story as it appeared the next day in Paris and New York in the *Herald-Tribune* bristled with that ominous word in italics, and consequently looked fully as disastrous for the Republic as the events had actually been. It also defeated the whole notion of censorship, since any moderately intelligent reader was able to tell from the context what had been omitted. I still think this was a perfectly legitimate way of overcoming censorship, and conveyed no military information not already abundantly known to the Fascists. But I heard with regret that it caused a row in the censorship office afterwards and nearly cost one man his job. I hadn't thought of all that; while the fever was on, I had thought of nothing but the story.

Late that night Hemingway came down to our room and joined my wife and me in a meal. He had, as a Catholic, been fasting all day (it was Good Friday). He had also been the victim of the same occupational disease as myself, and with even greater cause for exasperation; for he had been up since four in the morning, scouring the front, and had had his story of these events cut to ribbons by the censor. His fever had also evaporated thereafter, and I think he, too, was a little ashamed of it. These must be familiar phenomena to everybody who works for a newspaper, but when you have forgotten them for many years and they still arise and smite you, there is occasion for astonishment.

On the next day I was better able to contemplate the situation created for the Republic (and for, as I believe, the whole world) by the Fascist victory. Catalonia was now cut off from the rest of the Republic. Supplies would be difficult to get into the blockaded south; Madrid would be hungrier than ever. With the Fascists at Vinaroz, and the bridge gone at Tortosa, it would be necessary for the Republic to withdraw all its troops to this side of the Ebro immediately. The scales had been so turned that the Republic must be on the defensive hereafter, and a Fascist conquest of Spain could never again be ruled out as impossible. After eighteen months of a desperate struggle in which hundreds of thousands had died for the freedom of Spain, the lawless powers of Germany and Italy had poured in so much fresh material in artillery, aviation and men that they had been able to deal a blow which might be fatal. When I remembered the clenched fists and the grins on the faces of those boys in the line at Ulldecona I knew that the war would not end soon; there would be no surrender; but the crippled Republic would pursue it in future against overwhelming odds.

That was April 16, the day on which the Anglo-Italian Agreement, a first fruit of the diplomacy of Mr Neville Chamberlain, was signed in Rome.

THE EBRO

7

On Easter Sunday I went again to the Ebro, and for the last time in the spring, as the Republican army was withdrawn altogether that night and the Fascists occupied the whole right bank of the river. Nothing in particular happened on Easter Sunday—nothing, that is, that I could see —and yet it sticks in my head by reason of four or five minutes of thoroughgoing fright which descended on us when we went too far. There was about a minute of the time when we thought we were due for (at best) a Fascist prison camp.

We started late from Barcelona, thanks to the transport difficulty. It was impossible to get a car and impossible to leave off trying to get one; consequently I missed the Easter Mass of the Basque government, one of the Catholic ceremonies surviving in the Republic with undiminished pomp. By noon (when I might just as well have spent the morning with the Basques) Marthe Huysmans of the *Peuple* (Brussels) wheedled a car out of the Ministry and we started for the Ebro in it—she and I and Richard Mowrer (Chicago *Daily News*). The road to Tortosa showed signs of abnormal activity only down toward the end, where we ran into some columns of retreating troops and several caravans of refugees. At Tortosa we were not permitted to cross the secondary bridge with our car—it was reserved for traffic coming this way until half-past six in the evening. We left the car and crossed the bridge on foot, intending to find an Estado Mayor or a line or a front somewhere and wait for our transport. We had a long walk. There was little movement down here, and no sign of a military command or of a front. To the best of our knowledge Modesto and his staff were still somewhere down here, but they were impossible to find. Barcelona's information in such matters was always a day or so behind the facts, and I was rapidly coming to the conclusion that had long since been reached by Matthews and Hemingway: that you never knew where the front was until you saw it yourself.

The countryside, too, looked as if it had been evacuated. Near Kilometre 186 (I think), the point where Modesto's headquarters had been two or three days before, we saw one house which was still inhabited. The peasants who lived there had been sitting in the doorway on this warm spring evening, and one woman was leaning over the garden gate, looking at us with interest. On the off chance, we asked her if she knew where Modesto's Estado Mayor was.

"Oh, he left this morning, quite early," she informed us. "They have gone away with the whole staff. Some of them left yesterday."

We were surprised at such explicit information, and a little inclined to doubt it until a soldier on a motorcycle came along and told us it was true. We walked on, just the same, until our car arrived and we obliged the rebellious driver to take us to the crossroads at Santa Barbara. This, to the best of our information, had not yet been occupied by the Fascists.

We arrived there at about seven o'clock or perhaps a little later. The flat country around there was a dusty yellow gold in the evening light, with the sierra off on the right turning purple. There was a handful of soldiers stationed here and we stopped to talk to officers and commissars. We had a longish and rather misleading talk with one man whom I took to be a Russian (one of the very few I ever saw in Spain). I think he was amused at the idea of newspaper correspondents, one of them a woman, in such a place at such a time. At any rate he gave us elaborate theories of

[*82*]

what offensives could be based on the Ebro after this strategic retreat was completed. He had a quizzical grin all the time, and if he was thinking (as I believe) that ours was a rather comic trade, there is no doubt he was right.

But in the middle of our talk the commander of the post arrived from somewhere down the road. He was very young, with a white face and startling black eyes. When he broke in, it was in a voice hoarse and very nearly silenced by emotion.

"I am sorry I can tell you nothing now, comrades," he said, "except that you must go back at once. At once. The Fascists are moving up this road with tanks, and there is cavalry coming across country. You must go at once. Forgive me."

He said that two or three times ("Perdónemi, camaradas"). He had come from whatever front there was, a kilometer or so down the road, and no doubt the sights he had seen may have unnerved him—that, and the knowledge that the whole right bank of the Ebro must now be evacuated. He took Marthe Huysmans by the elbow and spoke to her in an undertone. Apparently what he said was: "Hurry. There is no time to waste."

We got back into the car and turned back to the Ebro by way of the delta road. (One of the roads at the Santa Barbara crossroads was the great Barcelona–Valencia highway, by which we had come; the other came from the west and continued round in a half circle across the delta to Amposta.) Our driver was loud in protest. He had not wanted to come so far, and he did not want to return on the unfamiliar delta road. The whole thing, he said, was *capricho* (whim, caprice).

Presently we flung ourselves headlong into the middle of a scene which silenced even our driver. There were extensive olive groves on both sides of the road. The sun had gone, and we were moving through a sort of pale gray light in which the olive trees lost their usual definition. A man in uniform, who looked like an officer, made signs at us as we passed—either telling us to stop or telling us to go on. We went on; it would have been impossible to stop that driver by now. For in the olive grove on the right we had all seen at the same time a startling sight. Every tree had a man behind it, and each man had his bayoneted rifle ready.

This would have been nothing extraordinary in such a place in broad daylight, especially if it had been accompanied by some healthy noise or other—a shout or the sound of firing. But those groves were as still as if we had dreamed them, and the gray evening light held trees and men in a sort of suspended animation. The rifles were not all pointing the same way: that was one thing I could make out.

For perhaps two minutes none of us knew whether these men were Fascists or Republicans. If they were *nosotros,* they were waiting perhaps for the cross-country advance of cavalry; if they were the Fascists, we had not much chance of getting through that grove.

These were minutes of complete silence. We could hear no firing anywhere, no voices raised, no shouts and no movement. The car catapulted along; there never was such a willing driver as this one now.

And that was all. Nothing happened. We got through the grove and drove on over the delta road to Amposta; the moment we emerged into open space we were sure we had seen Republican soldiers and no Fascists. But for the very brief extent of that episode I think we were all thoroughly frightened, not perhaps so much of death itself (although that is the base of all fear) but of the possibility of capture by Navarrese or Italians. For Marthe Huysmans, at

any rate, those must have been moments as terrifying as any
she had spent in the bombardments.

We ran into a false alarm of aviation at Amposta, where
there were large numbers of men gathered to cross the
pontoon bridge that had been thrown across the Ebro.
They all got across and the bridge was blown up that night,
although we did not know it for a day or so. Santa Barbara,
where we had just been, was occupied by the Fascists very
shortly after our departure—fifteen or twenty minutes later,
I believe. At Amposta our main desire (like everybody
else's) was to get across the river, but the alarm of aviation
left us without a driver for the car. He vanished at once. I
made for cover in the town (a foolish move), but Marthe
Huysmans, very experienced in such matters, walked
straight out onto the bridge.

She told me afterwards why she did this. Her experience
had been that the Fascists usually dropped bombs on
everything except their military objective. At Amposta
their military objective must obviously be the bridge;
therefore the bridge was safer than anywhere else. She
supported this thesis by examples. At Lerida she had been
in El Campesino's headquarters when the Italians and
Germans came over to bomb the place. That was the three-
hour bombardment on April 2, one of the worst of the war.
Marthe felt herself in the way at headquarters, which
was in any case rocking with bombs; she went into one of
the main refuges. Here there was such a crowd that she
nearly stifled. Considering the situation, she decided that
the bridge would be safest. She walked out through the
town and onto the bridge, disregarding the attempts of a
sentry to stop her (this during the bombing). She remained on the bridge for the rest of those three hours,
during which Lerida was bombed to ruins and many people

died. The bridge was untouched. By Marthe's logic, this proved the point.

When we recovered our car and driver and got across the Ebro we found Marthe already on the other side, talking to a refugee. The refugee was a peasant woman from down San Carlos way. She was complaining of the haste with which she and her family had had to flee. The burden of her complaint was that her husband's new suit and his Sunday gloves had had to be left behind. I had heard exactly the same kind of protest years ago in China; I was to hear it later in Austria and Czechoslovakia. The mind of the refugee, dazed and uprooted, concentrates upon the small, specific losses that it can cling to with understanding. To be homeless and without food or shelter as a result of the "policy" of foreign dictators and prime ministers—that is a state so terrible that it cannot be taken in all at once. The new suit, the Sunday gloves: these are the losses one can still comprehend.

There had been fresh bombings a little further along here, and severe ones. There was still blood in the ruins.

8

So, in the spring of 1938, while Mr Neville Chamberlain was negotiating his Mediterranean agreement with Mussolini, the Fascist alliance turned the tide of war in Spain. By means of overwhelming supplies from Germany and Italy the Spanish puppet generals on the Fascist side were able to drive the Republican forces out of Aragon and part of Catalonia, back behind the Ebro. In the next phase of the war the Republic, blockaded by the tragic hypocrisy of "nonintervention," cut into two parts by the Fascist armies, subjected to an embargo by the United States of America, and suffering cruelly from lack of food, was to fight against immense material forces with little to count upon except the force of its own spirit. I think it must have been clear to most informed persons in Barcelona last spring that a military victory of the Republic would only be possible hereafter if events in the international field obliged Mussolini and Hitler to withdraw their artillery, aviation, infantry and tanks from Spain. But it was also clear that this people, which had risked everything and dared everything for eighteen months, would not submit to the lash of the conqueror without prolonged resistance, whatever the odds.

That was what you got by these occasional and otherwise insignificant visits to the Ebro front in the moment of defeat—a sense of the vitality of an idea for which people will willingly die. The courage and endurance of the Spaniards were not characteristics to be deduced from patriotism alone or the heritage of their race. Spaniards in other times have shown themselves to be no more courageous or long-suffering than any other people. But in this prolonged crisis caused by the revolt of black reaction and sustained by the Fascist alliance, men who had been reluctant to fight for Alfonso XIII were ready and eager to die for the Republic. You were hearing tales of heroism all the time. Some of them were no doubt exaggerated by the imagination of a people who have always loved the picturesque and the brave. But it was true enough, and I saw the evidence of it often myself, that there was something indomitable in them. Even a Fascist victory and a Fascist terror could not conquer them, and if such a triumph does in the end come to Mussolini and Hitler, it will be the least permanent of their achievements. That it could ever come, even temporarily, or that we can put the possibility into cold print, is due to the unceasing efforts of those British and French politicians who have labored to make the course of Fascism easy. While they were thus engaged, either through stupidity, cowardice or something more infamous, in the network of treachery which constitutes the diplomatic year of 1938, men of simpler breed were offering their lives for freedom. The Anglo-Italian Agreement, like the other treaties between the trembling democracies and the rampant dictators, was violated before the ink was dry upon it; it was made to be violated, and not even a British politician can have expected anything else; but it served its turn in the rigmarole of hypocritical mystification under which half Europe was delivered to the Fascists. The Ebro was already a frontier of the human spirit when it was negotiated, and it was signed on a day when the Ebro ran red to the sea.

CHAPTER III

By the Rivers of Babylon

THE HEIGHTS OF EVIAN rise tranquilly from the shores of
the peaceful, domestic lake of Geneva. Lausanne lies directly
opposite; Geneva, that high-minded old city of whose
history the League of Nations was such a characteristic
episode, is just over on the left; the Castle of Chillon is
farther right on the Lausanne side, near Montreux. A
steamer connects all these noteworthy points with each
other and with Vevey, a town down at the end where they
make chocolate and operate girls' boarding schools. In
July the lake is a cool, brilliant blue, the sun is hot but not
at all unpleasant, and the gardens of the Hotel Royal afford
shade or *le tennis*, depending on your taste. The cooking in
this establishment is also excellent, and its cellars can com-
pare favorably with the best to be found in Paris, London
or New York. The champagne could have been a shade
colder, at times, but then, as is well known, the French do
not share our American passion for ice, and perhaps there
is something to be said for their view of the matter.

It would be ungrateful to go further without also mentioning the Casino, a building in which roulette and baccarat can be played, drinks drunk and dances danced until the last boat leaves for Switzerland. The reason why the Casino shuts up shop after the last boat is that most of its clients in ordinary times are Swiss. The Swiss have a good or goodish currency still, and they are forbidden to gamble with it in their own country. It is their laudable custom to cross the lake of an evening and lose their money on the tables in France. They gamble methodically, without apparent pleasure or excitement, and wear evening dress on Saturday nights.

The mineral springs of Evian are also—I believe justly—celebrated. Half of the town seems to be *établissements de bains*, and according to report you can drink the water, bathe in it, be pummeled by masseurs in it, or merely sit and look at it, and whatever is the matter with you, you will be cured. If you are able to move after your cure you will probably make your way back to the Royal at the top of the hill by means of a cab drawn by a well-fed, lazy horse, through lanes where wild flowers grow.

On the wide terrace of the Hotel Royal in July, 1938, and in its bedrooms, sitting rooms, drawing rooms, ballroom and suites de luxe, there was an international meeting to discuss means of dealing with the problem of Jewish refugees. It would have been called a conference in the 1920s, and was in fact a conference; but that word has grown into such disrepute in recent years, since every result of every conference was nullified, that another term was preferred on this occasion. It was called the Intergovernmental Committee. It was called into existence by Mr Roosevelt to propose means of absorbing the exiled Jews of Germany and Austria into the outer world. Twenty-six nations and self-governing dominions sent their representatives, and the Hotel Royal must have done very good business, even if you calculate that some of these gentlemen were not obliged to pay full rate for their rooms. What was lost on the rooms was no doubt made up on food and wine, not to mention the fact that there are shops in the hotel, too. When the full history of the occasion comes to be written, and studious scholars of a remote epoch ponder over the records of the Hotel Royal, it may be found that the hairdresser did about as well out of it as anybody. Most of the delegates brought their ladies, and most of the ladies had nothing to do most of the time except to get their hair dressed. The gentlemen might just as well have spent their time at the hairdresser's too, and then at least somebody would have profited.

The actual result of the meeting (the only concrete one) was the formation of a permanent intergovernmental committee, with its seat in London, to consider the question. Otherwise there were the usual pious resolutions, a great many speeches, and the hearing of a vast number of organizations and committees and subcommittees which had suggestions to offer. To the best of my knowledge and belief, no Jew who has escaped from the hell of life in Germany owes anything whatsoever to this meeting or to the intergovernmental committee which it set up.

But perhaps it had some slight sentimental and psychological value: it was at least a gesture of sympathy. Or so I thought as I was making my way to Evian from Vienna. That notion was upset on the first day of the meeting. A colleague (John Elliott, New York *Herald-Tribune*) succeeded in getting a ticket for me to attend the opening session at eleven o'clock in the morning, and I was wandering about the big terrace of the hotel with my ticket in my pocket, waiting for the magic hour, when I saw friends from Vienna. One was Dr Neumann, the nose-and-throat specialist, a rich and wonderful character; another was Dr Löwenherz, the head of the Jewish Community of Vienna, a lawyer who had been thrust into the position of responsible chief for his people during the most terrible ordeal of their modern history. They were rather agitated, and rightly so: for they had come to Evian to represent the Jews of Austria, the people about whom this meeting had been summoned, and they were barred from attending it.

As nearly as I can make out the secretariat of the conference (borrowed, I believe, from the League of Nations down the way) had prepared for a limited number of delegations, for the press, and for nothing else. It had never occurred to them that the persons most directly concerned might want to be heard, or at least to get the chance of listening. When the Jewish delegation appeared they were informed that they could not enter—there was no room at the inn. I gave my ticket to Dr Löwenherz, who thus passed into the conference room as a representative of the *Red Book Magazine*, the name I had given to the pert young lady who made out the cards. Dr Neumann and the other delegate (an economic expert) were unable to enter.

The incident was perhaps of no consequence, but it seemed to me to set the tone for the meeting. I went to two sessions after that, later in the week when the Jewish representatives had been given tickets. Both sessions reached a very high point in stupid, sanctimonious, heartless pomposity and boredom. Delegate after delegate got up and read a long speech saying his country sympathized deeply with the sufferings of the Jews but could do nothing to alleviate them. Reasons were always given—overpopulation; unemployment; economic distress; the overcrowding of cities. Usually the delegate would include one long passage detailing all that his country had already done for the Jews, which seemed to be a great deal until you thought about what the words meant. When the speech was over it was solemnly translated into French and English. The chairs were hard and so were the voices. There was sunlight outside. I went to no more of the sessions.

In the private meetings things were not quite so cut and dried, I believe, but the results were the same. A large number of Jewish and non-Jewish relief organizations were heard; data was collected; suggestions for action were received and discussed. There were arguments. But it was perfectly apparent from the first day that no serious attempt was being made or would be made to take action: to accept into a freer world those men, women and children who were being tortured, robbed and driven out of their homes by German Fascism. There existed no reason why America, the British dominions and South America, all of whom had plenty of room, should not accept Jewish immigration: the only reason offered was economic, and it was not valid because the Jewish organizations stood ready to guarantee that no Jewish immigrant would be a burden upon the state which accepted him. Since this was true, there must be other reasons which were not avowed —either anti-Semitism or the fear of anti-Semitism, and in either case a reason beneath contempt.

I very much preferred the Casino to the conference. You saw a good many of the same people down there, and it was much better to win their money than to listen to their speeches. It was even better to lose money to them. There were thousands of people dying tonight because of the "problem" these men had met to solve: dying the slow deaths of hunger and humiliation or the quick deaths of the club, the machine gun and the knife. But at least at the

Casino you were not pretending to do anything to help them—you were squandering energy, and wasting time, and losing money, and generally making a fool of yourself, but frankly, frankly. You were not glossing over a living horror with dead and empty words. Down at the Casino there was some kind of reality, a stupid and vulgar one, but it was there; up at the conference there was no reality at all.

Perhaps I might not have been so disgusted at the Evian Conference if I had not come to it straight from Vienna. In Vienna these things were real.

2

The Judengasse in Vienna is a street which dates from beyond the sixteenth century, perhaps from the middle ages. The buildings are not ancient, but there has always been a street there—a street of shops and lodgings, crowded and shut away from the main life of the town, a sort of ghetto street with thin tall houses and cobbled pavements. You can reach it in less than five minutes' walk from St Stephen's Cathedral. It lies behind the Rotenturmstrasse on ground rising to a sudden but not high hill.

From the time when the Germans came in (March, 1938), the Judengasse has been the resort of as unhappy a population as you could find on earth. They come here from all the districts of Vienna, from the suburbs and from the country. They come even from far away—from the Burgenland, down on the Hungarian frontier, there have been some thousands. The headquarters of the Jewish Community (the Jüdische Kultusgemeinde) are still here in the Judengasse, and it is here that Jews come to put their names on the register of those who want food, shelter and a chance to escape to some happier country.

BY THE RIVERS OF BABYLON

The Jewish Community of Vienna has enjoyed considerable self-government for centuries. The emperors used occasionally to make sudden demands for money upon the organization, but otherwise they left it free to direct all the religious and charitable enterprises among the Jews, as well as education. In the nineteenth century, when the barrier between Jew and Gentile began to crumble, the Kultusgemeinde lost some of its authority over the minds of its own people, but retained its direction of the special Jewish religious and cultural life. In March, 1938, when the German Fascists took over Austria, they dealt with the Jews of Vienna—insofar as they ever dealt with them—through the Kultusgemeinde, issuing ultimatums and edicts by direct communication with the chiefs of the Jews themselves.

The people come to the Judengasse all day long. Here is a brawny young workman who can no longer work; there is a mother with three children whose father is in the concentration camp; the next is an old woman with the suffering of a thousand years in her eyes. They crowd the dark staircase of the old building and stifle in the airless corridors as they wait for their turn to come. Children go one way; widows and women whose husbands are in jail or concentration camp go another; Burgenland refugees go to a different office; men who are still at liberty but deprived of all means of support go to a still different one; all have taken sanctuary in this rabbit warren which has once again become the capital and the only hope of Austrian Jewry.

The Kultusgemeinde, by a miracle, continues to operate, continues to give money and food and shelter to thousands of the victims of German Fascism. Aid from abroad (particularly from America) has made this financially possible. But the actual administration is endangered every day by arrests, and a worker there (like other Jews in Vienna) cannot know when he gets up in the morning whether he will not spend the night in jail or on the train to Dachau. To keep the people alive and, whenever possible, to help them to escape is the aim of the work done here. No other hope has existed in all Austrian Jewry since the Nazi horror descended from the north.

The Kultusgemeinde had maintained orphanages, old people's homes and other charitable institutions for many years. These were now crowded, and were conducted against every sort of difficulty that could be invented by Nazi officialdom. The Kultusgemeinde had also maintained a few soup kitchens for relief of the destitute, particularly in winter; these were now besieged, and others had to be opened. When I visited the soup kitchens there were seventeen of them, and others were planned if the funds would stretch so far. All seventeen were crowded for the midday meal, the only one which could be supplied by the strained resources of the Community. Twelve to fourteen thousand destitute people were maintained by this single daily meal at the soup kitchens; upwards of six thousand families were receiving supplies to be taken home and cooked; over ten thousand were receiving relief in cash. All these figures have risen sharply since then, with the aggravation of the persecution which came in the autumn after Mr Neville Chamberlain had flown to Munich. In those halcyon days of July there were only twenty thousand Jews in the concentration camps and jails in Austria; hardly more than three or four hundred had been beaten to death or accidentally killed by machine guns; the synagogues were intact and there had not been much destruction of Jewish property, only confiscation under the "commissar system." After the triumph at Munich all this was to seem mild.

BY THE RIVERS OF BABYLON

We used to think at that time in Vienna that Austria was being treated to a much more thorough and inhuman enforcement of the Nazi policy than Germany had ever seen or ever would see. There were various theories put forward to account for the ferocity with which Jews were being persecuted here: one, that the proportion of Jews was higher in Vienna and the Nazi desire to get rid of them consequently keener; another that the Führer himself, Adolf Hitler, took a special interest in Austria because it was his fatherland; another that Austrian anti-Semitism was naturally hotter than the German variety, and that the regime was undertaking a popular task by flaying the Jews alive. None of these explanations, in retrospect, seems the correct one. The persecution in Austria was a rehearsal: that was all. With the knowledge of ways and means thus gained, the National Socialist party was able to engage in its large-scale operation against the Jews in November, and thus gaining technique with each operation, will in time, unless civilization as a whole finds means of arresting its course, be able to exterminate whole myriads without disturbing the normal life or temperature of the Fascist state.

The thing that puzzled me then, has puzzled me since, and will no doubt continue to puzzle me as long as I live, is how this particular kind of persecution can be executed by modern Europeans living at a fairly advanced level of culture. I understand the passions and necessities of politics: that Hitler must exterminate the enemies who threaten the life of his regime is comprehensible. He rose to power through fraud and violence, and he must rule by fraud and violence to the end, extending his political base (if or when possible) by means of a fraudulent philosophy concocted out of ill-digested hunks of other men's theories. But the

Jews en masse are not a political phenomenon. Every kind of political opinion is to be found among Jews; there would be thousands of Jewish Nazis if the regime admitted them; there were Jewish Fascists in Italy, and very active ones, before Mussolini accepted anti-Semitism as a creed. There is nothing in the general line of Fascist doctrine which is repugnant to Jews as Jews. If the anti-Semitism were removed, the rich Jews of Central Europe would probably tend to become Fascists and the poor ones Social Democrats or Communists. That tendency was already apparent before Fascism adopted the anti-Semitic program as its principal form of diversion and began startling the deluded and bewildered people with it. Now that Fascism has rejected the Jews and persecutes them with every device of ingenious sadism, it is naturally impossible for a Jew to be a Fascist; but I personally know a number of Jews in various nations who regret the impossibility, who accept every item of the Fascist doctrine except anti-Semitism, and who have to the full the social and economic outlook of the confirmed Fascist.

With Hitler, as can be seen in his book, the lines of logic are terribly confused; he believes in all sincerity that the Jews are a race bred and trained to evil, and therefore his natural enemies. In some obscure way which a psychoanalyst might be able to trace out, the shocks and disturbances to which he was subjected in his youth were associated with Jews in his mind. It seems clear that Hitler himself is the prey of every legend, every invention, every pernicious bit of ignorant folklore that the ages have accumulated among Gentile peoples against the alien Jew. No Gentile altogether escapes some of this heritage: it is in our literature and tradition, like innumerable other relics of the dark past, but we shed it as we grow older. Few among us believe in the stories of ritual murder which once horrified our ancestors; and yet these exact stories (the same old tales of Christian babies murdered so that their blood could be used in Jewish sacrifice) circulate in Germany today with the approval and, as I suspect, the ardent concurring belief of the President and Chancellor. Hitler shows in *Mein Kampf* that he holds the Jews responsible for almost every great event of modern times: the World War, the Treaty of Versailles, the Russian Revolution, the reparations system, the policy of France on the Continent. He accuses them in the same breath of being capitalists and of being Communists; of being religious fanatics and of being irreligious; of anti-German nationalism (when they are French)and of internationalism (when they are German). The simple truth, that the Jews are all these things and a great deal else besides, as other human groups are, does not seem to have dawned upon that rigidly simple mind which surmounts the most complex emotional character of our time.

But all Austrians and Germans are not like Hitler. Few, indeed, possess anything like the fire of his own belief. We hear the cackle of the cynic in every word of Dr Goebbels; there is burlesque in the slightest phrase of the ineffable Field Marshal Goering. Hitler may inspire the Nazi organization with his own assurance that the Jews are responsible for every misfortune, and may even generalize a part of that belief among the German and Austrian people by dint of unceasing propaganda through a period of years; but he cannot give all those millions of people the same simple faith in a scapegoat that he himself possesses. They are modern; they cannot help knowing better. If you try to talk to any ordinary Austrian or German he will make out a very lame case for the persecution of the Jews. I always had the impression (in Vienna and Munich, and later in Berlin) that the ordinary German was ashamed of this aspect of his glorious regime, tried to bolster it up with a number of halting arguments about the financial acumen and unscrupulousness of the Jews, and was immensely relieved if the subject could be changed to something else. Any German I have ever known at all well has regarded the anti-Jewish policy as the mania, or aberration, of National Socialism rather than its strength; and among cultivated people of the upper class the embarrassment of the subject is avoided by saying that "the whole thing has been greatly exaggerated by the foreign press." (I am speaking of people who are not on the whole inimical to National Socialism, of course.)

How, then, can these things happen? Supposing a large number of Germans and Austrians do dislike the Jews (as I believe they do). What of it? So do large numbers of Americans, and yet they do not go out and smash their shops, beat their women, haul their men off to jails and concentration camps on no charge whatever. How can the ordinary mild form of social anti-Semitism, which was prevalent in Central Europe before Hitler, have been transformed into this vicious and bestial attack upon a whole defenseless population?

Somewhere in the mystery of mass suggestion the answer could be found, and can some day be analyzed upon dead material by the psychologists of the future. Now that the material is living, it is almost impossible to trace the process of transformation. A German goes into a Nazi meeting one sort of man—sentimental, even tenderhearted at times, in his immediate relationships; convinced that Germany has been ill-used by all other nations; uplifted by the hope that Germany may yet dominate a regenerated continent

in National Socialism; and by means of songs, cheers, in-
flamed speeches, flags and orgiastic mass emotion, is so
worked upon that he comes out ready to kill the Jews, to
beat them up, to take their goods or to plunge them into
starvation as homeless refugees. That is a simple enough
transformation, perhaps; but it happens often to all members of the Nazi party; often enough to make the hysteria
of the mass meeting no longer a phenomenon, but a condition of life. Thus it becomes possible later for a Nazi
to be called out of bed at three in the morning by a telephone call from his superior officer, to climb into his clothes,
get his club and go out in cold blood to attack the Jews,
even when there has been no preliminary drugging of his
mind. The Nazi is conditioned (as the behaviorists say) to
brutality against the Jews, and by now his superiors can
call upon that fact as often as they like.

It remains, just the same, an incomprehensible thing to
persons who are not so conditioned. In Vienna I once saw
an S.S. man (of the Schützstaffel—Himmler's gang) standing in the Kärntner-Ring feeding the pigeons. He was
gurgling at them without the slightest self-consciousness,
and obviously entertained the warmest feelings toward the
creatures. The same man might have been breaking into a
Jewish house the night before to arrest the father of a
family, beating him into insensibility if he resisted, knock-
ing the women down if they got in his way. He could shoot
a Jew whom it was thought desirable to remove, and then
report solemnly that this happened by accident; he could
steal Jewish property, torture Jewish children, swear to
incredible and impossible lies against Jewish organizations
under oath in the courts; he would be capable of every
variety of murder, arson, perjury, robbery, blackmail and
physical sadism so long as its victim was a Jew; and yet

there he stood, positively drooling over the pigeons in the Ring, and without a doubt convinced in his own mind that he was a loyal, admirable citizen of the Third Reich, a heroic soldier in the new crusade which was to regenerate the world.

There are more Nazis in Germany than there are Jews; and, ghastly as the treatment of the Jews has been, it has a counterpart which is as bad for the balance of mankind. That is the degradation of the Nazi himself, his bestialization in these successive pogroms. What Hitler has done to young Germany—the youth which he trains and from which he recruits his gangsters—is even more horrible in the long run, as will be abundantly proved during the lifetime of this generation, than his persecution, spoliation and expulsion of the Jews. For in a transaction of this kind, a mass crime with a mass criminal and a mass victim, all must suffer: the victim immediately in blood and spirit, the criminal by his rapid and irretrievable degradation to savagery, and the remainder of the species by the necessity of either subduing the savage or submitting to him.

3

The most striking thing in my casebook from Vienna was the harmlessness of the cases, considered from the point of view of a dictatorship. That Communists should be jailed, tortured or killed was understandable: they were the implacable enemies of the Nazi regime, the only ones who would never recant and never give in. That Catholic Socialists, Social Democrats and aristocratic Legitimists should go to jail, lose their jobs, have their property seized or be subjected to personal indignities was also quite logical under the theory of divine inspiration for Hitler and his party: they were enemies and must be either converted or expunged. But the Jews—?

A poor woman was going along the street in the Fifth District when she tottered and fell. She was pregnant and her time had come. The policeman who picked her up did not know that she was Jewish; she would have asked him to take her to the Rothschild Hospital, but she could not speak; he sent her to the public hospital, now reserved for Christians. She gave birth to her child and remained there for a week. At the end of that time she was informed that she must pay her bill (fifty-four marks) or be taken to jail. She had no money to pay the bill. At the Rothschild Hospital she would have had no bill to pay. She went to jail.

What danger did she represent to the regime at any point in her story?

A rich woman was arrested and taken to jail, where she was made to sign papers "voluntarily" surrendering her two Vienna houses to "Aryan possession." After two and a half months in jail she was examined by a slightly more human official than those who had preceded him; he restored one of her houses to her, and upon her release she returned to live in it. She was then confronted with arrears in taxes (calculated on the German scale, not the Austrian one) for not only the smaller house where she lived, but for the large property which had been confiscated. Her money had been so exhausted by the expenses of getting out of jail that she could not pay, and returned to jail.

It is easy to see that this woman's money was wanted by the Nazi party; but what danger did she represent to them? Why was it better for her to be in jail than out of jail?

A watchmaker was arrested, and his small business confiscated ("transferred to Aryan possession"), so that his wife and children were obliged to depend on relief from the Kultusgemeinde. His jailers discovered that he had a brother in America .They made him sign a paper, therefore, declaring that he would leave the Reich by June 1. On this, and the payment of a ransom, he was released. He was unable to obtain the American visa by June 1, or any other visa, and the authorities gave him a "prolongation" of two weeks. At the end of the two weeks he still had no means of leaving the country, so he was arrested again and taken to the concentration camp at Dachau.

How was this man an enemy of the regime? In what way were the interests of the regime better served by keeping him at Dachau?

I could go on giving these specific instances by the yard, and to each instance the response of any non-Fascist mind would be—at first—sheer bewilderment. We think there must be *something* else, some definite reason, some political or antisocial activity, which marks out these apparently blameless citizens for punishment. After the cases pile up, and the German authorities themselves make their position in the matter quite clear by official statements, we must accept the fantastic truth: that the whole machinery of a mighty state is thus set in motion to crush its Jewish subjects not because of anything they have thought, said or done, but simply because they are Jews.

It is Hitler's conviction that the whole Jewish race is infected, that its plans are inimical to all other groups in the modern world, and that there is no solution for the problem thus postulated except the *extermination* of the Jews. (*Mein Kampf*, official unexpurgated German edition, p. 372.) The anti-Semitism of Hitler is obviously a diseased condition amounting to mania, since it disregards all evidence and expresses itself in terms of the most violent hatred and ignorance. The Führer is an uneducated man of limited intellectual power and tremendous emotional intensity. His emotional intensity is what has given him dominion over the German people, for he stirs their depths by expressing at the whitest heat what they have felt in a lukewarm way, half consciously, for centuries. But so far as any system of thought or collation of evidence is concerned, *Mein Kampf* and the speeches of the Führer are both raw nonsense. The Führer had read the *Protocols of the Elders of Zion*, a fabrication of alleged Jewish plans for world domination, produced by a Russian anti-Semite, on their appearance in Germany in 1919. He apparently has never read, or never deigned to notice, the able analysis and disproof of this document published by *The Times* in London in 1921, and in many other periodicals in and out of Germany. None of Hitler's statements about the Jews in *Mein Kampf* (1926) shows a calm or balanced mind; and for none of them does he adduce evidence. The book is animated throughout by the most passionate hatred of that people with whom Hitler associates everything else that he hates in life—Marxian Socialism, international capitalism, France, England, the democratic system of government, the theater, sexual activity of any kind not designed to produce German children, and all literature which departs from the narrow limits of patriotic and edifying themes. His hatred for the press is in part based on his lifelong conviction that it is dominated by Jews: "Almost every writer was a Jew and every Jew a writer," he says. All of his prejudices and hatreds, evolved by an extremely complex and thwarted emotional nature out of poverty, obscurity, fierce racial patriotism, and an obvious cloud of inferiority-superiority interactions, have been crystallized around the figure of the Jew, and in destroying the Jew he believes

he will destroy the objects of them all. Some men are molli-
fied by power and success; but Hitler's mind, as he tells us,
was formed in his childhood, adolescence and early man-
hood, and has never changed since. He has read scarcely
anything since those far-off days before the Great War: "I
have not had to add much to what I then learnt; I have had
to alter nothing." (*Mein Kampf*, official German edition,
p. 21.)

A man who has learned scarcely anything, and has
altered nothing in the furniture of his mind, since the year
1912: that is the Führer according to his own statement.
And all these adolescent hatreds, conceived in the secret
bitterness of his youth, are formalized into a system which
now must be professed by the whole German nation: for
Mein Kampf is studied as a required text in every German
school, college and training camp. Naturally so, for the
Führer is ridden by a messianic mania of the most virulent
kind, and the book is his Bible and Koran.

"I believe that I am acting today in accordance with the
intention of the Almighty Creator," he says in the official
text of *Mein Kampf* imposed on the German nation, "and
when I attack the Jew I am fighting for the work of the
Lord."

Therefore it does not matter what the Jew does: he can
be a benefactor of humanity or an artist of the rarest value,
he can be a scientist or inventor of unique quality, and he
is still on exactly the same level as a criminal, merely by
virtue of having been born a Jew. In this view of things the
obscurest of Jews—the poor woman who was pregnant, for
instance—is an "enemy of the state" equally with Walther
Rathenau, who did so much to help Germany win the war
and save the wreckage of the peace. Jewish children are also
"enemies of the state" because they are Jewish. Christians

born and bred, to no matter what generation, are "enemies of the state" if they have a racially Jewish grandparent. "One single drop of Jewish blood," according to the rabid anti-Semite Streicher, "is poison to the race." Karl Marx was born and brought up a Christian; he was, in fact, an anti-Semite; but because he was of Jewish race his whole economic doctrine is a Jewish invention which has poisoned the world, and all Jews are held equally responsible with him for it. These and similar beauties of Nazi logic stun the imagination of the foreigner; it is immensely difficult—requires a real effort of *Einfühlung*—to realize that grown-up human beings can believe such an idiotic farrago even under the pressure of ceaseless propaganda and ruthless terror.

But they do believe it. Not with the furious intensity of Hitler, of course: most men and women have something to do in life besides hate. Very often they want to eat, go to bed, take a walk down the street and look at a shop, or sit in a movie theater and munch peanuts. Sometimes they like to stand and look out of a window. Sometimes they want to sing or dance or whittle a new stick. Hitler does none of these things, has no ordinary human interest by all accounts, and can concentrate all the venom of a phenomenally powerful hate machine on sheer hatred twenty-four hours a day. He has thus inspired the Nazi organizations with enough of his passion to make Jew-baiting a primary interest of the National Socialist party and acceptable (if nothing worse) to the non-Nazi mass of the German and Austrian peoples. A generation is growing up in Germany which has never heard a word to contradict all the Nazi doctrine and legend about the Jews, a generation which has been given a scapegoat to sacrifice and knows no reason in the matter. When that generation is the dominant one, it will be perfectly pos-

[*107*]

sible for the Nazi regime to order a general massacre of the Jews, and the rest of the population—terrified, half believing, uncertain—will be glad to forget it in a week or so and say that it was "all greatly exaggerated by the foreign press."

4

The devices used by the Gestapo in the persecution of the Vienna Jews—since wholesale massacre was not considered expedient—were many and complicated. The main objectives were the spoliation and expulsion of all the Jews of Austria, concentrated chiefly in Vienna. By a series of decrees, the new authorities made it impossible for a Jew to direct his own business or derive profit from it; to retain possession of real estate; to own a motorcar; to engage in any profession; to sell industrial shares; to send his children to any except specified schools; to walk in the parks or sit on benches, etc., etc. All of these decrees did not come out at once, and some were a little ambiguous in language. As the law was slow, the Nazi party invented its own ways of dealing with the Jews. Wholesale arrests, operated on the system of rotation of crops, kept about twenty thousand Jews in jail or concentration camp at the same time. Before they were released, all those who possessed property or industrial shares, houses or art works or other valuables, were made to sign papers "voluntarily" surrendering these possessions in whole or in part (depending on the whim of the Nazi official) to "Aryan ownership." Very often they also signed a paper "voluntarily" promising to leave the country by a certain not very remote date.

Of the Jews who were not arrested, but who lived in hourly terror of the jail and the camp, it was easy to obtain acquiescence in these and other schemes of spoliation. The "commissarial" system of administration in commerce and industry was invented to keep Jewish businesses going without giving the profit from them to their owners. The banks, shops, factories and offices which once belonged to Jews were put under *"kommissärische Leitung"* ("Commissarial control"). The "commissars" were young Nazis, many of whom had just emerged from jail themselves and were in great need of recouping their fortunes. They knew little of business, were ignorant of the simplest methods, and the money scattered with a splash all over Vienna. The waste and inefficiency (not to speak of the plain stealing) that went on under this system were so flagrant that while I was in Vienna in July the Nazi authorities themselves had to arrest a hundred or so of their bright young men and put them into a concentration camp to think it over; otherwise the system of commerce and industry in Vienna might have collapsed altogether.

The technique of punishment was simple, as it is throughout Germany. No search warrant or warrant for arrest is required; the agents of the state secret police—Geheime Staatspolizei, abbreviated to Gestapo—can enter any house at any time and arrest anybody, without saying why. The same powers were exercised during the early days of the terror in Vienna (March and April, 1938) by the S.S. men (Schützstaffel), but later on the Gestapo took over all the mechanism of persecution and operated it with quiet efficiency. When I was in Vienna street incidents had ceased, and it was perfectly possible for a casual foreign tourist to visit the city and say that "everything looked normal," especially if he had never known Vienna before the German conquest. Arrests took place only at night, and for the most part in Jewish or working-class quarters which the foreigner would not see unless he went to look for them.

But they took place every night, and there were two heavily loaded trains every day to Dachau, the great concentration camp in Bavaria.

The man arrested could buy his way out, providing the Gestapo felt sure he was not holding back any part of his wealth, and providing he would sign an undertaking to leave the country within a specific length of time. Among the poor Jews there was no money to be obtained, or hardly any; and there was little assurance that they could be expelled, since foreign countries had become so reluctant to grant visas. Consequently the imprisonment and physical maltreatment of these people (the majority) would appear to have been sheer sadism, the exercise of strength over weakness, and the release of pent-up hatreds created by National Socialism's long campaign against the Jews.

An arrest in a wealthy Jewish house was a carnival for the S.S. and Gestapo men. They could take anything that caught their fancy, and would never be held to account; they could maltreat the inhabitants of the house at will. There were never any criminal trials; the only trials were the civil ones, about property or arrears of taxes or other items in the spoliation scheme. Consequently a squad of S.S. men sent to arrest Dr X, for example, were at liberty to take the household silver, Dr X's wife's jewelry, some gold picture frames and all the cash they could find, and there was never any question of restoring it. This happened wherever there were arrests for the first two or three months: the S.S. men, in particular, had keen eyes and capacious pockets. This was, of course, simple individual robbery, and the proceeds did not even go into the party's funds.

The other forms of robbery disguised under the phrases "voluntary surrender" and "transfer to Aryan possession" were for the direct benefit of the Nazi party funds: they

[*110*]

did not benefit the Austrian state or the German national treasuries. I accumulated some of the curious documents used in these operations, with their pseudolegal phraseology masking a process of confiscation. Here is one:

According to the decision of May 23, 1938, taken by the State Commissar for Private Property, Mr X. Y. Z. has been appointed as Commissar for your bungalow in the bathing station of Kritzendorf on the Danube.

According to Law Number 80, Paragraph 2, concerning the nomination of commissarial administrators, the Commissar is entitled to undertake all legal actions, and therefore all rights that you had concerning your bungalow are canceled.

According to the disposition that Jews are no longer allowed to enter the bathing stations on the Danube, the transfer into Aryan possession shall be arranged at the sum estimated, or the bungalow will be destroyed, and you will be informed in due course.

(Signed) THE COMMISSAR, X.Y.Z.

Later on the owner of this bungalow was asked to sign a paper reading:

I herewith certify that I voluntarily cede my bungalow to the Community of Kritzendorf at the price of three hundred marks.

This particular owner had spent ten thousand marks on her bungalow at Kritzendorf, and refused to sign for some time. She then received a printed postal card from the local authorities saying:

You are hereby warned that you must send in the bungalow keys which you have retained to the Community of

[*111*]

Kritzendorf within forty-eight hours. Otherwise change of locks at your expense.

THE COMMISSARIAL DIRECTOR, X.Y.Z.

The owner of the bungalow, making the best of a bad bargain, signed her "surrender" in the hope of getting at least the three hundred marks out of it; but these were never paid. Nor was I able to discover any case in which the Nazi valuation (absurdly low though it always was) had been actually paid to the former owner of property.

All this was long before the decree imposing the two-thousand-million-mark fine on the Jews of the Reich; that came in November. What was happening in Austria in the spring and summer was an attempt by hitherto untried methods, the inventions of Himmler's Nazi desperadoes, to rob the Viennese Jews and drive them into exile without any of their property. Every device of the law was used, but when the law did not go far enough the party officials "interpreted" it to suit themselves, and were safe because no Jew would dare to bring a legal action or would find a lawyer to direct it if he did. (Non-Jewish lawyers were forbidden to represent Jews by one of Goering's April decrees; and although they did so, for exorbitant fees, in the ordinary business of property, taxation, etc., they would not go into a court as representing a Jew. Jewish lawyers were forbidden to practice.)

The result was as the inventors of the system expected: the Jews of Austria, harassed and terrified at every turn of their ordinary lives, unable to work or use their own property or send their children to school, penalized by a thousand humiliating devices such as the "No Jews" sign on cafés, park benches or theaters, were in an appalling state even when they still retained their liberty. A very large proportion of them either had been in jail or would soon go when their turn came; thousands were in concentration camps; some hundreds certainly had been murdered. In such conditions of life they came to be dominated by one idea only: escape. This was the result the persecutors had desired to achieve. They were now able to say to the whole Jewish population of Vienna (nearly two hundred thousand): "You can go when you have your papers in order and have paid your taxes. Arrange to suit yourselves. We don't want you. We will be glad to get rid of you."

Then began the long torture of preparation for escape. I never heard of anybody who was able to leave Austria after the new methods really came into operation (after about mid-April, that is) without an agony of many weeks, often three or four months; thousands who began their attempts to get out last April or May are still midway in the attempt. The difficulties were and are almost innumerable. The simplest ones are those concerned with taxes. Twenty-five per cent of the total capital of a Jew had to be paid in the form of *Reichsfluchtsteuer* (tax on "flight from the Reich"). Ten per cent had to be paid for the relief of the poor Jews of Vienna—a tax which never reached the persons who were supposed to benefit by it. Income, profits and corporation taxes, as well as taxes on real estate, had to be paid in full on the German scale (not the Austrian), and for the last fiscal year as well as the present one. The past records of the Austrian fisc were combed to find irregularities or some justification for claiming arrears of taxes; these were often claimed when they had been paid in full before the German conquest. Persons whose property had been confiscated could not leave the country until they had paid full German taxes (for this year and last) on that property. With all this, the stock exchange was closed and the Jews were not allowed to sell industrial shares except by arrangement with the Nazi authorities and at absurdly low prices. Under such circumstances it was most often impossible for a Jew to pay all these taxes; and if he could not, he was not entitled to a passport.

But if, after weeks of struggle, he succeeded in paying his taxes and still had enough money to buy a ticket to some happier country, he entered a new phase of torture. This consisted of standing in line for day after day, week after week, at the passport office. The crowds here were dense at all times, and every non-Jew, no matter how briefly he had been present, was taken ahead of any Jew; the same people went back to that line for weeks on end without ever reaching an official who could deal with their request. Once they had made their application for the passport and had proved their fiscal purity, they had to repeat the ordeal at the Devisenstelle, the office where foreign currencies can be bought for purposes of emigration. Here the questions asked, the proofs demanded, were ingenious, complicated and numerous. The business at the Devisenstelle occupied a friend of mine for nearly three months, although he had the double advantage of being a Christian non-Aryan with only one Jewish grandparent, and of having established residence abroad some years before.

If the passport and Devisenstelle operations were successfully carried through, there existed no further obstacle to emigration under German law and Austrian Nazi decree (which often differed from German law during the first six months). The émigré might be robbed of his money and belongings at the frontier—as happened fairly often—but at least he was legally free to get out of his stricken country and try his luck elsewhere. But before he could do so he had to obtain the visa of some country which was willing

to accept him as a resident or visitor, and of whatever intervening countries there might be over which he had to pass.

This was in many cases impossible, and the effort at
escape ended there. All the consulates were besieged; the
Jews of Vienna were ready to go anywhere, even Italy, to
get out of Vienna. At the Czechoslovak Consulate, for example, there was a mass of people waiting all day every day,
filling the street outside, roughly marshaled into submissive
order by the German green police—and this although everybody in Europe knew that Czechoslovakia was the next
nation to be attacked under Hitler's program. In the American Consulate and all along the street leading to it there
were lines waiting from March until the German quota was
exhausted, and even after it had been exhausted at the end
of the summer. The Americans gave some of the people,
particularly women and old men, chairs to sit down on, but
the waiting was the same, the results for the most part not
good. Thousands of applications had to be turned down because the applicants knew nobody in America who could
guarantee them; other thousands were received and filed for
months without action being taken. It seemed to me that
half the Jews in Vienna must have applied for American
visas, and only a small proportion of them could ever hope
to obtain them under the quota laws. The French, having
granted too many in the beginning of the terror, suddenly
ceased granting any at all except to visitors who had money
and could prove that they would not stay in France. The
British granted visas on a very small scale, preferring to give
temporary visas to people who could prove that they
would eventually be admitted somewhere else. In the American and Czechoslovak consulates the press of work was so
great that extra staff had to be engaged and volunteer
workers brought in; both of these consulates had to close

their doors for a few days in June to catch up with the filing and forwarding of their applications.

The Jew who, upon his release from jail or concentration camp, went through all this struggle to emigrate and did finally succeed in doing so was a singularly lucky man in spite of everything, for most of those who tried did not succeed. At some point in the long ordeal of emigration the money would give out, the formalities would become too great to be coped with any longer, or the susceptibilities of some Nazi official would be offended; and all hope ended there. The Jew who gave up subsisted, in the end, on relief —the half starvation of the soup kitchen; or he went back to the concentration camp when the time allotted him by the Gestapo had expired; or he committed suicide. There were seven thousand suicides in Vienna during the first four months of the Nazi regime. Some of these were Catholics and Austrian patriots, but most of them were Jews.

5

How is the mind to conceive what this suffering must have been? It passes any other known to me because there is no hope in it. The Fascist bombs that destroyed the lives of children in Spain were a crueler and bloodier expression of Hitler's will, but they were an infamous accident in a land which was alive with hope. Moreover, the determination to impose Fascism on Spain is a political determination, and there has been no period in which wars of this kind have been humane. But the persecution of the Jews, even in its mildest forms—even in those which involve only confiscation of his property and humiliation of his person—is a subtle and profound moral degradation for everybody concerned. It subjects a helpless minority to the deepest in-

dignity that a human being can suffer: the assurance that
he and his kind have no right to live. There had been a
considerable influx of southeastern and eastern European
Jews to Vienna during and after the war, it is true; but they
were still not the majority, and most of those who suffered
had been Viennese for generations. Their parents and
grandparents had helped make Vienna what it was: they
were builders, scientists, artists, men of business and the
theater. The university, the opera and the orchestra, those
three most beloved of Viennese institutions, were particularly indebted to Jewish talent and energy. The Austrian
Jews loved Vienna and had been absorbed in it for at least
a hundred years, so that most Viennese even of the oldest
Austrian aristocratic families seemed a trifle Jewish and
most of the Jews had taken on the softness and the graces
of the society in which they lived. It was a decaying society,
that Austrian world before Hitler, and there were many
absurdities in it, but it maintained throughout its economic
layers some special character which assured a man almost
without his being aware of it—merely by the inhalation of
the air—that life was made to be enjoyed when possible.
There are many thousands of the Viennese Jews who can
never survive transplantation—even if they achieve it—in
an alien land: will never, that is, live fully again. When all
the horrors of the jail and concentration camp are over, and
the humiliations of those months of struggle to escape have
faded a little, the emigrant from Austria still faces the new
world (if he is lucky enough to face it at all) with a heart
and mind grown colder, with an important part of his vital
imagination deadened by the thought that he will never
see Vienna again. This is the final and permanent unhap-
piness of the Viennese Jew: that he is likely to be an exile
forever, since there is no spot on earth that can possibly

seem to be his home. Because they were not so blessed in the past, the Jews of other areas held by the swastika may be less cursed in the future—that is, if they have a future.

Sometimes in Vienna it seemed that there was no future possible for them except to be *abgerottet* (torn out by the roots, exterminated) as Hitler had proclaimed in *Mein Kampf*. The difficulties put in their way were too great to be overcome except by very exceptional patience, fortitude and good luck. A hundred thousand, a hundred and twenty thousand, more perhaps, must continue this death-in-life for months or years to come; for those who escaped were relatively few. The American quota for Germany was soon exhausted: is now exhausted, I believe, for five years in advance. The British have no quota, but in principle they are unwilling to admit anybody who must work for his living in England. The French adopt the same generous principle. South America, the British dominions—little or no hope. And in Vienna, what? The soup kitchen and a lodging (if one can be found which will take Jews); no air, no freedom, no chance to live and work—the existence of the outcast, rejected and despised of men.

In every family there is at least one member who has gone to jail or to the concentration camp (often to both). The family at home in Vienna receives a postal card from the camp at Dachau once every two weeks. On these cards a man is allowed to say nothing except that he is well and that the weather is good or bad. Hundreds of Jews have died "of natural causes" or been "accidentally" killed by machine guns, either en route to Dachau or at the camp itself: their bodies are returned to their relatives in sealed coffins or else as ashes in an urn. It is forbidden to open the sealed coffins, and the ashes might be those of anybody. The relatives of those who die at Dachau are never able to say that the corpses have been correctly identified—and in many cases an obstinate, agonizing uncertainty subsists for weeks before the widow or children admit that death has taken place. Jews vanish—as Catholics and aristocrats do also, although in lesser numbers—and are never heard of again.

And this, I would say, going along the street, this is Vienna. This is the place where you waltzed. At the big, ugly Rathaus, across the square from the Burgtheater (remember the Burgtheater? It was very good), is the solemn and ridiculous black-draped room where they marry people; I was married there. The Burggarten is green in the summer and the children play with their nurses. There is plenty of beer still in the beer cellars (if you can stand the constant heil-Hitlering) and the night places up on the hill at Grinzing are still open. Im Prater blühn wieder die Bäume. Out on the Danube there is an aquatic life of the utmost energy going on, all among simon-pure Aryans, and the boys and girls who can prove their racial purity are entitled to go where they like in regional dress, *Tracht*. Not a word of the daily and nightly horrors is allowed to be printed in the Viennese press, and there are hundreds of thousands of people living here who know nothing about them. All they know is what happens to their neighbors; a few stories which they listen to and discount at once; and official statements which, in the long run, they must believe because they hear nothing else. The disaffected (or anti-Nazi) population, which must on any reckoning be three or four hundred thousand, can hear news of Vienna and of the world only in one way: by tuning in on the *Strasburg-sender*, the nightly broadcast of news in German from Strasburg. But the mass of the people is too timorous or too apolitical to risk this forbidden fruit, and sinks, in time, into acceptance of everything the Nazi authorities may choose to publish, no matter how impossible it may be—and perhaps, by Hitler's principles, precisely because of its impossibility. "For the broad mass of the people in the primitive simplicity of its heart more readily falls victim to a big lie than to a small one." (*Mein Kampf*, p. 252.) This is what Hitler calls a "very sound principle," and it has guided him with immense success since 1933 as before. And moreover, people can even be happy, after a while, in whatever conditions, since they will believe anything if they are told it often enough. "The skilful and unremitting use of propaganda can persuade people to believe that Heaven is Hell or conversely that the most miserable existence is Paradise." (*Mein Kampf*, p. 302.)

This is Vienna.

6

Up in the ballroom over the lake of Geneva the gentlemen made speeches of varying length but uniform content. The delegate of Switzerland spoke eloquently for twenty minutes about the regret with which Switzerland recorded its inability to do anything. The delegate from Paraguay spoke at even greater length about the economic necessities of his country, which would permit of no Jewish immigration to its cities, but would admit a limited number of carefully chosen immigrants with special qualifications or training who could go on the land. The delegate of the Irish Free State, with admirable brevity, stated that his country as a whole had deep sympathy for the Jews of Austria but was incapable of accepting any number of them however small. And so it went.

Down at the Casino the bored croupiers raked in money and chips at the green tables. Swiss gentlemen from across the lake made complicated calculations in their notebooks and played with businesslike skill. The Conference of Evian (begging its pardon, the Intergovernmental Committee at Evian) went on for a week, and the Hotel Royal had to take on some extra waiters.

7

Some months later the balance of Europe had changed. Mr Neville Chamberlain had made his expedition to Munich: the dilapidated and uncertain democracies were henceforth unable to exercise any influence, even by the flow of public opinion, upon the course of Fascist Germany. There is the strongest presumption that a new persecution of the Jews had been arranged, and all its details settled, by the end of October, both as a sop to anti-Semitic passion in the Nazi party and as a means of extracting money for the bankrupt state. Germany had monopolized the capital market inside its frontiers all year long, forcing some eight milliards of marks in loans (about fifteen hundred million dollars, or three hundred million pounds) upon the people able to invest. The arms and munitions programs, the mobilization and the Austrian and Czechoslovak enterprises had been costly in the extreme, and all the wizardry of the Reichsbank was required to keep even this artificial economy with its rigid controls from collapse. It was no longer possible to squeeze any important sum out of the Austrian Jews; the Jews of the old Reich, who had so far fared considerably better than their Austrian brethren, were in better case and it was their turn now.

At the correct moment a young Polish Jew named Grynszpan walked into the German Embassy in Paris and shot a secretary by the name of Von Rath, who died a day or so later. Von Rath was a professional diplomatist belonging to a family known for its liberal ideas; he had been a Nazi and had not long before resigned from the party. His loss was therefore not felt too keenly in the upper circles of that organization; but to make him appear a national victim of greater importance, Hitler promoted the unfortunate youth to counsellor of embassy on his deathbed. The individual act of violence became a mass act by all Jews against all Germans, or was so presented to the German people.

Two days later (on Thursday, November 10, 1938) the Nazi youth organizations and chosen adult members were summoned from their beds at three to four in the morning to execute vengeance. At the same hour throughout Germany, in Berlin, Magdeburg, Frankfurt, Munich, Vienna, Leipzig, Düsseldorf and hundreds of other towns, the brown shirts and the Hitler Youth, aided by Nazi party members not in uniform, set fire to synagogues, looted houses, smashed shopwindows and carried off their contents, destroyed furniture, beat up Jews and in some places committed murder. Some hours later, while the looting of shops and houses continued unabated in broad daylight under the benevolent eyes of the German police, the wholesale arrests began, and in two days and nights about sixty-five thousand Jews were arrested throughout the German cities and taken to jail or the concentration camps.

The story of November 10–12 is so well known throughout the world that it scarcely needs repetition. By the time I reached Berlin it was all over, and the hour of the worried Aryan comment—"It has all been greatly exaggerated by the foreign press"—had arrived. But from persons who actually saw these events, and there were many of them, it was possible to reconstruct the scenes of fire and horror in that wintry dawn. Men scurrying along the street with cans of kerosene said to friends of mine: "We've got them now. They won't forget this." Germans who had never believed any of the *Greuelmärchen* (atrocity stories) before this day were the stunned witnesses of an organized outrage which was not over with the daylight, but continued until late afternoon. They might, if they chose, refuse to believe anything except what they had actually seen, but enough of them had seen enough to send an electric shock through Germany. There are, after all, many millions of Germans who are neither Nazis nor Jews, and who have not yet been completely brutalized by Fascism. One of the few rays of hope in the German nightmare was the frequency with which one heard, in Berlin, of movements of sympathy toward the helpless and persecuted people during those dreadful days. Some hundreds of non-Jewish Germans, simon-pure Aryans, were dragged off to jail for attempting to defend or protect their Jewish neighbors. And in nearly every specific outrage of which I was able to obtain a description from somebody who had seen it, there were these signs that the conscience of Germany is not yet altogether lost. It was little enough, in a nation of eighty million people, but it was better than nothing at all.

In the Prinzregentenstrasse there occurred one of the most horrifying episodes of the day. The Fascist contingent arrived there at dawn, equipped with kerosene, straw, etc., to set the great synagogue on fire. The synagogue in the Prinzregentenstrasse was one of the finest in Berlin, built before the war of 1914–18 at great cost. Its pipe organ had been a present from the Kaiser Wilhelm II. Neighbors who saw the preparation for the fire came out into the street and told the Nazi in charge that he could not burn this building without rescuing the sexton and his wife and children, who lived at the top of it. The Nazi in charge replied: "Lass die jüdische Sauen schmoren [Let the Jewish sows roast]!"

And the synagogue was, in fact, set on fire at once, without any attempt to warn the sleeping family on the top floor. The neighbors telephoned to the fire department; three or four calls were made before there was an answer; and later—much later—the firemen did come. They extinguished the flames first, leaving the great synagogue gutted inside, and then rescued the sexton and his family. The man was dying, and did in fact die the next day. The children suffered very severe burns; the wife went insane.

You could see those synagogues of the West End, and humbler ones elsewhere, their shells still standing as evidence of the pogrom. You could go along the Kurfürstendamm or any number of other streets and see the smashed windows of the shops, most of them now barred or boarded up. In poorer districts there had been wanton destruction, not simply looting or stealing; the furniture of poor Jews had been broken up and thrown into the street. German children carried off what they liked from Jewish shops on November 10 under the eyes of the Nazi gangsters and of the benevolent police. One Protestant pastor in the West End spoke to his children's class on the following Sunday and told them that stealing was stealing, under whatever circumstances; he received an official visit before the day was out, with the warning that if he spoke again in this vein he would find the way to the concentration camp. Wherever you went in Berlin you heard of nothing but the pogrom and the innumerable incidents that had taken place during those two days; of the arrests that followed; of the thousands who had gone to jail and concentration camp; and of the hunger and misery of the people. In that population which is so severely rationed for its milk, butter and vegetables, where fruit is almost unknown and meat exceedingly rare, where the ordinary egg has apparently ceased to exist, shock follows shock until the responses of human nature become too feeble to count; for the pulse of Germany as a whole is very low, and the country has been bled white to create its military force. It is for this reason—the beaten, devitalized bodies and terror-ridden spirit of the people—that thousands of Germans possessing the normal humane sympathies looked on, with horror but in silence, as the Nazi party's thugs attacked the property and persons of the helpless.

And when it was over the decrees began. They were like the decrees of some months earlier in Austria, except that in some particulars they were worse. Jews could no longer go into parks, theaters or concert halls; in Munich they were forbidden to buy food for several days; all over Germany they were forbidden to sell property; after due reflection, Dr Goebbels and his colleagues decided to impose a collective fine of two thousand million marks (four hundred million dollars) upon the Jews of the Reich as punishment for the "disorders" they had "provoked." If they were covered by insurance for the destruction of their property, the insurance money was the property of the Reich. The Nazis distributed *"Judenverbot"* signs in restaurants, hotels and other public places, Jewish tenants in places owned by Christians were given notice to leave, etc., etc. Both by public decree and by private animosity, the Jews were reduced in a few days to an even more unhappy state than had been the lot of their Austrian brethren a few months earlier.

Again, as in Austria, these people dreamed of only one possible life: exile. And, as in Austria, they faced the heartbreaking difficulties created by a government which was

[*125*]

willing enough to let them go, but only after it had been thoroughly proved that they were leaving all their possessions behind. The same taxes and the same restrictions entangled their steps as they tried for weary weeks to escape; and once they obtained passports, they began the same endless procedure of application and waiting for the foreign visas. Austria had, indeed, served Hitler's Reich well: it had provided the dress rehearsal for the great operation contemplated since 1933, the spoliation and expulsion of all the Jews.

8

Twice during my brief visit to Berlin I drove out to Sachsenhausen, the concentration camp on the other side of Oranienburg. On the first occasion a colleague and I tried to get in; the guard trafficked with us for ten minutes or so, peering with beady eyes into the car to see if we had brought anything besides ourselves. He had the Nazi sense of humor, a faculty which depends chiefly upon brutal reference to the victims of the regime. "Have you come to put somebody in or to take somebody out?" he asked us as we drove up to the gate. We had, of course, no chance of entry, and it was merely to catch a glimpse of the place that we made the attempt.

On the second occasion I drove there at three in the morning and made the circuit around it, on the off chance that something might be observed at such an unguarded hour. The white walls were silent under the blaze of light that beats on them night and day. The turrets which rise at regular intervals showed their machine guns; the inhabitants of the place—overcrowded like all concentration camps this year—were sleeping in their close-packed rows inside, trying to keep warm. Jews and Social Democrats and Catholics and Protestants were huddled together there, several thousand of them, but most of them just now were Jews: some of Berlin's thirty thousand Jewish prisoners. There were others at Dachau in Bavaria, and at Buchenwalde in Thuringia, and in the cellars of the Brown Houses, and in jails, or in the new concentration camps that are springing up everywhere. They would be all asleep now, if they were lucky, all huddled together in their worn-out army pajamas with their single worn-out blanket each. At five o'clock in the morning they would be wakened again to the day's work in the fields. Near Sachsenhausen they were employed in breaking up stone for road repairs.

Sachsenhausen (which looks very much like the photographs of the camp at Dachau) is a huge rectangle walled in white stone. Along the top of the wall run three electric cables, charged so that electrocution will be the fate of anybody who attempts to crawl over them. Inside the wall the pitiless lights beat upon a space which is forbidden for inmates. Any prisoner who steps into the forbidden space near the wall is shot at once. ("Scharf geschossen!" as the signs say.) Further inside are the buildings and the space provided for prisoners: these I have not seen.

Numerous accounts of life in the concentration camps have been printed, and the routine of brutality and privation is well known by now. Death "from natural causes" is frequent, being brought on by floggings and other forms of punishment as well as by the diseases incident to undernourishment, exposure and strain. Death "while trying to escape" is also very frequent, and constitutes a recognized form of suicide as well, since anybody who goes beyond a certain line is shot on sight. In the early days of the Hitler regime, before the camps were so hideously crowded, the S.A. (Sturm Abteilung) men who guarded them derived much pleasure from torturing the prisoners, beating them with rubber truncheons, stripping them naked for amusement in various clever and obscene ways, making them march in a circle for a day at a time, chaining their wrists to their ankles, and the like. The events of 1938, particularly after "Peace with Honour" had been made at Munich, filled the concentration camps to overflowing, and the guards had no time to indulge in their earlier pastimes. In the stories I was able to collect from Sachsenhausen, which is the camp where a large proportion of the Berlin prisoners go, there is no evidence of the kind. The Sachsenhausen prisoners were treated brutally, but without any special inventions of sadistic subtlety. Aside from the deprivation of liberty and the absence of hope, the chief suffering seemed to come from cold, hunger and fatigue—that and, of course, sanitary complications. The Nazi sense of humor, a monstrosity in itself, particularly delights in practical jokes about the water closet; and as no camp has adequate plumbing, the fun in this respect is practically continuous.

Buchenwalde, in Thuringia, has the reputation of being the worst of the camps for ingenious ill-treatment of the prisoners, for bad equipment and for general cruelty. It is even more crowded than Sachsenhausen and Dachau, so that this winter a new device had to be invented to accommodate all the inmates at night. Like all such devices, it served also as a form of torture. Big cagelike boxes were constructed with shelves in them, so that four or sometimes eight inmates could sleep in a vertical space which had been wasted hitherto. The wood used was one which bent easily, so that the inmate had his neighbor hanging over him like a sword of Damocles all night. Sometimes these shelves broke and there was trouble and injury; but even if they did not break, they were narrow perches in the crowded night of the camp, when the darkness was filled with sighing. One man who had the good luck to stay at Buchenwalde only a few days (his family were rich and could buy him out; also he had his passport and visas ready for escape) told the story of his time there before he left Germany forever. He had been among a group of about a hundred and fifty Berlin Jews who were taken down to Buchenwalde after the arrests of November 10–11. In the tunnel at Weimar, when some delay was caused in the movement of the crowd, the S.S. men who were guarding them beat them all over the heads with their rifles. This was after a journey of many hours during which no man had been allowed to go to the water closet. (It is one of the greatest pleasures of the Nazis to force prisoners to foul their clothing; numerous systems are used to bring about this admirable result, including Mussolini's old weapon, castor oil.) Thus weakened by fatigue, their beatings, and in some cases loss of blood, the men arrived at Buchenwalde and were made to stand in line for twelve hours. At the end of this time, when each had been entered in the books and had passed the official scrutiny, they were all taken to what their guards said was the "latrine." This was a ditch with a wooden rail along one side of it. The ditch had been used often before for this purpose. The rail had been cut nearly through in several places, so that when the exhausted men attempted to use it they fell through into the filth below. The episode was one eminently characteristic of the humanity and wit of Hitler's regime, and the S.S. guards howled with laughter.

There were said to be forty new concentration camps under construction when I was in Berlin. The classic type is that of Sachsenhausen (also called the Oranienburg camp; it is just beyond Oranienburg) and Dachau, a walled rectangle with machine guns mounted in square turrets, cables for electrocution, and guards with rifles. If the Hitler program is to be carried out, and we cannot doubt that it will be, all forty of the new camps will be needed as well as those already in use, for there are about six hundred thousand Jews in Greater Germany, as well as several hundred thousand "political enemies" or other non-Jewish victims of the regime; twenty-seven million Catholics, of whom thousands have already found their way into the concentration camps; and over fifty million Protestants who have also contributed to the throng of the victims. Pastor Niemöller, for example, the celebrated preacher of Berlin who would not be silenced, was in Sachsenhausen when I was last in Germany. There are trades union leaders, clergymen, professors, members of all the learned professions, bankers, engineers and men of great talent in the arts imprisoned in these places, without trial or hope of a trial, without a chance of escape except at Hitler's pleasure. The "brutal ruthlessness" which the Führer enjoins upon his followers is put into execution here upon Jew and Gentile alike—perhaps the only way in which the regime recognizes an equality between the human beings who come beneath its sway.

9

What is Hitler going to do with the Jews? There are six hundred thousand of them in Greater Germany, and there are another three or four hundred thousand "non-Aryan" Christians who have enough Jewish blood to attract varying degrees of persecution. It is clearly impossible for even the German National Socialist Workers' party, in all the pride of its absolute dominion, to murder so many people. They do not fear the opinion of the outside world, at least since the surrender of France and England in September, 1938; the German press has made it quite clear that the influence of the democracies upon their thinking ceased at Munich. But what the Nazi party probably does fear (if it still has any elements of common sense) is the German people. Germany is subdued, dispirited, bled white; the young and the foolish are for the most part taken in by the regime's unceasing propaganda; and yet my impression in Berlin was that the pogroms will have to be arranged differently the next time. They must be organized so that ordinary Germans do not see them, do not look out of their windows to see helpless Jews being chased by gangs of Nazi thugs, do not wake up at dawn to hear the crashing of glass and the screams of beaten women. If the mass of the Germans do not actually see the pogroms, it will be perfectly possible for the regime to tell the people that none have taken place, and the people will believe—or if they do not fully believe, they will at least remain in doubt, which has been their normal state on all matters since 1933.

But the pogrom of November 10 did shock the German people who saw it. There can be little doubt about that fact. Another such, or two or three such, might arouse such indignations that the dominion of the Nazi party could be, to some degree at least, shaken—its hold on the masses weakened, its moral prestige severely impaired. It may seem strange to foreigners who have not visited Germany that the Nazi party has any moral prestige left; but it should be remembered that every question is presented to the German people in one way only: the way which makes the Nazi dictatorship the virtuous and heroic defender of its people. German aviators who were taken prisoner in Spain, when asked why they had come so far to fight against the Spanish Republic, invariably replied that they came "to defend

the Fatherland against Bolshevism." They went to Czechoslovakia to "free" the German-speaking citizens of that
state (and incidentally to put a hundred thousand or more
of the others in jail and concentration camp, although this
is never mentioned). In disputes with the United States,
that country is represented as a Bolshevist colony under
Jewish dictatorship; Mr Roosevelt is said to be Jewish, his
real name Rosenfeld; and Julius Streicher even offered
(in a public speech) to produce proof that Pope Pius XI was
Jewish. The Nazi mass meeting with its incredibly elaborate paraphernalia, Herr Hitler playing on the crowd as
you play on a pipe organ, with one electric signal for one
sort of shout and another signal for another, is always
crowned by words of patriotic virtue and heroic self-
abnegation. Millions of Germans believe these things because they hear them constantly and they never hear anything else. *Funkwarte* (radio guards) haunt the streets to
keep them (not always successfully) from tuning in on the
Strasburg or other radio stations from which they might
hear the truth; loud-speakers infest every park, square or
public gathering place; the press and the wireless are rigidly
controlled and the land pullulates with spies. It is practically impossible for a German under the present regime
to have any idea of the world he lives in. This is in accordance with the principle Hitler stated so clearly in *Mein
Kampf:* "The German has not the slightest notion how a
people must be misled if the adherence of the masses is
sought." (This was in the first eleven editions of *Mein
Kampf*, but after Hitler had sufficiently misled the people
to obtain the adherence of the masses, it was suppressed.)

Moreover, having heard it so often, the German very
probably believes that most of his national misfortunes have
been due to the Jews; that the Jews are a parasitic and

[*132*]

inimical growth; that Germany will be in a healthier state without them. But from this state of ignorant acquiescence —comforted, if he hears "atrocity stories," by the reflection that they have all been invented by the foreign press—to the state of stunned astonishment in which many ordinary German citizens found themselves at dawn on November 10 is a considerable psychological journey. I believe that the Nazi leaders will arrange their next pogrom in such a way that this particular danger may be avoided; and if they do, the German people in general will never know how bad it has been. For as Hitler himself has repeatedly pointed out in *Mein Kampf*, this people is extraordinarily sheep-like, phenomenal above all things in the ease with which it can be led; and unless they see horrors with their own eyes they will accept whatever story their Leader chooses to give them.

The pogroms in future, therefore, may be different in the details of their arrangement, but there will certainly be pogroms again and again. Nothing else is possible to the Nazi regime under Adolf Hitler. The ideal, as Hitler has stated, is the extermination of the Jews, but as there are so many of them a downright massacre presents the gravest difficulties from the technical point of view. Successive pogroms to gratify Nazi sadism, terrify the Jews, bring in money and signalize Germany's independence of the humanitarian prejudices of the outside world will be organized from time to time when occasion seems to warrant, and each of these pogroms will spur on the movement of expulsion a little bit. That is, more money will come from abroad for Jewish relief—money which goes directly into the Nazi pockets in the form of foreign currency and passes to the Jews in the form of paper marks—and more visas will be, or may be, granted to Jews, after each such demonstration of the will of the Führer. Dr Goebbels will blandly call the demonstrations "spontaneous," and blame them on the "*kochende Volks-seele*," the "boiling-over soul of the people," but nobody would be more surprised than himself if anybody believed him. In this system of fraudulent thought and lying statement, millions of Germans do not know what to believe, and they will not find out in time to be of any use to their Jewish brethren. The democracies gave up any chance they had of exercising an influence when they paid their homage to Hitler at Munich in September, 1938; the United States is too far away; the Jews of Germany must suffer again and again and again until such time as the freer world beyond the German borders decides to admit them all.

And for my part I cannot understand why there has been any delay about it. The existing Jewish communities in the United States, the British Empire, France, Holland, Switzerland, the Scandinavian countries and the South American republics would unquestionably assume the expense, heavy though it would be, of resettling as many exiles as possible throughout their extent.

There is also the Soviet Union, which has not been consulted in these matters and is in a peculiarly difficult position with Germany openly threatening to attack one of the Soviet republics. But if Jews could be found in Germany who wanted to go to the Soviet Union, who could be assimilated into the life of a very different form of state, and who were willing to accept the principles of the Soviet organization (including the disappearance of the Jew as a Jew), the Soviet Union would probably accept them. In this case the political difficulties would be enormous: nothing could prevent the Nazi regime from slipping a few trusty spies into the ranks of the refugees, just as no infallible system has yet been devised for differentiating between a Jew and a non-Jew. Even so, in a settlement of refugees on any large scale it would be stupid not to consult the Soviet Union, which has great spaces, great opportunities: yet this is one of the stupidities committed.

There is room in the world for the German Jews; to deny it is not only silly but malevolent. The United States could take fifty thousand without noticing it; the British dominions could take another fifty thousand between them; South America could accept another fifty thousand or more. Scandinavia, Holland and Switzerland could absorb the same number. And the British colonies (not the dominions) and mandated territories have space for easily another fifty thousand. Among the mandated territories I do not include Palestine, for the Jews who emigrate to Palestine are, or rapidly become, Zionists—a political aberration which has done as much as any other single factor to make the problem of this section of the human body so difficult. There is no use attempting to settle Jews into a place where they will have to displace another population which has been there for centuries; the idea is crude romanticism at its best, sheer insanity at its worst, and constitutes such an unnecessary complication of the problem that one wonders how any mind favorably disposed toward the Jewish people can have considered it for a moment. It is not at all surprising that the Gestapo wishes to see Jews settled in Palestine and has actually smuggled several shiploads of them there from Trieste: for Zionism is obviously a useful aberration for the Nazi schemes. The introduction of Jews illegally into Palestine (without proper immigration papers) is a first-class Gestapo trick; it embarrasses the British, gives the Zionist Organization trouble, incites the Arabs and makes the Jews miserable, besides exposing them to the danger of death from the moment they land on those barren shores.

I have counted countries which seem to me able to absorb two hundred and fifty thousand Jews at once without difficulty, providing the expense of their resettlement is borne by the organizations which stand ready to do so. The other two hundred and fifty thousand would either have to wait in that death-in-life which is theirs in Germany, or could be resettled in a new country if one could be found suitable; in any case they would undergo hardships, but no worse than they are undergoing now. To accept six hundred thousand at once is, according to all the experts, impossible. (I don't see why, but that is what they say.) Granting that this may be so, why is it impossible to take half of them? Nobody can pretend that fifty thousand Jewish emigrants would make any appreciable difference to the hundred and thirty million people who live in the United States, especially as the fifty thousand would not become a public charge. Nobody could seriously contend that Canada, Australia, New Zealand and South Africa, in the vast unoccupied areas they possess, have no room for fifty thousand hard-working people who pay their way. What, then, is the trouble?

It seems to arise chiefly from either anti-Semitism or the fear of anti-Semitism, but the pretext given is usually the latter. "If we accept a whole block of Jewish immigration from Germany we are going to have a crisis of anti-Semitism in a few years"—that is the way I have heard it phrased a good many times. The German quota for America is exhausted for five years in advance: that is another statement. But is the German quota fixed by a law of nature? Is the immigration law itself immovable?

The fear of anti-Semitism in democratic countries is very

nearly as contemptible as anti-Semitism itself. These wretched democracies, we wonder, which are unable to defend themselves in any field of foreign politics, are they also unable to defend their own principles inside their own frontiers? Are they afraid to make it clear that their fundamental principle, the equality of citizens, applies to Jew and Gentile alike? And that anti-Semitism, wherever and however it appears, is inimical to the genius of their institutions? To hear the talk of comfortable, well-to-do Frenchmen, Americans and British, it would seem that the acceptance of even a modest proportion of these tragic exiles would provoke pogroms worse than those of Germany.

The argument is absurd. The German pogroms were neither provoked nor spontaneous; they were arranged very carefully, as the evidence overwhelmingly shows. Even in czarist Russia pogroms seldom took place without official patronage. The Jews of the whole world are used to a certain sort of anti-Semitism (the mild social forms of that disease) and they are prepared to endure it. To argue that any more savage forms of the malady would or could be produced in the democracies by immigration of the stricken German Jews is to argue that democracy has failed more signally than we yet believe—has failed even in its deepest roots, the minds and hearts of those who support it. If this were indeed true, we might as well all accept the slavery of the swastika at once, for there would be no hope against the conquering march of Fascism. Things have not yet gone so far, at least in America and the British dominions, and what seems more probable to me is that the fear of anti-Semitism is merely a new and fashionable dress for that ancient beast itself, a certain sanctimoniousness taking the place of the ferocity which characterizes your

plain common-or-garden anti-Semite. There are also re-
moteness, pomposity, self-importance: nothing seems urgent
to these people with stiff white shirts and double chins;
they will meet and discuss, and meet and discuss, and write
notes to each other, and think up fine speeches, while the
lifeblood of our species drips cruelly away, and the bones
of our dead are strewn from China to Spain on fields where
Fascism has conquered.

10

There is, then, so far as I could ever tell, no hope for the
Jews of Germany except in escape from the Reich. Even
if, at some stage of his triumphant career, Hitler encountered an unexpected resistance from the democratic powers,
and a war ensued, the Jews would suffer: in the passions of
wartime it is almost certain that there would be massacres,
particularly as any war would certainly be blamed on the
Jews. There may be massacres even in peace, for the Nazi
party has inculcated "brutal ruthlessness" with such success
that the rising generations steadily approach savagery in
their insensibility to suffering. When total insensibility is
reached the lives of half a million Jews will make no more
difference to the Nazis than the lives of six flies. The whole
German population has not yet been anesthetized: that is
the only deterrent I can perceive at present. But short of
wholesale massacres, anything in the range of starvation,
torture, arson, robbery, blackmail and physical assault is
possible at every moment. And the day of mass murder may
not be so far off as we now think.

If it comes, the democracies will have their share of the
responsibility before the conscience of mankind, which
must someday break through the clouds and assert its do-

minion, at least in retrospect, over the conduct of nations and prime ministers. Summer, autumn and winter have passed since that meeting was called at Evian on the lake, and nothing has yet been done to receive the victims of German Fascism into the world beyond the swastika. Worse: whole new populations have been added to those already bereft of every possession and every hope. Jews who fled from the swastika when Hitler entered Czecho-slovakia have been sent back to the newly annexed territories in batches of a score or two at a time, there to be murdered outright or sent to the concentration camp. At every hour of the day there are thousands of Jews suffering torture in Germany; week by week hunger and fatigue and humiliation weigh them down; with the ticking of the clock they die, tonight and every night; and the men with stiff white shirts and double chins write notes to each other about it.

Down at the Casino in Evian the croupiers still rake in money and chips every night up to the time the last boat leaves for Switzerland. The conference up on the hill was over a long time ago, and business has not been so good since.

CHAPTER IV

Madrid

Valencia was a pleasant place. There was a good deal of food there in the spring, as all the crops of vegetables and fruits had been excellent in the rich coastal plain of which it is the capital. We had meat in the Hotel Metropole twice a day, and one vegetable (cauliflower or the like), with oranges to follow. They even had wine at the Metropole, and it tasted like wine, although possibly it may have been synthetic. Each person had one round roll of bread, and there was a sort of black preparation of roasted beans which served as coffee. I never ate so well anywhere else in Spain.

There were air raids every day, some of them extremely destructive, but they did not come over the center of the town at any time when I was there. They seemed to concentrate chiefly on the Grau, the port district, and I never went into the Metropole without running into a few angry British seamen who had just been bombed and never intended to go back to their ship again, no, sir. (They always did go back.) Perhaps the British ships were particularly singled out for attack. This seemed probable, for there were, after all, a good many French and Spanish ships in the port too, and they were not often hit. I suppose the Italians were simply being mischievous: they dearly love to tweak the lion's tail. The British seamen were not, on the whole, appreciative of the joke. Too many of them had paid for it with their lives or limbs.

Inside the city of Valencia there was no excessive show of war, or even of warlike spirit, except during air raids. All the shops seemed to be open and you could buy almost anything you wanted. I once even bought some sweet cakes with orange paste in them. Such a thing was unknown in Madrid or Barcelona or anywhere else in the Republic. The fact was that the fertile land around Valencia produced food in great plenty, and transport was not well enough organized to take much of it away to the less fortunate areas. The whole population had food, and good food, too (their own, not the government's). Bread was rationed, but that was all. If you had energy enough to go to market you could buy food at prices which startled anybody from the other parts of Spain.

This was in May, and the front was up beyond Torreblanca on the coast road, and beyond Mora de Rubielos on the road to Teruel. I visited the fronts there by the hitch-hike method, which was very useful down in that part of the world as there were no foreigners and your casual friends along the road were all Spaniards. I had credentials from the foreign press office in Barcelona and it was surprising to see with what deference they were treated. The Fascists had cut through to the sea on April 15, the month before, and it might have been reasonable to expect some weakening of the Barcelona government's authority down here in the districts which were cut off from communica-

tion with it. Not at all: in the southern zone of the Republic
I found my official press credentials to be even more politely
treated than in Catalonia—perhaps because there were fewer
correspondents wandering about down there. One time I
went off to the front for three or four days by myself
(rather against the advice of the local press attaché) and
never had a moment's trouble. The boys who drove trucks
of food or munitions were always ready to give me a lift;
the military commanders were affable and informative; I
could always find a place to sleep and a blanket to cover
me. The Fascists were shelling and bombing pretty intensively along the front and for miles down the coast (they
had started their offensive to the south on April 23), and
the Republicans were inclined to assume that anybody who
came up to the front at this time must be a friend. I never
heard of a war in which a stray foreigner could roam about
so freely, even with press credentials. One of the curiosities
up there near the front was the way in which soldiers
would offer you a chunk of their bread. It had happened
once or twice in Catalonia, and up at Puigcerdá, but it
seemed to be a regular occurrence down here where there
was even less bread. Sentries and such, to whom you had
not even spoken: it was very generous and also (by the way
in which it was done) very Spanish.

I shall remember some of those conversations up on the
Levante front for a long time. The driver of a munitions
truck who picked me up on the road near Beni Casim, for
instance: he was a Basque, twenty years old, and had
fought throughout the war. He had been on the Madrid
front and then in Euzkadi (that's what they call their
country) until the Fascist conquest there; he had seen
Guernica. He got out through France and came down to
Catalonia to enlist again. This youth was a fire-eater indeed,

but he did not belong to any of the Left political parties:
he was a Basque Catholic, a nationalist, and although he
was a fierce Republican, he wasted no love on Socialist,
Communist or Anarchist. "When the war is over we'll take
care of them," he said. He admitted that the Communists
made good soldiers, but his opinions with respect to the
Anarchists (especially the Catalan Anarchists) could
scarcely be printed in any language. He was chock full of
regional prejudice, disliking Catalans, Andaluzes, Estre-
meños and pretty nearly everything else except his own
people and the people of Madrid, but his dislike of these
non-Basque populations was as nothing to his virulent hatred
of the Fascists, the Italians and the Germans. A bold fellow,
I thought, and characteristic of his own people in the part
they have played in this war.

There were a couple of *enlaces* (couriers? messengers?)
somewhere below Torreblanca who had brought dispatches
to the front. Their motorcycle had then collapsed under
them and had to be left for some days to be repaired. They
were hitchhiking back to their unit somewhere up the road
to Rubielos. They pressed food on me: bread and corned
beef, very good if you were hungry. They also told stories
(I spent some hours with them on the road, hailing trucks
and waiting for trucks). One was a Madrileño and the other
from the south; both had been in the army since there had
been a Republican army, and in the volunteer militias before that; and they had the Spanish trick of boasting. It is
the most inoffensive boasting in the world—is, in fact, a
delight to hear—because it is done without self-consciousness,
without restraint, and in a wonderfully florid language.
This particular trait always reminded me of the Arabs, who
do just the same thing in the same way: talk of their
prowess. One of the *enlaces* got a little melancholy at one

moment, just the same. He took a shiny new hand grenade out of his pocket and held it up to be admired; then his face saddened and he said, "That is all we have to fight with now. No tenemos otro!" This was an exaggeration like the earlier boasting, but he knew that I knew what he meant, and it was essentially true: the disparity of war material between the Republican and Fascist armies was indeed very great.

But the civilian population up in that part of the world did not show the slightest intention of retreating. Even at Torreblanca (which was then under shellfire and bombing every day) the houses seemed to be inhabited and the ordinary life of the place had not been interrupted. Even more surprising were Castellón de la Plana and Sagunto. Castellón had been bombed from the air every day and every night for about three weeks, and more occasionally before then; one third or more of its houses were in ruins; and yet people still lived there in large numbers, and the children played games in the rubbish heaps. Fragments of bombs were especially sought after, and colored glass was highly prized. When I first arrived there a bombing had just taken place, the streets were full of fresh ruins, and yet nobody living in the town had been hurt. (At the Provincial Civilian Hospital there were some wounded and killed among the patients who could not be moved.) This relative immunity to bombings was due to the fact that Castellón had the best system of deep refuges in Spain. The soil there was particularly suitable for digging, you struck water only at forty-five feet, and it was possible to make refuges forty feet deep, with connecting galleries. Every house in Castellón had a refuge, and there were big general refuges in the Plaza and other centers. In spite of the terrific bombings to which the place had been subjected, there were seldom any casualties, as the plane detector was vigilant and the sirens were always obeyed.

When I went to Castellón I had never been inside a refuge. I had been in a few bombings out in the country (a very bad one at Puigcerdá, for instance), a lot of the Barcelona raids, and a disastrous bombing at Alicante only a few days before; but in all these cases there was no reason for taking to the *refugio*. The planes came too quickly in the country, and there were usually no *refugios* there anyhow; in Barcelona the bombings were never directly over the center of the town; in Alicante, where the raid had taken place at five in the morning, I had been too lazy (or too scared) to get out of bed. Here at Castellón things were arranged differently.

I had been given the last available room at the inn, but had to share it with a captain in the C.R.I.M. (Cuerpo de Reclutamiento y Instrucción Militar), a fellow traveler from Valencia. He went to the C.R.I.M. mess for dinner, and when he returned at ten o'clock I was already in bed. In the dark room (there were no lights here, of course) I heard him come in and search for his bed.

"Where have you left your clothes?" he asked—probably after falling over some of them.

"I don't know," I said. "All over the place, I suppose."

"You must get them together," he said severely, "and put them on the chair beside your bed. There are several alarms a night here."

"Well," I said, "I don't believe in the theory that you're safer in one place rather than in another. I never get out of bed for the alarms."

He used that extreme and universally popular blasphemy which has been the Spaniard's favorite oath since Isabel la Católica.

"When there is an alarm in Castellón," he said, "you will get out of bed and you will go to the refuge. There is a big refuge right here in the Plaza, not three minutes away. You will have plenty of time to get to it. It is stupid to stay out of the refuges in a place like this. They are very good refuges."

"I don't doubt that they are good refuges," I said, "but I don't believe any refuge is safe against a big bomb in a direct hit, and there is no reason why there should be a direct hit on this bed more than on a refuge."

"Tontería!" he said, getting angry. "You don't know what you are talking about. There were seven alarms last night in this place, and five of them were bombings of the town. They will certainly come tonight. Why, at any moment the sirens may sound——"

And at this precise moment, just as he was saying it, the sirens sounded. It seemed such a direct proof of his competence that I got up obediently, put on my coat, shoes and trousers and followed the C.R.I.M. captain out to the stairs.

"Besides," he continued in reproof as we made our way down to the Plaza, "you are a journalist. You ought to see the refuges. It is part of your professional duty."

The refuge was, as he had said, within three minutes of our room. It was immense—the biggest and deepest I ever saw, although not so elegantly accoutered as the new "modern art" refuges in Valencia. It was a sloping gallery into the bowels of the earth. Steps had been cut into the slope, and below these it turned into another gallery, another crude flight of steps, and a very deep room which was already occupied by a number of women. These people all made jokes and talked in apparently high spirits as they made their way into the depths. They were dressed rather peculiarly, in whatever they had snatched up first, and this gave rise to some very pointed remarks. There were a few men, and perhaps half a dozen young boys. No crowding: there were so many refuges in Castellón that none was ever crowded. Most people had deep shelters underneath their own houses, so they did not even have to go into the streets when the Fascists came.

We stood about the mouth of the refuge for a long time, looking at the sky. There was moonlight, plenty of it, and the town was clearly designed against the luminous dark blue. We heard some antiaircraft guns, and we could also distinctly hear the airplanes, but they must have been on other errands tonight, for they dropped no bombs on Castellón. (Perhaps they were frightened off by the anti-aircraft, although I doubt it: all they ever had to do to avoid antiaircraft was to fly above its range.) After a while the sirens sounded again and we returned to our hotel, the captain in the C.R.I.M. explaining, rather apologetically, that *if* there had been bombs it *would* have been far better to be in the refuge. Even without the bombs, he had made his point, and I had a high opinion of refuges after seeing the big one at Castellón. It was surely invulnerable even against five-hundred-kilogram bombs, and against the fifty-kilogram bombs which were the usual Fascist medicine it was as safe as the grave.

Sagunto was another extraordinary place in this Levante area. It had been bombed even more often than Castellón, and for many months: it was almost as ruined as Tortosa. This was because there was a big munitions factory at Sagunto and the Fascists—well served by spies, as always—had known it for a long time. They clearly knew all about it, as they showed by their bombings; but the censorship would never allow us to mention the munitions factory in dispatches from Spain, even months after the Fascists had spoken of it in their own press. I thought this, on the whole, a stupid use of censorship, since the story of Sagunto was in fact one of the most remarkable of the war. The workers there were members of the U.G.T., the Socialist-and-Communist trades union, and they were offered relief if they wanted to retire to a less punished area: they voted to stay. This had been months before, when the Fascists first started bombing the place during the operations of the winter at Teruel. Since then Sagunto had taken gruesome punishment; the town itself had been blasted again and again; hundreds of people had been killed and wounded, the women and children as much as the men, or even more, since they were the ones who lived by day in their houses; but by some fantastic freak of fate, not one of all these myriad bombs had landed on the factory. One alone would have done the job, and all the workers there would have been dispersed indeed; for the factory was crammed with explosives. Shortly before I was there the munitions workers had again been offered the chance of retirement, to change places with workers in a safer place for a while; and again they had voted to stay where they were. It was one of the grimmest of episodes, lacking even the excitement or the transitory "glory" of action at the front, but what soldier could have been more determined than these workers? And, when you thought it over, did it seem possible that such a people could ever be conquered?

2

One day in Valencia two men came and sat at the table where I was having lunch. They did not speak to each other or to me. One was small, dark, very thin, with flashing black eyes. The other was built on a larger scale, was lighter in coloring, and had a comfortable breadth in the middle. I decided that they were dissimilar enough to have dissimilar views, and made an attempt to get them started.

"When was the last bullfight in Valencia?" I asked, nodding at the Plaza de Toros across the street.

"Last December," the comfortable fellow said reflectively, "or was it in November? No, I think December. It wasn't very good. There has never been one since."

"We have better uses for bulls now," the cadaverous man said, his eyes snapping.

"When I first came to Spain about fifteen or sixteen years ago," I said, "the first thing to be noticed in any town was the bull ring and the second was the church. Those were the centers of all life. Times have changed since then."

Both men laughed—the comfortable man comfortably, the little dark fellow with a certain bitterness.

"The priest and the bullfighter!" the little man said. "Between them they ruined Spain."

"Yes, that is perhaps so," the big man said, "but it is true that there have been good priests."

"I never knew one," the small man said. "My truth is simple. It is this: in the Church everything is bad."

His eyes flashed and he held his head very straight. He repeated it: "En la Iglesia todo es malo."

"I don't think we can say that," the big fellow remarked. "After all, as you know, liberty of conscience is one of the things guaranteed in the Thirteen Point program of the government of the Republic. You can't deny that."

"Liberty of conscience!" the little man said. "What is liberty of conscience? Do you know what it means? Does it mean to take small children and fill their minds with black superstition, to keep them from learning to read and write?

Does it mean reaching out and grasping at the land, the railroads, the mines, everything that controls the life of the people? Does it mean forbidding a workingman to belong to a labor union, or to vote except for the priest's candidate, or to own his own house?"

"Certainly not," the comfortable fellow said, getting a little heated in his turn. "It does not mean any of those things. The Church has done those things. The Church can never do them again. But liberty of conscience is guaranteed to all citizens of the Republic, and let me tell you that I am as good a workingman and member of a trades union as you are."

With this he pulled out his papers from his pocket and showed them. He was a member of the U.G.T. (Unión General de Trabajo), which was the great trades union body controlled by the Socialist and Communist parties—although this man, by my guess, was neither Socialist nor Communist. The other fellow, not to be outdone, produced his papers, too: he was a member of the C.N.T. (Confederación Nacional de Trabajo), controlled by the Anarchist party. All workers in the Republic belonged to one or the other of these labor federations, although not necessarily to the political parties which had organized and now controlled them. The small fellow was an Anarchist, or an Anarcho-Syndicalist, for he also showed his membership paper in the F.A.I. (Federación Anárquica Ibérica). They were so intent on these paper-showing operations, and upon the argument that now promised to break out between them, that they forgot all about me; I was able to listen as at a public meeting.

"*Claro, claro,*" the C.N.T. man said, his thin, dark face working with excitement. "I do not deny your right to speak as a member of the working class. But I am sorry to hear any member of the proletariat, however misled ideologically, saying a word in defense of the Church."

"I did not say a word in defense of the Church," the U.G.T. man protested. "I know what the Church in Spain was. All I say is that liberty of conscience is guaranteed by the Republic and must be respected. My mother is a Basque Catholic and she still devoutly believes everything she was taught when she was a child. Am I to forbid her to believe these things? Moreover, if you or one of your F.A.I. committees were to break into my house one night——"

"Hombre!" the little fellow interrupted. "Is such a thing likely?"

"Well, it happened a year and a half ago, and it might happen again. Anyhow, if you broke into my house you would see my mother's Virgin Mary hanging alongside the picture of Karl Marx. Would you think I was a traitor to the Republic for that reason? Would you want to shoot me——"

"Hombre! Who talks of shooting? We are discussing liberty of conscience."

"I am telling you that there is a shrine of the Virgin Mary in my house and that it will continue to stay there. I do not believe in shrines and images, but I believe in the liberty of conscience, and my mother shall keep her Virgin Mary. Moreover, I am as good a citizen of the Republic as you are, and as good a member of the proletariat. I believe in the Thirteen Points of the government, and I don't think you do."

The C.N.T. man was a little put out at this.

"It is necessary to win the war by collaboration with all the democratic forces," he said. "I would collaborate with any force against Fascism. But I do not believe either in the Virgin Mary or in Karl Marx, and no government can oblige me to do so. We are discussing the liberty of conscience. I believe the true liberty of conscience is only possible when every individual spirit has enough enlightenment to choose what it wishes to believe."

The big fellow grunted angrily.

"Anarquismo!" he muttered.

"Yes, I am an Anarchist, and we do not believe either in Marx or the Virgin, and if you know what liberty of conscience means you will not try to oblige us to do so. I say that your notion of liberty of conscience is so false that you would restore the Church to its power in Spain—yes, in time you would. That is the way you would begin, with your mother's shrines and images, and afterwards you would let the Church take such control over the people, and especially over the children, that no liberty of conscience would be possible. You must first abolish everything in the Church before you can pretend to create any form of liberty of conscience, because the Church is fundamentally opposed to the exercise of freedom in the individual mind. I tell you: in the Church everything is bad, everything, everything."

"I am not defending the Church," the big man said loudly, almost in a shout. "Do you not understand that I am talking about conscience, worship, religion? People believe these things. They have the right to believe them under the Thirteen Points. I would not bring back the Church as before, to rule Spain; but I insist that we have the right to believe whatever we do believe in such matters. After what the Basque Catholics have done for the Republic, you are a very poor anti-Fascist if you deny them the right to believe what they like. It is not a question of the Church: the Church, in the old sense, has gone forever. It is a question of conscience only."

"Conscience, conscience!" the little fellow fumed. "You do not know what the word means. The conscience of mankind is so darkened and befuddled by people like you, with your Marxes and your Virgins, that it is unable to decide clearly what it does believe. There is a mountain of rubbish to be cleared away before we can even see into the mind of man. I tell you all that must go, and must go for a long enough time to see what people really are like underneath, before we can talk about liberty of conscience. Such a thing is impossible now and does not exist anywhere. Nothing is free. Children are brought up to believe from their earliest years in a large number of things that are not true. Of all these things the worst is the Church. Everybody knows that the Church arranged and financed the rebellion against the Republic, and after nearly two years of war you can still defend it."

The big U.G.T. man appealed to me.

"Señor," he said, "you are a foreigner and a witness. Have I said one word in defense of the Church?"

"No," I answered, "not exactly."

"Not exactly," the little C.N.T. fellow agreed, still breathless with disputation. "Not exactly. But by means of your so-called liberty of conscience, which is no liberty of conscience because you don't know what the conscience is or might be if it were really freed—by this means you would admit the priests again to batten on our women and children, to steal our land and factories, and to rule our government."

"I would not!" the U.G.T. man declaimed. "If the priests ever come back to the Republic it will be for religious service only."

"Ha! Beautiful! Wonderful! That is the way it begins.

You do not understand. *Everything* in the Church is bad—everything, everything."

They were still at it, hammer and tongs, when I left, and may still be arguing so far as I know. I had an appointment and could not stay. Whatever else they said, I feel certain that they did not come to a permanent agreement on the subject of the Church. When I went into the street the Plaza de Toros was directly opposite, the vast amphitheater of red brick, the biggest thing in Valencia: deserted and forgotten now. The two men in the restaurant had not even thought it worth arguing about, although its one-time rival still had enough vitality to bring on interminable disputes.

3

At six o'clock in the morning of May 21 I got out of bed and made my way across to the Carabineros office on the other side of the railroad station to get the bus for Madrid. The Carabineros operated buses all through the Republic, and with a letter from their central command in Barcelona I was able to ask for transport anywhere in the south.

There was a crowd waiting here, not all for the Madrid bus: there were buses also to Albacete and Murcia. Men, women and children, with bags, bundles, packages and shawls, they stood in the street and talked. Half the talk seemed to be about bombings, as was usual in Spanish crowds; there had been two bad ones the day before. The people I found myself with seemed to be mostly Madrileños, and I made my first acquaintance with a fact which was to seem commonplace thereafter—that the Madrileños, having lived under shellfire for two years, pitied Valencia and the other coast districts for their frequent Fascist bombings. "Ay, ay, I will be glad to be back in Madrid!" one girl said,

[*154*]

and several of the others took it up. She was a pretty girl in a *mono* (blue overalls, like the ones the men wear), with her full lips brightly painted and her hands cracked and worn from work.

A trim *carabinero* came to the door and read out his list of names. As our names were called we passed him, one by one, and traversed the hall to a courtyard. Here the Madrid bus was waiting. It was a Ford truck, fairly new, with benches installed in it. There was room for exactly forty people, five on each bench.

There was double daylight saving in the Spanish Republic (an extra hour of it) so that six o'clock was in reality four in the morning. The sun was just breaking through, and the sky first paled and then flamed with red and yellow light. We took our places on the benches—which were very hard, made of slats—and waited. At some time between seven and half-past seven the crowded truck drove through the gateway; many of the people in it gave a slight cheer; there was much laughter. You never saw a crowd of people happier to be on their way: they were mostly Madrileños and they were glad to go home.

It was very cold at this hour of the morning, although in another hour or so Valencia would be warmed by the sun. But by the time the sun was well up in the coast district we had already begun to climb hills and go through a cloudy area where the sun was not to be seen. It was very cold. I had no overcoat—I had expected various things down here, but not cold—and before we had been out half an hour I was chilled to the bone. Most of the people in the bus were well muffled up. The man sitting next to me had a huge collection of flowers in a shapeless paper wrapping which was always coming undone. He kept them on his lap part of the time and part of the time on the floor behind his feet.

"They are flowers from Valencia, for my *novia*," he explained to the neighbors. "I could not come back to Madrid if I did not bring them. I am afraid they will be frozen."

One of the women volunteered to wrap the flowers more efficiently, and did so, but from then on until we arrived in Madrid more than eleven hours later, the flowers continued to fall out and get lost and get stepped upon, until I doubted whether there would be much left for the waiting beloved.

Eleven hours and a half from Valencia to Madrid on this bus, and bitter cold all the way: at first it was cold because of the early hour, and later because of the high cloudy hills, and still later because we were crossing the great Castilian plain in a gale. And yet no amount of cold, discomfort or fatigue seemed to have any effect on these people. I never traveled in such a merry company. They talked all the time, made jokes, laughed without ceasing. There was one elderly woman on one of the benches further back who became the recognized humorist of the bus. She was quiet to begin with, but her rather strident voice individualized itself sharply before the first hour was over, and by the end of the day she was a familiar character to all her thirty-nine fellow travelers. She was a worker in a factory up the Guadalajara road from Madrid somewhere; her husband had been killed at Madrid; she had three sons at various fronts; she wore the red star; and she had the most wonderful Spanish vocabulary I ever heard. Her language was the rich, lusty language of the people, full of references to the physical organs and functions, to sexual activities, to fear, courage, hunger, work, death; it was also brilliantly funny. This woman had a real wit, which she put into the language she knew at its coarsest and brightest. Unfortunately all these Spanish expressions, so full of life when spoken, are not at all the same thing in print; nor do they translate into anything remotely like the original. The woman with the red star had an argument with a peasant at one of our stops along the road; she wanted to buy eggs from him; the conversation was so funny that I laughed without stopping for about fifteen minutes. The man sitting next to me—some sort of government functionary or clerk, very respectable— was shocked, above all because these things were said in the hearing of a foreigner.

"That woman talks very bad language," he explained to me in an undertone. "You must not think that other people talk like that. She is very bad."

"I don't think she is very bad," I said. "I like to hear what she says."

He stared at me, puzzled.

"But it is very bad," he protested. "Such things should not be said."

The same man turned to me with an air of importance when we reached Tarancón late that afternoon and said: "The second husband of Isabel II was born here. He was a Spaniard." The town was half ruined by bombs, and there were innumerable things of interest to be said about it, but the second husband of Isabel II (who was a Spaniard) overruled them all.

The road from Valencia to Madrid, in spite of its importance to the Republic, seemed to have drawn very little of the Fascist attack. We saw no airplanes all day, and I gathered that the road below Tarancón was never bombed. In some of the towns along the way through the provinces of Valencia and Cuenca it was quite possible to imagine that the country was at peace: there were even cafés open in some of these places, selling coffee and (in one place) anis. At Valverde de Jucar, latish in the afternoon, we stopped for lunch at a roadside inn where there were eggs, bread and red wine. There were enough eggs for all the passengers who wanted them—the only eggs I saw in southern Spain. For breakfast we had eaten what we could on the bus. I had some corned beef; my neighbor, the respectable gentleman, had some oranges; a woman on the same bench produced some bread.

The Castilian plain was an ordeal: dead flat country over which a gale was blowing steadily, monotonously, bitter cold and sharp. One of the passengers, an old woman, got out of the bus at Valverde shaking her shoulders and shawls like a hen getting rid of water.

"Qué aire!" she sighed. ("What a breeze!" or, literally, "What air!"—this after hours in the biting gale.)

The woman who had given us bread was a housewife, tidy and competent. I asked her if there was wine for sale in Madrid.

"It is very difficult to obtain good wine just now," she said. "I paid eight pesetas forty centimos for one liter of good wine about four months ago. Imagine! Eight pesetas forty centimos! And you can't get it now—there is some wine at three-fifty, but it isn't good."

My respectable friend, the functionary or clerk, saw a chance to show his knowledge of the world.

"The Señor is a foreigner," he pointed out, "and pesetas are cheap for him. How many pesetas do you get for a dollar nowadays? It is a hundred and fifty, is it not?"

"I don't know what the Black Bourse pays for dollars," said I virtuously. "I bought my pesetas at the official government rate for tourists, and it is the same as the French franc."

My respectable friend thought this either a barefaced lie or a piece of sheer lunacy, and he continued to argue about the exchange rate for some time. He had an eminently businesslike mind, and could go off into long calculations about the peseta, the dollar, the franc and the pound, in much the same way as a musician improvises, with the flowers for his *novia* forgotten under his feet as he gazed into the sky and counted.

At Puerto de Cabreras, the pass in the sierra, our papers were thoroughly examined. The government had by this time despaired of getting any large numbers of people to evacuate Madrid, for the experience of the previous year had shown that it was impossible; but even so every effort was made to keep the population there from increasing, and nobody could enter the Madrid area without a special pass. For women two passes were needed: the ordinary one from the Seguridad, for entry to the Madrid area, and another from the police of Madrid saying that the woman's presence was necessary for some specified reason. Twice afterwards, before we actually entered Madrid, the bus was stopped by road guards and the women's papers were gone over carefully.

We left the main Valencia–Madrid road somewhere in the neighborhood of Perales and made a detour to the north: the main road was under the Fascist guns, and all the Valencia traffic had to be shunted around to the Guadalajara highway. Thus we came into Madrid from the north, and it was wonderful to see how the whole busload of weary people, silenced by fatigue and cold, roused to life again after we passed the last barrier of guards.

"Madrid! Madrid!" they said. Pronounced that way ("Mathree! Mathree!") it sounded like an amorous address. The girl in the *mono* laughed and chattered: she had been in Valencia for a week, she said, away from her work, and she never could get used to the bombings; she would be glad to get back to her own place. My respectable friend rescued his flowers from the floor and began to go over them anxiously, pulling off rose petals which had been frayed or frozen in the day's journey. The tidy housewife bent over and relaced her shoes.

The Carabineros office, where our bus came to its final stop, was in a busy street which I did not recognize. I had not been in Madrid since 1931. I consulted my respectable neighbor.

"Hotel Victoria?" he said. "That is easy. Go straight across the street here and take the Metro to the Puerta del Sol. From the Puerta del Sol it's a short walk up the Calle Calletas, and you'll see the small plaza on the left, with the Victoria in it."

"But the smallest money I have left is one hundred pesetas," I confessed. "Can they change that in the Metro?"

"No, certainly not," he said. "Here, let me give you two pesetas."

He did so, and was never paid back, either. I fished out my bag at the terminus and went across a street which looked rather like the Paseo de Gracia in Barcelona, with trees down the middle. The Metro station was under the trees.

When I got down into the subway I found that even one peseta was difficult to change. The woman behind the ticket window said: "You will have to wait a minute. I have no change." The price of a ticket to the Puerta del Sol was fifteen centimos—a sum so small that it would hardly buy a short tram ride in Barcelona. It was too small to wait for, but I was undecided. I did not want to treat the currency with alien disdain. I stood back; a young man in a yellow *mono*, whom I had not noticed before, thrust fifteen centimos at the woman and told her to give me a ticket for it. I thanked him, astonished.

"De nada, camarada," he said with a quick gesture of his hand before he vanished down the stairs to his train.

So, I thought, taking my way to the train for the Puerta del Sol, that is the way they do things in Madrid. "De nada, camarada [It is nothing, comrade]." Nothing at all: the guns for eighteen months, the starvation, the cold in winter and the heat in summer, the ceaseless indefatigable epic struggle against overwhelming force, all nothing at all; here's your Metro ticket, you're welcome to Madrid.

The subway did not seem to have changed much since I had last taken it years before. It was crowded, but so had it always been. In Madrid (as, for that matter, in Barcelona and Valencia) the younger women seemed to have the knack of making their clothes sit attractively upon them, although they could have had no new supplies for a year and a half; they managed to get lipstick even if food was scarce; and they chattered away in high spirits. The younger men were mostly in *monos*. Otherwise the subway looked the same as always, and even some of the same advertisements infested it, although the actual products advertised were no longer obtainable. At the Puerta del Sol I got out and climbed to the street.

It was some time between six and seven in the evening, and the big square had a fair number of people in it. There were not many idlers (the Puerta del Sol used to be packed with idlers who stood about there for four or five hours every night); all seemed to be going somewhere; yet they had no hesitation in crossing the square through the middle or diagonally, in spite of the fact that it was the most dangerous place in the city. Shells very often fell there; it had been shelled for three hours the night before, as I was to learn soon; and yet you could not have guessed it

from the look of the people. I walked around on the right
to the Calle Calletas.

Here the whole street was crowded; a car or a tram had
to progress slowly, for the crowd took up all the space
from one side to the other. It was the evening hour when all
the Madrileños like to go out and walk. Girls walked arm
in arm, four and five abreast; there were young men in
monos to eye them, and there were innumerable uniforms.
The Calle Calletas had been shelled countless times, and
there were some big gaping holes in the pavement that had
not yet been repaired. This did not seem to matter; the evening stroll was more important. I thought a lot of the girls
had unusually pale faces, but then, as I remembered, the
Madrileña was always rather pale, so perhaps undernourishment was not the only cause. My suitcase was heavy with
sardines, tuna fish, tinned ham and butter; I wondered what
kind of riot there would be if I opened it then and there in
this crowded street. They might have passed it by with a
look: for I knew them to be even prouder than they were
hungry. The Plaza de los Angeles was off to the left, and
there, down by the church, was the Hotel Victoria. It
seemed a quiet enough backwater, and although I had heard
some firing down at the Puerta del Sol, nothing was to be
heard here at all. The porter assigned me a room on the
third floor (which was actually about the sixth, Spanish
nomenclature for floors being of the generous kind); and
when I got up there and started to wash I heard what
sounded like machine-gun fire from the bathroom window.

I opened the window cautiously and peered out with all
the elaborate precautions of a man in a front-line trench.
I saw nothing but the back of another part of the hotel,
with a courtyard between, and some washing hanging on a
line. The firing had ceased. I went back to the bathtub and

turned on the ice-cold water. You're going crazy, James, says I to myself; you can't hear machine-gun fire from this place; shells, yes, or maybe trench mortars or something, but you couldn't have heard machine-gun fire. Don't start imagining things.

For a while I doubt if I could have heard even a shell in the immediate neighborhood, so cold was that water. It made me feel a good deal better, just the same, and when I heard the machine-gun fire again a little later, while I was dressing, I ignored it firmly.

In the restaurant downstairs there were plenty of people (I had trouble getting a place) but there was little food. *Bacalao* and lentils, and that was all. *Bacalao* was the dried codfish which all foreigners and most Spaniards found it difficult to eat; it smelled to high heaven and had a bitter nasty taste; it was the main food of Madrid, as it had been for a year or more. I went back upstairs and extracted a tin of ham from my suitcase. Fortunately I liked lentils. I began to wish I had brought oranges from Valencia, for there were none here. All these important preoccupations filled my mind to the exclusion of anything else, and at first I did not even notice when a trio of colleagues came in and sat at the next table. Forrest (of the *News-Chronicle* in London) hailed me: there he was with Joe North (*Daily Worker*, New York) and Georges Soria (*Humanité*, Paris). We joined forces for coffee, and I made another trip upstairs to get some sugar for it.

Forrest, North and Soria gave me my instructions. They and I were on the most exposed floor of the hotel; there was one floor above that, but it was unoccupied because of the shellings. In case of a shelling in or near the hotel at night, it was the rule for dwellers on our floor to get out of bed and come down to this floor where the restaurant and lounge were. The Germans had a new electric battery on Monte Garabitas which had been operated for three hours the night before and had caused much damage, many dead and wounded. One shell had hit the church which made the angle of the little plaza with this hotel. Many had fallen in the Puerta del Sol. It was a very fancy battery which fired four times in a series, the last two closer together than the first two, thus: boom-boom-BOOMBOOM. And then all over again, indefatigably, to the extreme annoyance of all Madrileños, even those outside the line of fire.

I asked for some mineral water (being a newcomer). The boy who was handing out coffee in the lounge—he might have been twelve or thirteen—said: "Hombre! Why do you want mineral water? Here is the best water in the world, the water of Madrid."

It reminded me of our humorist on the bus, the woman with the red star. She had ended her argument about the eggs on just such a note. The peasant who had no eggs had said to her: "And who are you, anyhow, to insult me like this?" The woman said in accents that are impossible to describe, a mixture of cross references, a tone of pride and rebuke and humor all at once: "Hombre! Soy una de Madrid [I am one from Madrid]." Before long the accent with which they all said the words *"de Madrid"* became more familiar to me, but it was still astonishing how much the words could mean in their successive contexts, and how subtly they put everybody and everything else in the wrong when they were properly used. Madrid was, is and will always remain a rebuke to the world of our time, and it was in such ways that the Madrileños occasionally showed that they knew it.

After a while I got up the courage to mention my machine gun.

"I know it must be impossible," I said, "but while I was taking a bath I thought I heard machine-gun fire. What could that have been?"

"That's what it was. From your room on the back you can hear machine-gun fire. You can't hear it at the front of the hotel, or in the street. It's at the university. Don't let it keep you awake."

We went out and walked down to the censorship office. It was a soft, dark night in late May. There was an occasional burst of firing of various kinds, and sometimes there were shells to be heard. Between times the silence was unusually deep for such a great city; and you could get hours of silence at night in Madrid. There were no people in the streets, and of course no lights. Down by the Ritz we turned off to the street where the censorship was, and I met Rosario, the chief of the press office: severe, thoughtful and efficient. She had just come from Valencia a day or two before and said she was very glad to get back to Madrid.

"I live with my sister," she said, "and my poor sister was in terror all the five days I was away. She was afraid I might be hit by a bomb."

"I suppose she doesn't care about shells," I suggested.

"We are used to shells in Madrid. We know more or less what to do about them. But we are not used to bombing any more. The bombing is all down on the coast and at the fronts now. My sister was very worried."

Rosario was one of the people (there were hundreds of thousands of them) who would not leave Madrid. She had been offered the same sort of work at Barcelona in the press and censorship office, and at Barcelona she would have had better food or at least more of it; she would have been relatively safe from bombings in the center of the town;

and she would have had much more work to occupy her mind. There were not many correspondents left in Madrid, and those who visited (like us) did not stay long. But she refused to go. I had news of her from time to time during the year after I had left Madrid. She had fainted several times from undernourishment along about September; in November the censorship was shelled for the first time. In that month Rosario had been intending to go with a friend of mine to a Red Cross dinner, and the two of them had elected to eat at the hotel instead: the Red Cross dinner was the one where a shell fell and all the guests (thirty-five) were killed. Death was always just around the corner in Madrid, even in the so-called "quiet" times and places, but most of the Madrileños preferred to end their struggle where they had begun it. I thought of Rosario after that as one of the types of the struggle: unobtrusive, severe and rectilinear as a schoolteacher with a crowd of refractory children, but possessed of such fixity of purpose that no difficulties could affect her inner sureness. Among the women of the war and revolution there must have been many who, like her, had no spectacular quality at all except their determination to do their job well. She had a calm, nunlike face, and in the intervals of her work she sometimes knitted.

4

It was now May, 1938, and Madrid had been closely beset by the Fascists since November, 1936. The Moors and the Foreign Legion had crossed the Manzanares then and had reached the lines where they were stopped, inside the University City and the Casa del Campo. There had been desperate fighting in the defense of Madrid all that first winter, and the Fascists had rained bombs on the city as well as the eternal shells. Thereafter the main tide of war had turned elsewhere, and except for the Brunete operations in July, 1937, no principal campaign had been in the Madrid neighborhood; but the siege was always on. The city, founded by Philip II in a vainglorious whim, had no natural reason for existence; its food came from afar; if the Fascists had captured Guadarrama it would have had neither water nor electricity. It received supplies of food and munitions only from the coast, for the Fascists were on the other three sides. It still had factories and shops, theaters and schools and a life of its own, and the population—in a huge majority— would not go away. Such children as could be taken were moved to the coast, to the colonies in Valencia, Murcia and Catalonia, but their parents frequently refused either to let them go or to go with them. Women whose husbands had been killed could sometimes be persuaded to move to the country somewhere, but even they usually preferred to take their chance in Madrid. The government had made a determined effort to get them out, all through 1937; that effort had now been abandoned. I saw some of the old posters urging them to go: "Confide your children to the Republic. Evacuate Madrid!" And "Madrid for the cannon! Evacuate Madrid!" And "The Republic asks you to leave Madrid to the army."

Madrid was regarded with the utmost pride by all Republicans, I believe, for its heroic resistance had amazed the world. Even the Fifth Column, those thousands of Fascist sympathizers who were supposed to be so busy at all times in the capital, probably had some trace of perverse pride in the phenomenal tenacity and courage of the Madrileños who were their enemies. But the Communists in particular, among the political parties of the Popular Front, had the unquestionable right to claim leadership here, for the glory of Madrid was in great part theirs.

The role of the Communist party in the Spanish Republic has been systematically misrepresented on all sides for the past two years. In the Fascist press of all countries the Republic is supposed to be a Communist revolutionary state; in Italy and Germany the word used to describe the Republic or the Republicans is "Red". This is, of course, absurd, and the people who write it do not believe it themselves; but it serves to befuddle the unhappy subjects of the Fascist despotisms. The ordinary word used in the press of Germany to describe Republican Spain is *"Sowjetspanien"* (Soviet Spain). The adjective used is *"rotspanisch"* (Red Spanish).

In the press of the democratic countries the situation is better understood, but even here the word "Communist" frightens writer and reader alike. Nobody seems to have the common sense to say the plain truth, which is that the Spanish Communist party has been one of the most powerful influences for discipline and order in support of the bourgeois Republic. Without the Communists Madrid would have been lost in the winter of 1937; without the Communists the Republic would have fallen into anarchy, an infinitesimal subdivision of civil wars; without the Communists it would have been impossible to create either the militias or the Popular army, it would have been impossible for a long time to maintain order in the streets or to guarantee the operation of the necessary systems of food rationing, factory work and transport.

And in spite of this, the Spanish Communists were a minority party who could not, even now, count much more than three hundred thousand members out of a population of twenty-six millions in Spain. They had never "controlled" the government; for a long time they were not even represented in it; in 1938 they had one ministry (Agriculture). Their parliamentary representation was tiny in comparison to that of the Socialists and the liberal Republican parties. In the most revolutionary layers of the population, especially in the factory districts of Catalonia, they were always outnumbered by the Anarcho-Syndicalists, diametrically their opposites in every point of doctrine and tactics.

How, then, could they come to be so active in support of the Republic, and how did they assume such importance in all discussion on Spain?

They did it by the best of their qualities: devotion, courage, self-abnegation and discipline. These are the most valuable of all qualities in times of desperate crisis, and they were not to be found in any other body in Spain. The Anarcho-Syndicalists were, by definition, opposed to every government, and have often been distinguished by an unwillingness to fight even for their own lives. The liberal Republican parties and the bourgeoisie in general had no organization that could call on them to go out and do the rough work, the digging, the fighting and the dying. Only the Communists could do this, and they did it not through their own party members (who were never numerous enough) but by their influence on the working class as a whole, and by their share in the control of the great trades union federation, the U.G.T. Among Republican politicians who have least cause to love the Communists, such as Largo Caballero and Prieto and their kind, it would never be denied that the Communist party saved the Spanish Republic in 1936 and 1937.

The Spanish Communists flung themselves into the breach, and they had the great advantage of international affiliation:

their friends took the lead in organizing the International Brigades which came before long to stiffen the resistance to Fascism. The brigades were more or less Communist, although they included men of many shades of opinion; and the only foreign power which gave any real help to the Republic during the first year of its struggle was the Soviet Union. These were the three great contributions of the Communists: their own courage and discipline, the aid of their friends in all countries, and the material help supplied during the first year and a half by the Soviet Union. This last would probably have come without the Spanish Communists, for Russia had the most powerful reasons for trying to head off a new Fascist dictatorship in Europe; but among the masses of the people the Communist party derived prestige from the guns and planes that came from Moscow, whatever may have been the political reasons that sent them. Consequently the influence of the Communists among the workers, and particularly in the great trades union body, the U.G.T., increased steadily from the time of the Fascist rebellion; and the membership of the party, which was 133,266 before July, 1936, rose to more than three hundred thousand during the next two years. Their influence on the youth organizations and the trades unions gave them at least a debating chance with a million or more of the revolutionary workers who were not members of their party. As a political power in Spain, they were created by General Franco's rebellion on July 19, 1936: before that they had been a small red tail to the Socialists' kite.

To understand any of these processes it was necessary to remember the nature and origins of the war in Spain. Feudal misgovernment had led Spain, in three centuries, from a position of great wealth and power to one of impoverishment, disunion and decay. Feudalism held the land,

and industry had developed only in spots (Catalonia, the Basque country, Asturias) with great corruption at the top and a rapid fixation into class war between employer and employed. In agriculture the thoughtless extravagance of absentee landlords had deforested huge areas and taken others from cultivation to support cattle and sheep; the great estates had grown greater, the number of landless peasants more enormous with every decade; peasants' unions, and the creation of a revolutionary peasant class, had been the result of conditions unparalleled elsewhere in Europe except, perhaps, in Hungary. The standard of living for over half the people was beneath what would have been considered enough for an animal in France or England. A peasant earned from one peseta (twelve cents) to one and a half a day in most agricultural districts; the average wage of a peasant throughout Spain was 810 pesetas (about $110) per year. Four per cent of the population held sixty per cent of the land. On the estates of the aristocrats feudal rights were enforced with vigor by the agents appointed to administer them, and the peasant population throughout the greater part of León, the two Castiles, Estremadura and Andalucía lived in effective serfdom.

The monarchy and aristocracy, which had brought the country to ruin—a country which had been one of the richest agricultural lands in Europe under the Arabs, amply irrigated and with rich, diversified crops—hung on to their tenure by various combinations and bargains with the new financiers, the army and the Church. The Church had become the largest landowner in Spain (and one of the worst) during the past century; it became the greatest capitalist in Spain during the present century. There was a huge movement of discontent among the masses, mostly influenced by Anarchist and Anarcho-Syndicalist thought; this took expression not in purposeful organization, but in acts of individual violence. Assassinations, street fighting, the dynamiting of railroads and the burning of churches and convents had been the characteristic forms of despairing protest among the people since the middle of the nineteenth century. Parliamentary politicians, for the most part dishonest careerists, brought the institution of parliamentary government into disrepute, and the vote of the people was bought and sold by those who controlled it. (The serfs voted as they were told to vote; if they did not, they starved for lack of land to work; the industrial populations were chiefly Anarchist and refused to vote or have anything to do with state politics; most of the political impulses that were real, and not simply conditioned by job hunting, went into the regionalist parties of Catalonia and the Basque country or into opposition to them.) The main struggle of principle through many years at the end of the nineteenth century and the beginning of the twentieth revolved about the questions of tariffs and subsidies. Catalonia was highly industrialized and paid most of the taxes, but was forced to see its industries penalized for the benefit of the Spanish landowners, whose products were protected by embargoes and received treasury subsidies besides.

The whole machine was extremely shaky, and threatened to fall to pieces several times (1909, 1917, 1920–23) before a temporary application of military dictatorship under Primo de Rivera arrested the processes for a while. The monarchy, which had been hated for decades, was deeply compromised by the Primo de Rivera adventure, and when the nine years of that interlude were over, its day was done. It lingered for a while under another military dictatorship (Berenguer's), but on April 12, 1931, the municipal elections throughout the country pronounced so emphatically in favor of a republic that Alfonso XIII took to his heels, leaving his wife and children to be escorted out of the country in a sealed train.

The republic that was then proclaimed tried to institute reforms which, although long overdue, ranged against it powerful reactionary forces from the very beginning. An agrarian reform law provided for the division of common land in the *latifundia* among the poorest peasants, the feudal landowners to be amply compensated; a parish law made the landowner hire his agricultural labor from his own villages, instead of importing cheaper seasonal workers from Portugal or elsewhere at will; the Constitution which established the Republic disestablished the Church, dissolved the Jesuits, and declared the principle that no child should be forced to go to a religious school if there was a state school available. Catalonia received its Statute of Autonomy at once. There were numerous reforms of a less urgent nature, and there were a great many declarations of democracy, peace and general all-round appeasement. The aristocrats, who had expected to lose their property, received instead a disproportionate amount of ready cash for the little that had been taken; and when they recovered from their surprise they went at once into an alliance with the financiers and the Church against these unexpectedly mild professorial Republicans.

There followed the attempt, at first very successful, of the reactionary forces to get possession of the Republic. The President, Alcalá Zamora, was under clerical influence; the estates of the nobles were practically intact and their influence on their voting serfs unshaken; the Church had millions to pour into the electoral battle; and the women— newly enfranchised by the Republic—were still hypnotized by the clergy and the aristocracy. The elections of 1933

[*173*]

gave a victory to the newly organized party of reaction (the C.E.D.A.) and its allies, who promptly canceled all the timid reforming legislation of the Republic's first year and silenced opposition by means of courts-martial and the firing squad. For two years the reactionaries controlled the government, while revolts broke out more or less all over the Republic and were savagely repressed. The greatest of these revolts was the united rebellion of the miners of Asturias in 1934—a movement of great historical importance in Spain, since it was the first in which all parties of the working class acted together. It was repressed with the most inhuman cruelty, and the reactionary Republican government (headed by Alejandro Lerroux, who had once been an insurrectionary leader himself) proved more expert in these matters than the monarchy itself. A series of frightened cabinets—frightened by the excess of their own energy; by the insolence of the monarchist parties; by the boiling discontent of the masses; by increasing disorder between political factions; by the rising fever of Fascism, which introduced the Fascist salute into the streets and cafés of Madrid in 1935—juggled the power about between them until elections could be postponed no longer.

When they were held (February 16, 1936) a wholly new force had entered the field. This was the Popular Front, made up of all the Republican parties which wished to establish the Republic on a firm basis and exclude the monarchy and the Church from control over it, *including* the Socialists and the Communists. Manuel Azaña and his Left Republicans headed the Popular Front's list, which was triumphantly elected in Madrid and throughout the country with some four and a half million voters as against about the same number for all the other lists combined. In this election thousands of Anarchists who had never voted before went to the polls, startled out of their "revolutionary" obsession by the danger to the Republic; the reactionary parties, which by now were openly Fascist with all the rigmarole of salutes, incitement to disorder, etc., were cut down to 144 seats in the Cortes against 265 for the Left and 64 for the Center. Among the Left deputies were fourteen Communists (there had been only one before).

When the Popular Front government took power it had no revolutionary intentions. Its program had been established after long discussion, and was formulated in the Popular Front Pact signed by the representatives of eight parties (one of them the U.G.T., the union federation). Azaña had kept the principles of the Front in a strictly Republican line, and it had the character of a temporary but wholehearted collaboration against the dangers of Fascist reaction.

That reaction had exercised its power for two years in such a way as to show the whole country what its intentions were, and in the elections just over the declaration had been made plainer still. The "corporative state" was the aim, with or without a restored monarchy, and the Church and the army were enlisted in its support.

From the time when the Popular Front government was returned to office the Fascist conspiracy gained momentum. All the intricate record of those journeys to Berlin and to Rome has not yet been published, and the financial transactions may remain forever in the dark; but between the politicians (Calvo Sotelo, Gil Robles, young Primo, Angel Herrera), the financiers (in particular Juan March) and the generals (Sanjurjo, in exile, and Franco, retired to Teneriffe under police surveillance) there was great activity during the spring of 1936. The Fascist militias were armed and their allies, the *requetes* (Carlists, many from the north) and the

J.A.P. (Robles' youth organization), were ready to support them. Disorder between them and the trades unions, especially during the strikes which multiplied through those months, was incessant. There was such alarm and anxiety in all sections of the population that the ordinary work of the country was almost suspended. The Left parties, particularly the workers and their unions, feared a Fascist coup d'état every day, and the reaction feared what they called a "preventive *putsch*" before their insurrection was ready.

There can be no denying that the Azaña government failed in the duty of maintaining public order. Its typical act was the request, stuck up in the parliamentary corridors, for deputies in the Cortes to leave their revolvers in the cloakroom as a contribution to "tranquilizing the spirits" of the legislative assembly. The Left was going more left every day and the Right more right. This splaying out of the violent and alarmed forces in the state left the bourgeois government of the Popular Front trembling with indecision and almost powerless. Azaña (who had been elected President of the Republic, but still governed through his closest friend, the Prime Minister Giral) thought at one moment of facing the storm out by means of a government of "national union," enlarged in the direction of the Right, but the maneuver was wholly unsuccessful; it infuriated the Left without gaining the adherence of the Right. Calvo Sotelo, the leader of the Right, openly threatened civil war from his place in the legislative chamber. Murders increased every night in the streets of Madrid; Barcelona was in ferment; the aristocrats, the landowners, factory owners and bankers were leaving the country in droves. At this moment the murder of Calvo Sotelo precipitated the inevitable disaster. The Right and Fascist groups had planned their insurrection, the evidence indicates, for a little later on (probably August 10); but after Calvo Sotelo was killed they hastened their tempo, and on the night of July 18–19 the signal was given for a revolt of the army in garrisons throughout Spain. General Franco, the ablest of the generals in the Right, flew from Teneriffe to Morocco, where he put himself at the head of his own corps, the Foreign Legion, and of the army of native mercenaries; this was the force he led to Cadiz. General Mola led four columns on Madrid from the north, boasting that his "Fifth Column" inside the city would make the task of capturing it easy. Azaña and the bourgeois government were left with no important military power outside the small air force and the divided navy. The streets of Madrid were filled with excited mobs of trades unionists, Socialists, Communists and Anarchists, demanding arms for the defense of the Republic. Azaña had either to give them arms or surrender to military insurrection. He gave them arms (or authorized them to take the arms from the Montaña Barracks) and the civil war was on.

The effort of the Madrid workers in the early days of the war was one of the strangest and most thrilling stories of the war. They swarmed out of Madrid to the Sierra de Guadarrama to meet Mola's four columns, and they held the regular army back—held the sierra with an undisciplined mob keyed up, for the moment, to the peak of mass heroism. The slaughter was great, but the workers here (as at the Montaña Barracks a few days earlier) flung their lives away recklessly. Even the Anarchists, who had never supported this or any other government, turned out to hold the sierra. They complained that the government was afraid to give them arms (which was indeed true), but they were willing to fight with anything they could put their hands on. Meanwhile Franco was advancing more slowly, but steadily, from the south, and in various parts of Spain the revolt of the garrisons was altogether successful. Seville and Saragossa, for example, were Fascist from the first week and were never wrested away from the military throughout the war.

It was in those early days that the Socialists and Communists came forward strongly to the support of the government. Theirs was the only force in the working class that could oppose sheer anarchy; they used it. Largo Caballero, the head of the Socialist union federation, had been building up the youth organizations for a year or two; in them the Communist influence was strong. From the earliest days of the war the Communists and Socialists both preached discipline, order and the sacrifice of every other principle or idea to the main objective of winning the war. The Socialist Prieto was the first to sound the warning that the war would be long and desperate. Lighthearted Madrid refused to believe him until the Fascist shells began to reach the city itself and the Fascist trenches were dug in the buildings of the university.

Madrid was saved by this phenomenal effort of the workers—which must have looked something like the First Crusade under Peter the Hermit, a mass action without organization or discipline but with a mighty fire in it—but also by the timely arrival of help from Russia in November, 1936, when the Fascists were already on the edges of the city. Help from Russia increased the prestige of the Communists among the masses, and it was invaluable to the government at that moment, but it served ever afterwards as the excuse for the open intervention of Italy and Germany in the war. It also alarmed foreign opinion unduly, and tended to make the government "Redder" in the general view than it actually was. These were inevitable processes;

the splaying out of Left and Right could never have been avoided in Spain; but the whole long battle has often lost its objective reality in the mind of the world because of the class passions and prejudices it was bound to arouse. The almost total collapse of public order during the first weeks of the war, during which excesses of every kind were committed on both sides and in all districts, still further contributed to the confusion in which the non-Fascist and non-Communist world (democracy, in short) tried to make up its mind. The nonintervention policy in Europe, a device of Léon Blum's, and the Neutrality Act in America, were alike the expression of a desire to "let the Spaniards fight it out themselves"—to "localize the conflict"—regardless of the world-wide nature of the problem and the openly international character of the forces involved. And under cover of these fussy and misleading projects, Italy and Germany steadily increased their aid to and influence over the Spanish Fascist side, while Russia, beset by enemies nearer at hand, withdrew from support for the Republic. That the forms and some of the spirit of a bourgeois democratic republic should have survived at all, under such conditions, is something of a political miracle. I believe this to be due chiefly to the Communists themselves, who steadily refused to be led into revolutionary proclamations or generalizations with the Fascist power pressing on one side and the Anarchist revolt forever surging up on the other. Factories in Madrid, deserted by their owners, were taken over and run by workers' committees (often, paradoxically enough, pure Anarchist in feeling); but the principle of private property was never renounced and outside of the great cities was not even attacked. The Socialists and Communists both had a hard struggle in the working class, among the unions and in the streets, to bring an amazingly individualistic people

[*179*]

into line, but they did it with such success that by now (1938) the Anarchists themselves were collaborating in support of the government and actually had one minister in it (Education).

Madrid now, at this moment (May, 1938), was under-nourished and still heavily besieged, but the anarchy of the first weeks had been completely conquered. There was order in the streets at all hours. Individual assassination, rob-bery and the like (the curse of the Republic's first years) had disappeared. The Anarchist committees and organiza-tions at last had exerted themselves to keep their people in line, and in fact most of the gunmen had been enrolled in the militias which had since become in time the organized and disciplined Republican army. It seemed to me likely that anarchism as a principle in Spain, which had been of im-mense power on the mind of the people since Bakunin, was likely to undergo great changes as a result of this war and would in time merge into some less wildly theoretical popular philosophy. The anarchist ideas that all states and all governments were wrong, that the only possible organi-zation for the masses was very loose and free trades unionism with a loose federation holding it together, could hardly survive such a struggle to the death in collaboration with people holding fundamentally different ideas. Some begin-nings of fusion and development must come from this tragic experience, even in a people marked by their bondage, the heirs of a thousand years of serfdom and the victims of a systematically maintained illiteracy. The bourgeois elements on the Republican side (lawyers, professors and the like, representing in a general way the petty bourgeoisie which had not yet gone Fascist) were able to survive and govern because the Spanish working class did learn something from the disasters of the war, and did come in the end to believe that the preservation of the democratic Republic was more important than the wholesale revolutionary experimentation which had been their dominating dream for seventy years. In this, too, as in the plain hard facts of digging and fighting, the government owed a heavy debt to the Communists, the most indefatigable workers, as they were the most objective and determined realists, among the leaders of the masses.

But all this "debt of gratitude" and so on, important though it was, had not made the government "Red". It seemed to me that it got less "Red" all the time, and the Thirteen Point program which had just been proclaimed a few weeks before was not "Red" at all. It made private property, liberty of conscience, universal suffrage and the other chief principles of democratic government the declared war aims of the Spanish Republic. You could always argue that this was only for purposes of diplomatic deception, and that victory in the war would be followed by social revolution on a national scale (and not simply in Madrid). I did not believe it, for I had seen too much of the army and people by this time, and knew how greatly the Communists among them were outnumbered. There were purely or nearly purely Communist units, such as the 5th Army—and these the best troops in the Republic—but they were not enough. The working class remained chiefly Anarchist, and the bourgeois elements in the Republic as a whole were still strong: were, in fact, dominant except perhaps in the two capitals. The conditions for social revolution would not exist in this exhausted country even in the event of a complete victory over Fascism. On the contrary, the war itself had moderated the rashness of the whole Left and had been a bitter lesson in historical realism. I thought the Republic, under Dr Negrin, would in fact try to put the clock back to 1931, whereas the Fascists would try to put it back to 1492: that was the difference. In this view the revolutionary parties, trades unions and youth organizations were seen to be in fact what the Republican government declared them to be—a mass support but not a control over the regime. The regime was fighting, therefore, for constitutional law and for democracy.

I found the strongest support for this view of the matter when I went to the opening session of the Central Committee of the Spanish Communist party on May 23, 1938.

5

Georges Soria of the Paris *Humanité*, a Communist colleague, took me to this meeting. It was highly irregular for a non-Communist journalist, representing an important capitalist newspaper like the New York *Herald-Tribune*, to be in these precincts at all. Soria took a chance, I suppose, with his guild instincts overriding his political orthodoxy for once. The meeting was the first plenary session of the Central Committee since the beginning of the civil war, and had a very considerable importance in the annals of Spanish Communism. José Diaz ("Pepe"), the general secretary of the party, was too ill to be present, and the session was to be opened in his place by Dolores Ibarruri, known as "Pasionaria".

It was as much out of sheer journalistic curiosity about this extraordinary woman as for any ideological interest that I wanted to go. Dolores, as her associates and party comrades called her, was one of the phenomena of the war. She had been a straight Communist revolutionary through a large part of her life, acquainted with the uses of dynamite and the technique of insurrection. In the February elections of 1936 she had entered the Cortes as a deputy from Asturias and the country as a whole woke up to her existence as an orator of terrific power. When the Fascist attack began, Dolores took the lead in bringing the Communists out in support of the government. She was brave and indefatigable; her influence with the masses was immense, going far beyond the limits of her own party; and throughout the siege of Madrid the government had reason to be grateful to her. Her talent for phrases had great moral value in the first year of the war: "It is better to die on your feet than to live on your knees" was one that was as powerful as artillery or aviation. She had greatly assisted in the work of restoring order and suppressing anarchy inside the Republic after the terrible excesses of the first weeks of war. Her political evolution had been so rapid that she was now one of the leading supporters of the government, and the one-time insurrectionary revolutionist had disappeared into a patriotic figure of symbolic value. Her nickname, "Pasionaria", had been a literary pseudonym to start with (she signed her articles in the press by the word for passionflower), but the Spaniards love sobriquets, and she was now known to the general public by the nickname alone.

The meeting was held in a theater, with the Communist delegates from all over Spain filling the house while the secretariat and the press occupied the platform. The audience sang revolutionary songs while it waited for the proceedings to begin. Soria got me a place at the press table and introduced me to Dolores when she came in. I saw a deep-bosomed Spanish woman of about forty or a little more, with a hearty laugh and a firm hand; she could not possibly have been anything but Spanish and proletarian in the modern world, although heads of her noble cast were usual enough among the Roman patricians who have survived in sculpture. There was a splendid earthy quality about her laugh, but her face was very sad in repose. She acknowledged the cheers of the crowd with a laugh and a shake of the clenched fist. After a formal opening by the chairman, she took her place behind a sort of pulpit and began to speak.

She spoke for three hours and a half and it seemed far from long. I listened to the first half of her discourse from the platform, and after she had paused to recuperate for five minutes, I found a place just beneath her in the body of the theater to hear the rest. Her speech was, of course, the official political statement of the Spanish Communist leadership, and must, therefore, have been prepared in committee: many hands had worked upon it. And yet it became wholly her own by virtue of the phrasing and above all by means of her extraordinary voice, face, hands, personality. The voice was not what is usually called "musical"—that is, it had no melodious tones and little sweetness. It was a little higher and lower than the average, had a greater range, but that was all. Otherwise it was not unlike other voices in actual sound quality. Where it became quite unlike any other voice I ever heard was in the effect of passionate sincerity. This expressive gift abides in Dolores' voice throughout, in her slightest remark as in the great sweeping statements, with the result that it is impossible to disbelieve anything she says while she is actually saying it. Adolf Hitler has a little of the same gift, but in his case it is ruined by the reckless disregard for truth in the text of his speeches. Dolores had a different sort of text—careful, analytical, closely reasoned, the work of a trained political committee filtered through her own exceptional heart and brain. And that text, in that voice, carried the very taste and substance of truth.

It was, for Communists at least, a bitter truth. She was confronting them with the terrible results of nearly two years' warfare, with the whole record of failures and mistakes. She made not the slightest attempt to minimize the gravity of the situation for the Republic. Sometimes she gave it to them so straight and hard that you could hear the gasp of the whole audience. Her purpose was, of course, to make such failures and mistakes rarer in the future. She criticized the government not at all, but her own and the other revolutionary parties came in for some terrific lashings. And then, having frightened the audience into breathlessness by her picture of disaster, she set out to prove that victory was possible, and on what conditions.

In this part of her speech (the main part) she went through the Republican government's Thirteen Point program point by point, with all the resources of cold analysis and fiery emotion, calling upon every Spanish Communist to give these principles wholehearted support. Without such support, her argument went, the war could not be won. But for Communists—people of fixed ideas for which they had struggled a lifetime—these were hard and bitter necessities. She was asking them to support the principle of private property, for example, and their whole philosophy was built upon an exactly contrary principle. She asked for liberty of conscience, when most of the people in that hall were convinced that the Church was responsible for the greater part of Spain's misfortunes. She told them they were suffering from "revolutionary infantilism" if they thought factories could be run without the help of middle-class people and intellectuals, or if they thought such people should not be paid more than an ordinary workman. (The notion of exact equality of wages, which is so dear to all Spanish revolutionaries with their general background of anarchism, was attacked with special violence.) To an ordinary American journalist in the front row of the hall it seemed that she was asking these people to stop being Communists altogether, at least until the war was won; and I suppose that was about what it amounted to. She made it quite clear that in her opinion any revolutionary impatience would only help the Fascists win; and against Marxian deviationists (the "P.O.U.M." and Trotskyists and the like) she was savage. She was less savage about the Anarchists, who were far too numerous to be dismissed with mere attack; her line seemed to be that all Communists should work unceasingly to convince these errant members of the working class and make them accept Marx and Lenin. By indefatigable work, endless sacrifice (including the sacrifice of Communism itself) and a determination to fight to the death, she declared that the victory over Fascism could be won and the Republic established on a firm basis under the Constitution.

Well, it was pretty much the whole hog. I did not see how any Communist could accept all this and still think of himself as a Communist. Unless, that is, it were done with "mental reservations"—a thing possible to a people trained by Jesuits, perhaps. But there was no suggestion of mental reservation about Dolores. She supported the bourgeois program with the utmost passion of sincerity. She obviously did not believe anything else to be possible; it was either that or a Fascist victory. I suppose the idea was that Communism must simply go into abeyance, not be permanently abandoned; but even so it was a tall order. I thought she was right, of course; the Republic was in far too bad a state to survive any revolutionary experimentation; but then I was not a Communist and all these people were. At first they seemed ill at ease, shocked and silenced by the extent of the sacrifice demanded of them. But afterwards the genius of Dolores—her unquestionable genius as a speaker, the most remarkable I ever heard—worked upon them its customary miracle, and she had the whole audience cheering with enthusiasm when she finished.

But what did it actually mean? I wondered. Was it merely a tactical maneuver in accordance with the resolutions of the Seventh Congress of the Communist International (1935) which had adopted the principle of supporting all democracies as against Fascism? It was that, of course, among other things. Did it also mean that Spanish Communism, being thus directed into the line of constitutional legality and compromise with capitalism, would in fact disappear, becoming merely a variant of the well-known middle-class Socialism we see in all countries? I did not know and still do not know, for the whole problem was completely dominated by the much more immediate problem of the war. Everything depended upon victory in the war; for in defeat the Communists would be slaughtered en masse, and the party must disappear with the Republic it was now supporting. The necessity of victory was the first fact, and every consideration of theory had to take a second place.

One thing I felt sure of, and that was that this retreat to capitalism was a fixed policy with the backing of all the Communist leadership in or out of Spain. Dolores was speaking in the name of the Central Executive Committee. Her discourse was interlarded with quotations from a notable to whom she referred as "*nuestra camarada Stalin*," so it was only reasonable to suppose that the Russian Communists approved of the policy. They would, of course, say it was only a logical development of the resolutions taken at the Seventh Congress, an extension of the principle of co-operation with the democracies; but it seemed to me much more than that. The resolutions of the Seventh Congress were, in fact, filled with conditions; they told the Communists of the world to support the democracies only under this or that set of circumstances, exactly specified; they did not tell Communists to support private property as a constitutional principle. What Dolores was putting forward was a program under which the Communists would cease to be any different from the Socialists or—in actual fact—the ordinary Republican liberals. Her program was Dr Negrin's program, and that was all. President Azaña would have had nothing to oppose to any part of it.

This, then, was the way they were facing reality. I thought there were two observations to be made: first, that they would never really convince the bourgeoisie of their sincerity, and second, that they would never reconcile the Spanish working class to an abandonment of the revolution even for a time. In the Newtonian laws of the intellect, inertia itself was not more terrible than momentum; and what the Communists were attacking here was the momentum of all postwar thinking the world over. The middle classes everywhere for twenty years had thought of the Communists as their most dangerous enemy; the proletariat, especially in Spain, had developed an unreasoning belief in constant revolution; and both currents of thought had acquired such terrific momentum by 1938 that this attempt to arrest them came too late. It was a gallant effort to face the facts, in a country on the brink of being conquered by international Fascism, but even the desperate urgency of the crisis could not overcome the headlong forces of division.

We came out of the theater into the starry dark night of Madrid where, as soon as the babble of voices died away, the sound of the firing could be heard again, implacable and very near.

6

One afternoon we went to the Teatro de la Zarzuela. The audience seemed much the same, robustious, rude, enthusiastic: they had been like this when I first went to Madrid in 1923. The most famous performer on the bill was Pastora Imperio, whom I had heard (and seen) in 1923, when she was already well past her prime. Now even the glory of her autumn had departed, and there was not a note left in her voice; she could not dance and scarcely tried; but even to see her walk across the stage or to hear her snap her fingers was to get some notion of the gorgeous insolent authority of the Spanish gipsy. Pastora had been a genius among the gipsies, for she never tried to learn any-thing from the arts of the theater: she had sung and danced exactly like all the other gipsies of Spain for centuries past, only better, much better. The Madrid public, which on this afternoon exercised its traditional privilege of being uproariously rude to younger artists, treated Pastora with affectionate respect, even though there was little she could do to entertain them. What they liked, I suppose, was that she still stuck to her own: that this, their favorite gipsy for decades past, the widow of their most beloved bullfighter, had not run away. Women like Pastora Imperio could have little notion of the war or revolution (I believe Pastora can neither read nor write); but she must have had the courage and loyalty of her caste, those fierce Andaluzes who pro-vided the swords and castanets of old Spain. They even cheered her on her entrance and at the end, and it was certainly not for her dancing.

There was another of the gipsy idols on that program, La

Niña de los Peines. I had heard her, too, fifteen years before; and she had grown no younger since. But she could still sing a rolling *flamenco* like no other you would hear in a year's journey. She had that same superb authority (like Pastora) so that when she walked onto the stage and clapped her hands everybody in the house was hushed. She sang only two songs, seated on a chair in the middle of the stage with a *guitarrista* beside her. Both were Arab ululations, delicate and complicated, delivered in that insolent or even contemptuous style which the Andaluza affects in singing. The second one had slightly modern words and it was easy to give them an anticlerical meaning; the audience cheered her frantically, but when she left the stage it was for good. This woman was so superb that one of my companions, a very "advanced" colleague who thought that "all that old stuff" of singing and dancing in Spain should be abandoned, was struck dumb and ceased arguing.

The rest of the performers were not very good, it is true. The supply of gipsy singers and dancers, as of bullfighters, depends upon Andalucía; Andalucía has had other things to produce since 1936; it is possible that the characteristic arts of the south are in decay. If this tremendous upheaval does make the bullfight a thing of the past, as is quite possible, the dances and the costumes will no doubt go the same way, for it is all the same culture and cannot survive by shreds. Even so, these things are deep in the people; they are not theater arts, but folk arts; you could hear any sentry along the hillside humming a *flamenco* as he goes his round; and in some form or other the singing and the dancing will survive if anything does. True, all these songs are the songs of famine, the cry of the oppressed, and would possibly assume merely antiquarian value in a reorganized society. But that reorganized society . . .

Well, when we came out of the theater we could hear the trench mortars and the hand grenades again, and before long there was a shell. The reorganized society was going to be drowned in blood, if the Fascist powers could arrange it; and in the Spain that would exist under Fascism—unimaginable though such a Spain might be—the dancers and bullfighters would be valued, if unconscious, collaborators of the regime. It is characteristic of Fascism to emphasize all the racial heritage of its subjects, partly for emotional diversion and partly to instill racial and national pride. Hitler makes peasant dress the badge of the faithful; Mussolini encourages traditional music, games and industries as he encourages traditional poverty and philoprogenitiveness. Keep them poor, make them procreate, and let them dress up and sing and dance and be proud of it—that was the Fascist line in such matters. It was easy to see how hollow and false the "blood and soil" philosophy might be, with its deliberate attempt to fuse the mind of contemporary man with the mind of his remotest ancestors; but the Communists and other theorists of the Left often made an opposite but equal mistake. In their anxiety to move fast, to create the brave new world, they were sometimes contemptuous of the arts and habits that had made a whole people through hundreds of years. Like my friend at the Teatro de la Zarzuela, they thought "all that old stuff" ought to be abandoned now. They would think this big, cheerful audience better employed listening to a lecture on dialectical materialism, or (more practically) in learning how to read and write. The universal fact, however, which defies all regimes, is that in such matters the people follows its own will, and neither Fascism nor Communism could ever destroy the *flamenco* until the whole culture that produced it had passed away.

[*191*]

I was reminded of a small cinema in the Plaza at Gerona, in upper Catalonia. The theater was called "Cinema Bakunin," but its front was ornamented with a huge poster showing Miss Joan Crawford pursing her lips at a guardsman. The film being shown at the Bakunin was probably being shown at the same moment in the Adolf Hitler Platz of innumerable German towns, as in the popular theaters of Moscow, London and Tokyo. The Madrid audience would have its own singers and dancers, whatever happened, and between times would inspect the romantic goings-on of Hollywood, and neither activity would be much affected by the clash of ideas—or even by the shells that sometimes came and perforated a theater.

7

The principal characteristic of Madrid was, of course, its life in proximity to death. This was what made it unique among the cities. The thing had been often seen, and I had often read descriptions of it—how the children played in the neighborhood of the trenches; how families lived in half-ruined houses; how the department store would be emptied for a shelling, and then all the shoppers would troop back again; how people walked on one side of the street because shells usually fell on the other. It was all true, and some little instance of it came under your observation wherever you went; all Madrid was a battlefield in which the ordinary people, attempting to live more or less ordinary lives, opposed their bodies and their collective spirit to the German and Italian artillery. It was a curiously one-sided battle, since the far-off gunners were in no danger at all. The Republic's supplies of artillery and ammunition were not great enough to be wasted in attempts on fortified positions;

almost all the firing one heard in Madrid came from the Fascists. This was true even of the small arms, since the Fascists had plenty of munitions and did not mind wasting them. But in this whole embattled city the nerve points were the university, up on the Manzanares where the Fascists had crossed the river a year and a half ago, and lower down at the Casa del Campo, the one-time royal park. Here were the front-line trenches of the two sides, the places where the Fascist lines had actually come into Madrid during that desperate November of 1936—and where they had ever since remained.

I went through the trenches of the University City under the guidance of a professional soldier—a staff major who had been a captain in the army before the war. Not many of the army officers had remained true to their oath of allegiance to the Republic, but occasionally you met some; they were to be distinguished from the new officers by the fact that they showed little political interest. They were ready to talk about the army at any length, and were eager to show you with map and pencil exactly what the positions were; but they never asked you what Chamberlain was going to do. Our friend at the University City was one of the best of the lot, a keen soldier who had had a lot to do with the development of the trench system there. He had fought at the University City in November, 1936, and had been there ever since, with one brief assignment in another field (Brunete, I believe). He was rightly proud of the whole system of defenses and shelters, the sanitary arrangements, the electric lights, telephones, homemade periscopes and deep dugouts behind the lines for rest. It took about three hours to go through all this, and during the whole time this officer did not, to the best of my recollection, mention any Spanish or foreign politician, any political party, or any particular doctrine or system of belief. I was almost as surprised at this phenomenon as I was at the trench system itself.

But the system was very fine. The Maginot and Siegfried lines are no doubt finer, as well they might be, considering what has been spent on them. Here there were no millions to waste, no endless supplies of concrete and steel. These trenches were first dug by the men who defended them in that epic November of '36, and had been made solid and habitable since then by months of effort in wartime, without great resources, always under fire. There were three such lines of trenches (the third not quite complete), all connecting, all with electric light, telephone, water closets and running water. They had been tunneled between and beneath the buildings of the University City which were the Republic's first line in November, '36, and ever since: the School of Letters and Philosophy, the Schools of Science and Law, and the three big connecting buildings which housed the Schools of Pharmacy, Medicine and Odontology. Most of these big buildings were a lacework of masonry by now, riddled through and through by shellfire, but their framework stood and their foundations were untouched.

We walked through five and a half kilometers of these trenches. They were a bit low for me; I kept hitting my head against the rafters. The roofing was made of iron sheets with wooden supports; the walk was of wood or (sometimes) of stone. Every fifty feet or so there was a round pillbox just off the trench, solid with brick, cement and iron, with emplacements for machine guns. There was a sentry in each pillbox, and each sentry had some sort of view of the enemy lines just opposite. In uncovered pillboxes the view was obtained by means of homemade periscopes, wooden troughs with mirrors at either end, made by the *chicos* themselves, and you could see the riddled Fascist buildings across the way very clearly (the School of Agronomical Engineering or the immense Clinical Hospital). At other regular intervals there were dugouts (*refugios*) opening off the trench on the other side, where the men rested, ate and slept. There were beds and tables in these, and some attempts at decoration with posters or bits of the wall newspaper. Covered pillboxes and dugouts (*fortines* and *refugios*) had roofing reinforced so as to stand a fire of 15.5. The lines here were so close to the Fascist trenches that nothing heavier than trench mortars or hand grenades was to be feared.

The Fascists apparently loved to waste their ammunition —which was but natural, considering that it was plenteous and came as the free gift of bountiful Italy. They could not possibly hope to make any impression on these trenches by rattling away at them with rifle and machine gun, but they did so all the time, as they had done for eighteen months. The Republicans, who had no such unlimited supplies to count on, never wasted time and money replying, although the sentry vigilance was unrelaxed at all times and the guns were ready. One sentry with whom we passed a few minutes amiably offered me his machine gun to fire—the courtesies of the house—but agreed when I remarked that it was a pity to waste the bullets. The Fascists were only forty or fifty yards away, but thoroughly protected by their trenches; no doubt they fired at us out of sheer boredom. Trench life was boring enough even for the Republicans, who had some reason for fighting, but for Moors and foreign mercenaries who were here to earn a monthly wage it must have been a living death.

Illiteracy and rats were the enemies most vigorously pursued in the University City. Each company had its school for reading and writing, and the record of achievement here was very high. The men contributed cartoons, poems and short pieces to the wall newspaper which ornamented every segment of trench. In those dark galleries beneath the earth the work of the university was going on in a way its founders could not have dreamed.

The Fascists occupied the ruins of the Casa Velasquez (fine arts: the scene of the most violent struggle in 1936), the School of Agronomical Engineering, the big sports field and the Clinical Hospital. The Clinical Hospital, a vast building perforated all over with shellfire, was their advance position: we saw it from almost every possible point of view, as it was faced on three sides by Republican trenches. Aside from the futile machine-gunning and rifle firing which went on all the time as an amusement for the Foreign Legion, which occupied the Fascist lines here, there were occasional outbursts with grenades and mortars, but seldom to any purpose. Even mining operations, although steadily pursued, had only local or temporary results. The deadlock was complete.

It was curious indeed to come out of this rabbit warren into the blazing sunlight of a Madrid May and see what I had often heard about before: the children playing just behind the trenches. My officer friend was rather embarrassed at this, and carefully explained that every effort was made to keep the children away; he chased a little boy off a rubbish heap that stuck up much too high for safety. The fascination of the University City for the children who lived anywhere within a mile of it needed no explaining. What was odder was that their parents would not move into another quarter of the city, although the houses in this neighborhood were frequently shelled and the streets were solidly barricaded. Houses were assigned in other quarters to the neighbors of the university, and at first many families did move out; but before the spring of 1937 they started moving back again, and now that they were used to the guns nothing would induce them to leave.

The Casa del Campo, Madrid's other permanent front, had been the private park of the former royal family. Its leafy tranquillity had never been disturbed by the rude touch of the people until after the Republican revolution of 1931. It became a public park then, and remained a public park until long after the Fascist advance of November, '36, had turned it into a battlefield. There were model trenches here, too, miles of them, and the zealous young commander in charge had undertaken to push the advance trenches out even further, so that in one place they were only ten yards from the Fascist lines.

In this advance post we had the ill luck to attract the special attention of the Moors opposite. (The Fascist trenches in the Casa del Campo had been held by Moors for many months.) We had stopped in an unfinished pillbox while our friend the captain (a highly political officer) asked the sentry there about conditions in Estremadura before the war. The Estremeño began to tell us, and got very excited over it; other soldiers crowded up from the trench and joined in; after about five minutes it must have sounded like a mass meeting. The Moors opposite heard it, of course, and threw us a hand grenade which exploded just outside the *fortín*. Our scramble for the trench was unanimous, and our friend the captain made things all right by explaining to his *chicos*: "These comrades are not used to fire, you know. They are journalists." I need hardly say that the captain had been the first through the hole into the trench.

The great park was as amazing as the University City: they were alike in affording opportunities for war that their designers could never have expected. The Casa del Campo offered all sorts of advantages in shape and forestation: it served its present defenders well. Not only were their trenches well placed and comparatively safe, but they had big fields under cultivation back of the lines and would eat well this summer. In no man's land between the trenches was the royal goldfish pond, where the *chicos* often went to fish in the evenings. We visited it and saw a fine catch of shimmering gold. The pond was just out of sight of the Fascist trenches around a hump in the land, but occasionally they tossed over a grenade or landed a mortar there for luck; it never discouraged the fishing.

In the Casa del Campo we talked to a man who was reading his first book. He had learned to read at his company's school, and had begun the book only the day before. He was proud of it: a military victory for the Republic. There was a club for the soldiers, clean and airy, in the building at the entrance of the park, and it contained a rudimentary gymnasium and a fairly good library. At night they showed movies in the club, and detachments were given leave from the trenches to go and look at them.

8

Not in the trenches was the glory of Madrid, although they framed it well. The theaters were part of it, the laden trams pursuing their clanging imperturbable way over streets plowed up by the shells, the factories where work had never ceased, the quiet bookshop where I found a literary and philosophical library presided over by a prim little lady with spectacles. Ugly modern streets—Alcalá and Gran Vía: had anything in early twentieth-century Europe been uglier?—possessed a sort of beauty in their dilapidation.

MADRID

The most squalid places in Madrid years ago used to be the pompous, expensive hotels, the Palace and the Ritz, where fat sleek ladies devoured innumerable pastries at teatime (seven o'clock) every afternoon, or sat down to immense dinners at eleven at night. Even these places were vulgar no longer: both were hospitals. Madrid, the mushroom, the parasite, created by a monarch's whim, an aristocracy's extravagance and the heartless ostentation of the new rich, had found its soul in the pride and courage of its workers. They had turned the brothel and show window of feudal Spain into this epic. Whatever the future might determine in the struggle against Fascist barbarism, Madrid had already done so much more than its share that its name would lie forever across the mind of man, sometimes in reproach, sometimes in rebuke, sometimes as a reflex of the heroic tension that still is not wholly lost from our race on earth. In this one place, if nowhere else, the dignity of the common man had stood firm against the world.

CHAPTER V

The Wayside Inn

WE USED to go hurtling along the road from Prague to Carlsbad at sixty-five or seventy miles an hour. There was nothing to delay us on most days: pleasure traffic had ceased altogether, and except during the mobilization and demobilization which succeeded each other with paralyzing rapidity later on, the road was almost empty. We had to be careful in the villages, where clouds of waddling ducks often blew across the road just in front of us, and women stood in the doorways staring, and the gendarmes picked their teeth as we passed.

There was always a colleague or two in the car with my wife and me. Often there was Walter Kerr of the New York *Herald-Tribune;* he was a friend of Jim Lardner's and was in Prague when we got there. Sometimes there was also Geoffrey Cox of the *Daily Express* (London) or John Whittaker of the Chicago *Daily News;* and once there was Maurice Hindus, with grave apostolic face and mournful eyes, forever comparing the Bohemian and Sudeten German villages with the villages of his beloved Slovakia. The dark forest and the rich farming plain swirled past us as we talked; for many miles there were hop fields, their monotonous framework giving the open country an industrialized look; at times there were long avenues of trees made gay with the scarlet splotches of the rowanberry. It was a rich, comfortable country, thickly peopled, closely tilled, with the frugal unspectacular domestic architecture and local culture of a small-holding peasant society. There were great aristocratic châteaux in Bohemia (belonging mostly to the Viennese nobles) but we saw none on the big road from Prague to Carlsbad.

We all thought the name Czechoslovakia was in itself a stroke of bad luck for these people. Bohemia was a fine old name, and meant something; Slovakia was a name too; Moravia was as pungent as a fresh-cut Christmas tree. But somehow or other when these three ancient lands and peoples had been thrown together at Versailles into a nationhood which corresponded, in fact, to their racial structure, the evil genius of that assembly had suggested for the amalgam a word which sputtered and crackled in the ear without euphony or associations—a word as new as a smear of fresh paint, a glaring brummagem kind of word, a cheap grinning toy from the bargain counter: Czechoslovakia. With a name like that, which had to be learned in 1918 by everybody including the inhabitants of the country, it was easy for the enemies of this people (notably one Adolf Hitler) to contest the reality of the thing, and to say that Czechoslovakia was no nation at all. The old names, Bohemia, Moravia, Slovakia, had their associations in every mind, the last least because it was too much overshadowed in the old days by its Hungarian seigneury, but all in some degree. The amalgam had acquired associations only of recent years, and they were, chiefly, concerned with cheap manufactured goods and a certain brand of postwar French politics. When you meant anything real (such as a man, a book, a language; music, theater, schools; the marks of a cultural entity or a continuous racial life) you used the single words Czech or Slovak, but not their combined form. The name Czechoslovakia was a Woolworth word.

And as for the French policy which that word called to mind, it was perdition itself. No part of the crazy framework of Versailles was more deplorable from the very beginning than this. Men of knowledge and good will had protested against it from the beginning—not against the creation of a Czechoslovak nation, since something of the kind was demanded by the people; but against the reckless dismemberment of the Danubian empire (Austro-Hungary) into uneconomic racial units designed to "set a fence" around Germany. Another system altogether might have been devised with the utmost ease, since it was in the tradition and habit of the whole Danubian world: there could have been a federation of these states in equal freedom, a sort of democratic grandchild of the Austro-Hungarian empire, without excessive nationalism, without economic barriers, accepting both Austria and Hungary as partners so that the prolonged unnecessary suffering of those countries (particularly of Austria) might have been avoided. Such a Danubian federation could not have been animated by anti-German feeling for long, because the Danubian Germans would have been important members of it. It could not have been dominated by the French general staff as Czechoslovakia was; it could not have taken its place in the League of Nations as an ultra-French instrument, ready to initiate proposals which were too strong even for the French themselves in the old strong days; it could not have aroused the resentment of north German political thought as these sudden new states did. Above all, it would have had a full economic life of its own, with a natural flow of agricultural and industrial exchange, systems of transport designed to complement each other, and capital markets which actually belonged to the productive units that fed them. Vienna would not have been isolated and starved out; there could have been no natural and inevitable process of union such as did in the end take place between Austria and Germany. The conquering thrust of Germany to the south and east would have encountered in Hitler's day what it met in Bismarck's—a perfectly natural barrier, a Danubian world which had its own social and political economy and neither needed nor desired to unite with Germany. Such a Danubian world would not even have been a "fence around Germany," since it was a natural growth and had taken much this same shape through the slow evolution of centuries; but it would have kept Germany within bounds better than any artificial system of fences.

Some years ago (in 1931 it was) the late Paul Painlevé told me that he had gone to see Clemenceau to protest against the dismemberment of Austria-Hungary. He was on the worst possible terms with Clemenceau, having been dislodged by the Tiger from the premiership in 1917 under very painful circumstances. The two old gentlemen made every effort to avoid meeting; when they did pass each other in the corridors of the Chamber of Deputies they bowed frigidly, without speaking. Painlevé was overlooked throughout the peace negotiations; his political star, never a powerful one, had gone into eclipse; he watched the doings of the Versailles junta through the newspapers, like any member of the public. When the Austro-Hungarian policy of Clemenceau and Wilson became too clear to be misunderstood any longer, Painlevé risked humiliation by going to see his old enemy. Clemenceau did not refuse to see him. Painlevé went in and spoke as briefly as possible. What he said was (according to his story in 1931) that the dismemberment of the Danubian empire was "*la plus grande ânerie qu'ait jamais fait la France* [the greatest asininity France had ever committed]." Clemenceau nodded grimly, bowed, and showed his visitor to the door without offering a reply.

The policy was, of course, difficult to avoid. Woodrow Wilson had come to Europe filled with high-minded and well-meaning liberal notions which were almost impossible to adjust to the complex realities of a very mixed continent. He seems to have believed that it was possible to draw frontiers according to the principle of "self-determination," and the general necessity of minorities was a painful surprise to him. He had also been sympathetically attracted toward the cause of Czechoslovak independence by Masaryk and the other exiles, thought well of the Serbs, and disliked the Austro-Hungarian empire as an illiberal survival (although from the "self-determination" point of view the old empire was much more liberal than most of its successors). His influence was overwhelming, even though the United States did not sign the Treaty of Saint-Germain. A general European settlement, whatever its details and whichever treaty embodied them, could only take place in accordance with the ruling ideas of Wilson, especially since these had been accepted and proclaimed by all the Allies as their aims in the war.

Clemenceau's job, therefore, was to translate the cloudy liberalism of Wilson into a language that could be understood in francs and centimes and supported by heavy artillery. It was easy enough to do this once the main lines of the technique had been developed, because Wilson was un-

familiar with the details and easily fooled. He would probably have opposed any form of democratic Danubian federation as being "the old Austria-Hungary in a new form,"
and his nineteenth-century mind had a rooted prejudice
against Austria-Hungary; but Clemenceau's alternative invention, the string of nation states on a racial basis, "self-
determination" as applied by French shrewdness and selfishness, seemed to both Wilson and Lloyd George to solve the
problems involved in a broadly benevolent sense without
material injustice to minorities. Wilson's conscience was
exercised over the minorities, just the same, and when he
discovered that it was impossible to invent a nation in Central Europe without some injustice to smaller national
groups, he wrote the discovery into the Covenant of the
League of Nations. (This was his solution for many problems which refused to be settled by professorial generaliza-
tion.)

Wilson's principle of "self-determination," in this case,
became Clemenceau's state of Czechoslovakia, an amalgam
of the old Austrian territories of Bohemia, Moravia and
Slovakia, deeply indebted at the outset to France, and dedi-
cated to the pursuit of an ultra-French policy throughout
its existence as an independent nation. The frontiers of the
new state were drawn in accordance with geographical and
economic necessities—all very arguable—and with "the historic frontiers of the kingdom of Bohemia," a concept so
absurdly unrealistic that it makes one think of Zionism. The
"historic frontiers of the kingdom of Bohemia," of course,
included districts inhabited almost entirely by German-
speaking people, the German Bohemians who had been
there since early medieval times and had contributed so
much to the industrial prosperity of Austria-Hungary.

No frontiers could have been worse than these. The Ger-

mans of northern Bohemia were not particularly Germanic
in race; they had been greatly mixed with other races in that
melting pot of Central Europe, and you found pure Slav
types among them very often; nor were they, up to now,
particularly Germanic in feeling. They had always belonged to the Austro-Hungarian empire and the earlier
kingdom of Bohemia; they had never enjoyed the blessings
of union with Germany. But they spoke German. They
had their share in the German cultural heritage, the German literature, tradition and domestic customs. They felt
themselves to be profoundly different from their Slavic
(Czech or Bohemian) neighbors, toward whom they had
always had the relation of superior to inferior in the past.
Now they were asked to accept membership in a predominantly Slavic nation ruled by the Bohemian Czechs in association with the backward Slovaks, a people only just
emerging from serfdom. Unpronounceable and incomprehensible Slavic names were given to their German towns
and to the streets in their German towns. They were represented in a parliament where most of the debates took place
in a language they could not understand, and which, in fact,
seemed to them ridiculous. Their highly developed industries and their intensive agriculture were to pay taxes for
the development of the inferior Slavic peoples to whom
they felt no kinship at all. Even if Czechoslovakia had been
an island in the middle of the Atlantic Ocean these facts
would have created an exceedingly difficult problem from
1918 onward.

But Czechoslovakia was far from being an island. It was
in the exact center of Europe, subjected to every current of
European racial and national feeling. And—the crux of the
matter—the German lands of northern Bohemia were cheek
by jowl with the German lands of Saxony and Bavaria.

Germany lay just over there, visible, tangible, ineluctable, working out its own troubled fate in its own way, pulling at the heart of the German Bohemians in misery as in success, and steadily becoming more real, more desirable, more vitally related, as the Slavic peoples of Czechoslovakia grew more alien.

Under the old arrangements before 1914 the Germans of Bohemia had experienced no desire to unite with the Germans of the Reich, and if some natural successor to Austria-Hungary had been accepted by the peacemakers, no such desire would have been created or pushed on by circumstance. As it was, the development of a desire for union was as natural as the growth of a plant or the revolution of the seasons. Even without Hitler, the emotions he exploits would have come to life in the Central European regions. And when the complicated miseries and diseases of the post-Versailles world did, in due course, produce their Hitler, a sort of race prophet thriving on grievances and inspired to visions of a magnificent future, it was no wonder that the disgruntled Germans of Bohemia turned to him as to a national savior.

All this is without regard for the details of Sudeten German grievances, which were extremely debatable. The Czechoslovak state began with promises of the utmost liberality to its minorities on all sides, and these promises were not fully kept. The democracy was real enough: all national groups were represented in the parliament, all had schools, free speech, a free press, and equal rights as citizens; but in fact it was the easiest thing in the world for the Slavic Bohemians (the Czechs) to dominate the machinery by sheer weight of numbers. The "cantonal" system, the "Swiss federal" idea, which had been much to the fore in discussions of the new state at Versailles, was heard of no more.

The Germans, Poles, Hungarians and Ruthenians in the new state were given full democratic rights but were always outnumbered, outvoted, outmaneuvered; the Slovaks, largest of the non-Czech groups, were in the main without political education or experience, and were easily led by their Czech cousins; the new state was, in fact, dominated by the Czechs from 1918 onward. It was not only a Czech-ruled state, but governed by a single Czech party and a single clique: it was Eduard Beneš who ruled Czecho-slovakia from the beginning. These were not necessarily bad things, and you could make out an unanswerable case for the statement that the Czechs had ruled with greater democratic justice and consideration for alien minorities than any other government in Europe excepting (always) Switzerland; but they were, good or bad, *alien* things to the German, Polish, Hungarian and Ruthenian minorities. And among all these the Germans, with their fixed convictions of superiority, suffered the most. Their pride was attacked every single day by the Czech language, the Czech police, the Czech officials in their German land; and with such real psychological grievances, such racial and national resent-ments perpetually at work within them, it was easy to blame all other misfortunes on the same dislikable state of affairs, so that economic distress and unemployment after 1929 (although in fact due to world conditions) were currently blamed by the Germans on their Czechoslovak government.

No special gift of intuition was needed to perceive how such a situation favored the plans of a supernationalism such as that invented by Hitler. Even other varieties of German national thought would have seized upon the Bohemian Germans (the so-called "Sudeten" Germans) as marked out for union with Germany. And in the old days Bismarck would have thought his fondest dreams come true if Austria-Hungary had melted away and given him German Austria and German Bohemia to claim as his own. This was not altogether for the sake of the mystic union of the German-speaking peoples, since Bismarck was too practical to be ridden by such obsessions: it was also, and supremely, because in this direction lay the road to the Balkans, the Ukraine, Constantinople and the East, the food and raw materials and markets which would make the Greater Germany irresistible. Bismarck had said that Bohemia was the key to Europe, and from any German nationalist point of view this was true. Hitler's German nationalism, although colored by the mystic imagination of its inventor, and full of nonsense about "blood and soil" and the Nordic race and other dream-creations of an ignorant and hysterical mind, was in practical politics grounded upon the same necessities, the same conceptions and the same appetites as all preceding German nationalism, so that Bohemia was not only a question of "blood brothers" coming "home to the Reich," but also one of the relentless expansion of Germany toward the goods of the south and east and over their prostrate peoples.

Strategic and political considerations of the first importance intervened here and changed the Bohemian question into one of world significance. You could see (as I did) that the Czechoslovak state was a steady irritation to its German minority members; you could admit that these Germans, since they lived on the borders of Germany and were treated more or less as stepchildren in their own state, must naturally in time turn toward the German Reich; but you had also to see that for them to do so at this stage of affairs was to destroy Czechoslovakia as an independent nation, to open the south and southeast to Germany's advance, and to threaten all Europe with a triumphant assertion of Nazi power. Czechoslovakia had been created with strategic frontiers, the north Bohemian hills and forests which opposed a natural barrier to advancing armies from the north; and these strategic frontiers had been heavily fortified since 1918. To have drawn the frontiers in such a way as to exclude the German population would have been possible in 1918: it would have meant making a weaker frontier, without the natural mountainous defense, but it could have been done. Now it was no longer possible without annihilating Czechoslovakia. To give up the present frontiers would be to surrender important links of the Czech fortifications to Germany, and the remainder of Czechoslovakia would be in no position to maintain an independent existence. This might have represented no very grave danger to civilization at large in another period—in the 1860s and 1870s, for instance, when Germany under Bismarck was as enlightened a state as most in Europe, if not something better than that. At the present time, when Germany was emerging from its postwar neuroses into a gigantic neurosis of the most perilous kind, called National Socialism, the conquest of such important new areas and the opening out of still further vistas for conquest must be a disaster for all mankind, bringing specific suffering (the jail, the firing squad, the concentration camp) to hundreds of thousands, the miseries of hunger, forced labor and legal tyranny to whole new territories, the strengthening of reactionary forces throughout the world, and a general darkening of the human spirit in the triumph of anti-Semitism, racial atavism, the doctrine of might over right, and the brutal assertion that no law could stand in the way of Germany's will.

This was the real trouble: that the world at large stood to lose by a transfer of the German areas of Bohemia to Germany. It might have been done in 1918, although, as I have said before, there was a much better alternative which was disregarded—a natural alternative, a solution with historical continuity and a tradition to support it. It could no longer be done without endangering the precarious balance hitherto maintained between democracies and despotism in Europe—without strengthening the powers of darkness throughout the world. And the *way* in which it was being done, by loud brutal threats from Germany and weak timorous shudders from the democracies, was in itself a humiliation to the universal conscience. For thousands of years western European man had struggled and died for the ideas of freedom under law; for orderly processes, the pledged word between nations, the rights of citizenship; for a whole complex of ideas, some extremely nebulous and some as precise as the right to get married and have children; for the progress of common humanity. The heritage of at least one thousand years of political progress was at stake for Europe in this case. To give Germany her way was to admit that all this had been in vain: that treaties, pledges, agreements meant nothing, and that "right dwells" (as Hitler said) "in might alone."

2

By the time my wife and I got to Prague the long crisis was reaching its height: on that day Mr Neville Chamberlain had flown to Berchtesgaden. We had left England on September 12 (the day of Hitler's speech at the Partei-Tag in Nürnberg), in accordance with a plan formed two months earlier. No crisis in my experience had been more openly worked up than this one. It was perfectly possible to foresee it for months in advance; in fact I (like most of my newspaper colleagues) had foreseen it almost exactly as

it took place. I had written to editors in America in July on
the subject, explaining that I was going to Prague in mid-
September for this crisis: and I had been told that "America
was no longer interested in Czechoslovakia." Hitler's statements and maneuvers had been so obvious since March 12
that it is difficult to comprehend how even an American
editor could have misunderstood them; and it is downright
inconceivable that the British or French Foreign Office
could have been taken by surprise at anything that happened.

We drove across Germany without particular haste, observing all the phenomena of a nation ill at ease, under
mobilization without either knowing or caring exactly why,
and profoundly worried. In Aachen we saw parades of soldiers at which only very small children lifted their hands in
salute; the adults in the town stared apathetically, no doubt
reflecting upon their nearness to the French and Belgian
borders and the dangers of bombing from the air. At Olpe
in Westphalia, where we stopped for dinner on the first
night, the radio was incessant in the hotel restaurant, and a
group of military officers and their wives occupied the
largest table, listening to it. At one moment the radio announced that the Czech soldiers and gendarmes were murdering the German inhabitants of Eger, and a fantastic
figure was given (three or four hundred, as I remember).
The officer who seemed to outrank the others at the table
made a dramatic gesture with his hand and said: "Jetzt
fängt es an [Now it begins]!" This misinformation of the
German people, judging by their newspapers and radio, was
something fabulous, passing anything that had been achieved
in this respect in the past even by the Nazis. The radio
belched forth lies at every moment of the day and night;
the newspapers carried streaming headlines about "Red

riots" in Czechoslovakia, the "murders" of the German citizens, and the "breakup" of the Czechoslovak Republic. There seemed to be a general line which presented Czechoslovakia as a Bolshevik state, and the efforts of the Czech police to restore order in Eger after the Nazi uprising there were represented as unprovoked attacks on a defenseless German population. Untruth could scarcely have been more systematically worked upon than in this case, with the obvious purpose of inciting the German people to a state of readiness for war; and yet, except among the aforesaid officers at the table in Olpe, I never saw the slightest evidence of warlike excitement in this jaunt across Germany. There was a slight increase in the normal German politeness; the people with whom one had immediate dealings were all very anxious to demonstrate how friendly they were to foreigners and how welcome the foreigner was in Germany. At the customs line between Belgium and Germany the guards made elaborate speeches to us (particularly to my wife) on this subject: "You are always welcome here," one of them repeated several times. In Aachen, Cologne and other places the efforts of the population to be helpful were at times embarrassing: no sooner did they see the "G.B." on our license plate (the car was registered in Great Britain) than they volunteered information and guidance.

We went on to Kassel, Weimar and Dresden. The roads at times were clogged with military trucks, blocked or in movement, and with columns of infantry and artillery. The general "maneuvers," which were, in fact, a full-dress mobilization, were in progress. The effort to whip up a pugnacious temper among the German people on the subject of Czechoslovakia had not been oversuccessful, but Hitler hoped (and with good reason) that the foreign powers would fail to appreciate this fact until it was too late, and meanwhile the mobilization threw the whole world into a state of anxiety. New signs had begun to appear on factories, indicating industrial mobilization. The chief of these seemed to be "Wir marschieren mit [We also march]!" This was painted in vast letters across the white walls of many a factory we passed on the journey.

At Dresden, where we dawdled a couple of days looking at pictures in the Zwinger and going to the opera, we got the first news of Mr Chamberlain's trip to Canossa. I had expected something of the kind since September 6, when the *Times* leading article had suggested that the German areas of Czechoslovakia be ceded to Germany. That leading article, a masterpiece of slyness, was easily explained away after its appearance, and it may indeed be true that it was not officially inspired, but the fact that it was printed at all proved the existence of such an opinion in the British governing class, and constituted a direct encouragement to Hitler to persevere in his plan of annexation. It was not necessary to be a Hitler to see in that monstrous paragraph a promise that England would assist in the dismemberment of Czechoslovakia when the time came.

That last evening in Dresden, and the next morning, we heard the Nazi *mot d'ordre* a number of times. It was: "Czechoslovakia is breaking up from within." The assistant manager of the Bellevue Hotel, the man in the garage, the porter—they all had it down pat, very glib and handy. This was the statement that had been reiterated a thousand times on the radio and in the newspapers during the past few days since the Partei-Tag at Nürnberg. It was no part of Hitler's technique to threaten war; it never has been. His system was rather to pose as the apostle of peace, but also as the apostle of union between German blood brothers, and

to throw upon all who opposed this union the onus of desire for war. With the control which the Nazis exercised
over all sources of information, it was possible for them to
convince their people that Czechoslovakia was, in fact,
"breaking up from within," that the Prague government
could no longer maintain order, and that the "Bolsheviks"
were running riot in the streets. (The actual fact, that Nazi
desperadoes made an attempt at revolt in Eger and were
driven out of the town with a loss of thirty men on both
sides, has never yet to my knowledge been printed in Germany.)

Upon these small curiosities of the time there supervened
the prize titbit, the astounding piece of news: Chamberlain's offer to go to Berchtesgaden. The Germans themselves could scarcely credit such an amazing voluntary in-
dignity on the part of the Prime Minister of Great Britain.
The tendency at first was to assume that this was, again,
some sort of trick or maneuver; either that it had not happened or would not happen, and was contrived either by
the British or by the Nazis to fool the people. It took some
hours of newspaper and radio screeching to make the Germans realize the extent of their Führer's triumph. To a
people which, like the Germans, has always regarded the
English as their principal enemy, rival and world-obstacle,
and at the same time as the proudest of European peoples,
the most worthy of imitation, this Berchtesgaden affair was
a tremendous psychological experience. Nothing that happened afterwards—neither Godesberg nor Munich—did so
much to open the eyes of the Germans to England's weakness and their own strength. Chamberlain's visit to Berchtesgaden in homage to Hitler was in this respect (for the
Volks-seele, the spirit of the people) the most important
event since the World War. It was also the proudest mo-

ment in Hitler's life, and one which even he, with his semi-divine pretensions, can never have expected. One saw the shoulders straighten in the streets of Dresden as this realization dawned upon all the people at the same time: that Germany was once again, and more than ever before, in a position to command the obedience of Europe.

We left for Prague on that day, followed by the solicitous recommendations of the hotel people to "take care of" ourselves. Like most other people in Germany they believed, by and large, what their government told them, and they therefore thought that public order in Czechoslovakia was no more. On this day Mr Neville Chamberlain was flying to Munich, to make his pilgrimage up the Ober Salzberg to Hitler's eyrie. I remember thinking as we crossed the Czech frontier that we were in all probability coming here to see the disintegration of a nation—not, as the Nazi password had it, "from within," but by the hammer blows of force and treachery from without.

There were no signs of military movement or other unrest in Czechoslovakia. We sped along the smooth road from Dresden to Prague without hindrance and without seeing anything out of the way. Teplitz, the big industrial town in the north which was a center of German agitation, seemed altogether normal, although many of its factories (I afterwards heard) had been closed. In Prague itself, sprawled out along the Moldau, there was the usual bustle and clatter of a busy modern city, but no sign of the "Red riots" we had heard about in Germany. We drove to the Alcron Hotel, which had been for some weeks the headquarters of Lord Runciman's mission of "mediation" between the Czechoslovak government and its German citizens. We did not choose this hostelry because of the glory thus shed upon it, but because Walter Kerr of the *Herald-*

Tribune was staying there. After an experience of some days we changed to the Ambassador, down in the Wenceslas Square (Vaclavske Namesti) where we lived for the remainder of our time in Prague.

The news of Berchtesgaden had struck the Czechs into incredulous bewilderment. On that first day and the next they did not seem to be able to take it in. They had been under the protection, tutelage and, politically speaking, the control of France and England since the annexation of Austria to Germany last March—and of France alone since 1918. They had mobilized in the spring at the bidding of their great allies; they had been psychologically trained all summer long to do as their great allies told them to do; they were ready now for peace or war as their big brothers might direct. They had accepted a long series of concessions to the Germans of Bohemia, the so-called Sudeten Germans, including by this time everything the Sudeten Deutsche Partei had ever demanded. Aside from the simple necessity of keeping order, which had obliged them to repress the armed outbreak of Nazi rebellion in Eger three days before, they had taken no action at all except to concede, concede and concede. They were now facing the extraordinary fact, wholly new to most of them, that France and England had been playing a cat-and-mouse game with them all this time, and that they would be sacrificed to Hitler without a qualm if he insisted strongly enough. It took over two weeks of grueling crisis and supreme disillusionment for this fact to penetrate the mind of Prague. The rest of the country did not realize it until the aftermath of October and November taught them that they were no longer free.

I made my preparations in good time: a store of petrol in the garage, another in the luggage space in the back of the car; a military pass; a letter from the Foreign Office; a military permit to buy gasoline after its sale would be restricted. All these, when the crisis actually came, proved of varying worth. My store of gasoline in the car was stolen by Germans in Carlsbad; my store in the garage was requisitioned by the soldiers in Prague; and the military permit proved of no use in places where there was no gasoline. In the end I navigated chiefly on bootleg gasoline bought from Nazi saboteurs in the Sudetenland, who were always anxious to disobey an order of the Czech authorities when possible. The military passes proved good throughout, for there was never a moment when the Czech soldiery did not obey orders from the center with unquestioning discipline.

And before we knew the full extent of Mr Neville Chamberlain's generosity at Berchtesgaden we set out to visit the German districts in the northwest. My wife and I and Matt Halton of the Toronto *Star* made that first trip over the road from Prague to Carlsbad and on to Elbogen, Falkenau, Eger and beyond. In Eger we saw the wreckage of the Nazi outbreak a few days before; in the villages beyond Eger, Rossbach and the others up in that extreme and ill-judged extension of Czechoslovakia, we were given the Nazi salute with cries of "Heil Hitler." The Czech police, walking by twos in the streets of the bigger towns, seemed to pay no attention to these manifestations of the Nazi feeling of the people. In the smaller villages there were no Czech police, and the swastika was scrawled on doors and walls. There was an ominous feeling about all those little towns and villages up there, an air of waiting. I reflected again—as often in the following two or three weeks—how insane it had been to include this particular area, the Egerland, in Czechoslovakia: for this district was about one hundred per cent German and was not necessary to the defenses of the country (the fortifications were behind it). And here, just here, had been the center of the whole Sudeten German agitation, Konrad Henlein's capital, with a guerrilla force of young men based on Bavaria just over the way. There might be a thousand reasons for including the mixed German and Czech areas of the Sudeten Mountains themselves, in northern Bohemia, but this Egerland was of no strategic value, contained no Czech population, and should never have been in Czechoslovakia at all. The insignificant Eger territory had been the sore spot since 1918, was now the focus of the whole Sudeten German movement, and would in due course provide the pretext for much more comprehensive cessions and annexations which would destroy the independence of Czechoslovakia as a whole. Among the many idiotic provisions of the peace treaties, this piece of map drawing seemed one of the worst.

3

In the following weeks, whenever I passed along the road from Prague to Carlsbad or back again—which was often—I had the habit of stopping for a glass of beer and a sandwich at a place which we called Horse's Neck. It was a village, predominantly German, about halfway between Prague and Carlsbad, and it possessed an inn where the villagers and the farmers of the district often gathered. The name of the village was Horesedly in German and Horsenec in Czech. The inn was called the Weisse Hirt (the White Hart).

The first time we became actively aware of the life and opinions of Horse's Neck was one morning about seven o'clock when we were chilled to the bone, having driven from Prague through a freezing white mist. We had left there sometime before six o'clock, and by this time Walter Kerr, who was with me, was loudly demanding coffee. We stopped at Horse's Neck to see what could be done, and the grim, black-browed mistress of the inn asked us into the kitchen.

It was a very warm kitchen with an immense stove all along one side. The mistress of the inn was ironing on the table in the middle. A sturdy girl clattered in and out on wooden-soled shoes, doing the morning's cleaning. There were three or four men sitting at the end of the kitchen with long Bohemian pipes in their mouths, listening to a radio which already (at seven in the morning) was pouring out news and propaganda in German. I had my first taste of the place's quality when I asked the mistress of the inn for beer. She gave it to me in a bottle.

"Why can't I have draft beer?" I asked. "You had draft beer the other day."

"The pipes are being cleaned," she said severely. "We clean the pipes here every morning. We do not let them stand dirty. We are Germans."

According to the same principle, the coffee had to be made fresh, which took a very long time. I sat down beside one of the farmers near the radio and attacked my beer. It was not easy to get him into talk. I asked what station he was listening to on the radio.

"Prague," he said.

I asked if he could get German stations on this radio.

"Yes," he said, eying me malevolently, "we get all the German stations. We do not depend on Bolshevik lies from Prague."

"What makes you think they are Bolsheviks in Prague?"

"We know," he said. "We know what they are doing in Prague. But before long that will be changed."

[*220*]

I asked if Horse's Neck was a German town.

"Ja, ja, ja," they all chorused. "We are Germans here. This is the frontier."

I was much interested in that statement, since I had never heard of any German claim reaching so far as this place (the maximum claim in the northwest had been the Carlsbad area).

"From here on," one of the men said, "everything is German. We are all Germans. Sudeten Germans. The Czechs have taken the land, but the people are German. Soon everything will be changed."

Even then I knew that this was untrue, as the population was in fact very mixed, with a predominance of Czechs, through most of the area up to Carlsbad. Interpreted, what he meant was that up to Horse's Neck the population had been purely Czech, with no German admixture; the German admixture began here; and it was certainly characteristic of Nazi logic to claim any mixed area—any area not purely Czech—as being rightfully German.

"What advantage would you have," I asked, "if you did join the German Reich? You would have forced labor, no freedom of speech, not enough food, and no liberty to organize in clubs or labor unions or political parties. Your schools wouldn't be free any longer. You could be picked up here and shipped off to Hamburg or the Rhineland to work on the roads. You couldn't vote except as you were told to vote. Your farm would have to produce what you were told to produce or you would lose the farm. You'd have spies and policemen everywhere. What do you want all that for?"

The man looked at me with narrow-eyed suspicion and rose slowly to his feet. So did the others.

"We are no Czechs," he said in a voice heavy with dis-

like. ("Wir sind keine Tschechen.") At that he knocked his
pipe out in a bucket of ashes and lumbered out of the room,
his heavy wooden-soled boots noisy on the stone floor. The
others followed him.

Walter and I perceived after this that we were not in
favor with the inhabitants of Horse's Neck. The mistress of
the inn looked gloomier than ever as she gave us our coffee.
No effort could draw her into conversation. We drank the
coffee, warmed ourselves thoroughly at the fire, and went
out by way of the front room, a beer parlor with tables covered in bright blue-and-white checked cloth. Here one side
of the room was hung with newspapers and magazines on
racks. We stopped to look at them: German, all German.
The *Völkische Beobachter*. The *Münchener Illustrierter*.
Simplicissimus. Die Wehrmacht. Der Stürmer. And in every
one, by headline, photograph and text, a screeching message
of hatred and untruth about Czechoslovakia. "Czech atrocities"—barefaced inventions, sometimes illustrated with pictures from Spain, actually pictures of the women and children killed by German bombs, now represented to be German women and children killed by Czechoslovak bombs. In
these German papers (and in fact in the entire German
press during September) there was a ceaseless iteration of
certain statements which had hardly a shred of truth to support them: that Prague was the "Jewish center" of the
world, that it was governed by the "Russian Bolsheviks,"
that the "international capitalists" (also Jewish) had col-
laborated in this curious enterprise, and that Czech soldiers
here, there and the next place were torturing and murdering German women and children. It was true that Prague's
Jewish population had increased since the conquest of Austria by Germany, as was only natural: the Jews who fled
from Austria had to go somewhere, and Prague was near.

But neither the "Russian Bolsheviks" nor the "international capitalists" had shown any great enthusiasm in the support of Czechoslovakia: the general cause of Western progress would have been considerably strengthened if they had. Moreover, the alleged "atrocities" of the Czech soldiery never took place, so far as I was ever able to determine, and I was in a number of the frontier villages during and after the disorders produced by armed insurrection of the Nazi gangs.

Such a press, containing such poisonous lies, would never have been allowed inside a country which was fully aware of its danger. But Czechoslovakia remained unconscious of the real danger until the worst had come. "We trust in our allies," was their motto: a blind, believing phrase which left them helpless against every device of calumny and bad faith.

The oddest thing, I thought, was the refusal of the Czechs to abandon the democratic structure even under such violent pressure. Konrad Henlein and the Sudeten Deutsche Partei had carried on their electoral propaganda last spring under the protection of the Czech police; freedom of speech, assembly and the press remained untouched until armed insurrection provoked the proclamation of martial law in the German districts; the whole assumption of the state was that the seditious German citizens were, in fact, loyal citizens of Czechoslovakia who had a perfect right to say and do as they pleased so long as they did not disturb public order. The Czechs, although dominating the state by their superiority in numbers, were faithful to democracy from the beginning to the end, and in the whole affair nothing was more striking than the ease with which the Nazi propaganda (itself controlled with an iron hand, and no nonsense about truth allowed to interfere) was spread throughout the German-Czech population for month after month without let or hindrance from its victims.

Henlein had declared on September 15, while Chamberlain was flying to Berchtesgaden, what he really wanted: "Wir wollen Heim ins Reich [We want to be at home in the Reich]." It was secession. Up to this point the Sudeten Deutsche Partei and its leader had always maintained that their demands—although these grew steadily greater—were not incompatible with allegiance to the Czechoslovak Republic. Henlein privately assured a number of English leaders, on his visit to London in July, that he desired no union with Germany or with the German Nazi party; to one of these leaders known to me he gave the assurance "on his word of honor." Either his word of honor had slipped, or his repeated visits to Hitler at Berchtesgaden had taught him that such things can be conveniently forgotten. Now there had been armed insurrection of the Nazi gangs at Eger; blood had been shed; the young men of the Sudeten districts were thronging across the frontier to Germany to form militias for attack on Czechoslovakia; and at the present moment, a day or so after September 15, Henlein had fled with his immediate associates to the protection of the swastika. And yet, at such a moment, the whole lying German press hung on the wall there at Horse's Neck, to be read by any Bohemian farmer who wanted to fill his mind with venom and confusion.

There is no truth that matters anything at all to the people involved in such a conflict once the forces of unprincipled propaganda are let loose. That woman, the mistress of the inn at Horse's Neck, was no more German than I am. She had the typical broad cheekbones and flat head of the Slav, with dark coloring and a heavy jaw. She

was probably of pure Czech-Bohemian race. But by one of
the accidents which are so frequent in that part of the world
her family had become German-speaking at some time before her birth—one, two, three generations before—and she
was now a "German," prepared to go to any length in
support of the union with Germany. Hitler defines this
process of unreason, which he regards as compulsory for
any German, as "thinking with your blood." In the case of
these mixed peoples of Bohemia it was not even that: it was
thinking with your language, if at all. And the language,
that broad thoroughfare to the mind, had been used for
such a traffic of appalling misrepresentations that no Bohemian German during these days could form an idea of
what was actually taking place. Again and again they said
to me: "The Bolsheviks are in control in Prague; the government is taking all its orders from Moscow now." This
was what they were told by German radio and press a
thousand times a day, and it was quite useless to tell them
the statement was not even a misrepresentation but a pure
lie. (A pure lie in that it had no basis of any sort—the
Czechoslovak government erred in exactly the opposite
sense, by refusing to maintain communications with the
Soviet Embassy or the Soviet Union at a time when Russia
could have been of great help to them.)

How beautifully Hitler understood Horse's Neck! This
was his strength, I thought: he was one with that dark-
browed Bohemian woman, those sullen farmers, those
people whose answer to anything and everything was "Wir
sind keine Tschechen." He knew that no truth mattered in
the least where their fundamental likes and dislikes were
concerned, and that by the unremitting use of simple lies,
highly colored and calculated to arouse indignation, likes
and dislikes could easily be transformed into a burning pas-

sion. Again and again in *Mein Kampf* Hitler reveals to us how thoroughly he scorns the truth and how valuable he believes the political or propaganda lie to be in the awakening and regeneration of "his" German people. Never has his system worked better than among these poor, industrious and uneducated, but proud and stubborn inhabitants of German Bohemia. He judged them well, being one of them. "The little Bohemian corporal," as Hindenburg called him, who so narrowly escaped being called by his father's Sudeten name of Schickelgruber, has often failed to understand the Germans of the north; but among these mixed peoples of old Austria who are his blood relatives his system of passion, intuition and blind assertion has been infallible. In the inn at Horse's Neck, his true intellectual habitat, not the wildest of his statements would be questioned. That the Jews were, simultaneously, the capitalists and the Communists of the world; that one drop of Jewish blood was poison in the veins; that the Czechs were murderers and torturers, the British, French and Americans dishonest profiteers and warmongers dominated by the Jews, and that the Spanish Republic was a Jewish Communist attempt to conquer Europe for Bolshevism—all these assertions of the conglomerate Hitler lie were accepted in Horse's Neck with the sighs and moans of the true believer. And underneath all these lies, beneath this burning passion of hatred, was blood and iron: the machine gun, the big cannon, the bombs. This was the true tragedy of Europe: that power and black murderous atavism had come together, and that the ideas of the inn kitchen at Horse's Neck could thus storm over the world.

4

Carlsbad's heights and hollows, lovely in autumn, enclosed a city under martial law, but even so there was no curb on the speech of the German population. They talked with ease as soon as they saw that we were not Czechs. "The German soldiers will be coming in tomorrow or the next day," they said. I think the first time I heard this statement was about September 18, long before the British and French had openly adopted Hitler's plans. The local Nazi party officials—undisturbed in their homes—issued proclamations, two of which I saw, calling on the Germans of the area to remain quiet and wait for "the day of liberation." Shops were closed; there were no factories; the guests of the Carlsbad water cure had long since taken their departure, and there were only two or three of the smaller hotels open. The Jewish Home for the Aged, on the slope leading down to the town, was still open, although about half its inmates had been transferred to a less threatened area. Czech soldiers had a camp along the Müllerbrunn, and there were gendarmes patrolling the streets, two by two, but the town was, and remained throughout these weeks, without disturbance. It was—like most of the area—confidently waiting. By this time all the Germans of the Sudeten area were perfectly assured that their annexation to Germany would be accomplished without trouble and in a short time. They acquired this assurance on the day Mr Neville Chamberlain flew to Berchtesgaden, and no incident thereafter materially disturbed it.

Elbogen, Falkenau, and the other towns on the road to Eger were also patrolled by the Czechs, with a curfew at eight o'clock and a general air of tension and waiting. There had been some clashes between the local Nazis and the Czech police, with casualties in several villages. At Eger, Henlein's capital, a very abnormal state of affairs prevailed, with hardly any of the inhabitants abroad in the streets. The little block by the railway station where the Nazis had attempted their uprising a few days before was still full of the signs of combat, and the whole front of the Hotel Victoria, where Henlein had his headquarters, was wrecked from the attack with hand grenades. The extent to which the Nazi rising had been prepared was shown by the underground passages here, through which the local Nazi gang escaped to the open country and across to Germany. The galleries underground made a system of communication between the buildings in that block and the railway station, and a means of escape behind, all dug without arousing any suspicion on the part of the Czech police.

We visited all that area so often afterwards that I thought I could probably drive from Prague to Eger and back again in my sleep. Other German-speaking areas of Czechoslovakia were at least as interesting as this; north Bohemia, with its superb French fortifications, and the Böhmerwald on the other side, toward Austria, were essential parts of Hitler's plan of dissection, and had played their part in the agitation which led to this crisis. But the real capital of the Sudeten German movement was the Eger-Carlsbad area, the most German district of all, and it was here that the Führer's triumphal entry was expected from the earliest days as soon as he could arrange it with Neville Chamberlain.

The sense of the population was never in doubt for one moment. They were all Germans, and a majority of them (two thirds or more) wanted union with Germany. This was shown in dozens of small ways, as well as in open speech. A week later, when the crisis was at its height and

Czechoslovakia was mobilized, gasoline was unobtainable almost anywhere along the road. But from the local German stations it was always possible to extract gasoline, sometimes as much as the car would hold. This was primarily a tribute to the "G.B." on the license plate of my car: English cars and English people were supposed to be the allies of the Germans during those days, thanks to Mr Chamberlain's efforts. The station owner would peer at the car and at us, would say, "You are not Czechs," and then would make cabalistic signs. Sometimes we had to back into an alleyway behind the garage, and sometimes the gasoline was openly delivered in the public road with an accomplice watching to see that the Czech gendarmes were not too near. The delivery of the illicit gasoline was always accompanied by information (usually false), reminiscence and statements of opinion. Like this:

"Ah, yes, the dirty Czechs don't want us to sell any gasoline any more. They are afraid it will be used for friends of our side. We have our stores, just the same. Do you know that the Czechs have been murdering the people at Heinrichsgrün? Our poor people. The Bolsheviks are in complete control at Prague now, and they have Red riots in the street all day long. We hear about it on the Leipzig radio every night; it is enough to make your blood run cold. We shall be glad when the day of liberation comes. They say the German army is coming in tonight or tomorrow morning early; I have heard that the Führer will march in with them. My two boys are both away in the hills. They joined the Freikorps first thing. One of them is in Bavaria somewhere now, I think in Bayreuth. I hope they will march in with the German army, but I haven't heard. Almost every family in our village has somebody who has gone away with the Freikorps. Ah, well, it won't be long now. Our Führer has promised us."

Henlein's Freikorps, a sort of militia of the young men from this area, had been rapidly organized after September 15 out of his former youth organizations. It trained in Germany and was designed to assist in the armed attack on Czechoslovakia when or if that came; but events were so accelerated, and the whole process was so eased to its culmination by Mr Chamberlain's haste to surrender, that the Freikorps were never used at all.

The desire of the German population for union with Germany was not, even so, unanimous. There remained about one third of the Germans who dreaded the torture and jails of Nazi despotism. These were the members of the German Social Democratic party, once the dominant political organization of the German-speaking citizens in Czechoslovakia. The rise of the nationalistic Sudeten Deutsche Partei, under Nazi influence after 1933, had been at the expense of the old Social Democratic solidarity. It was particularly noticeable at mass meetings and other gatherings that the youth of the German areas was attracted to Nazi ideas and not to Social Democracy: and after the conquest of Austria in March, the process was speeded up by every means known to Nazi technique and experience. The Social Democrats were outnumbered in almost every area, and in some they had practically ceased to exist. But there were determined anti-Fascists among them who were marked for death in the event of a Nazi victory, and the organization continued its struggle to the end.

Maurice Hindus took me to visit a group of some three hundred Social Democratic refugees at Chodau, not far from Carlsbad. These were factory workers and their families from Graslitz, near the German border. They knew themselves to be outnumbered by the Nazis in the area, and they believed that at least half of their number were on the death list. A couple of nights before, when Henlein had proclaimed his bombastic "six-hour ultimatum" to the Czechoslovak government, these people knew their time had come. They were too near the German border to escape the Nazi terror no matter how temporary it might be. They left Graslitz in the night, on half an hour's notice, taking with them only such belongings as they could easily carry—a few clothes, a few family valuables. Men, women and children made the trek across the mountains in the cold autumn night, carrying their sick with them, and when they reached Chodau they threw themselves on the generosity of the local Social Democratic co-operative. The co-operatives throughout German Czechoslovakia had been greatly weakened in the past two years, but they still had funds enough to help their unfortunate brethren from the areas of Nazi terror. They arranged soup kitchens and shelter for the three hundred people from Graslitz, and took care of them until the terror culminated in the catastrophe at Munich and all refugees had to be moved out of the Sudetenland.

The shelter provided consisted of one private house and the village inn (two big rooms, altogether). The people lay at night on heaps of straw with their belongings in bundles beside them. There were several sick among the women. They had the staring eyes of terror victims, uncertain of what might come next. For many weeks past they had been subjected to the nightly alarms of a Nazi-ridden area, their men dragged out into the street and beaten with rubber truncheons or sometimes murdered, their women and children brutalized. They had stuck to their homes so long as any hope remained that the Nazi would not be given undisputed possession. These were the people whom Nazi propaganda always called "Jewish Communists," but there were no Jews at all among them, and only three Communists. The rest were ordinary German workmen who had belonged to the Social Democratic party all their lives. The Communist party had no importance in any of the German Bohemian districts, and in fact could hardly be said to exist there. The Jews were fairly numerous in the cities, but not among factory workmen such as these.

Some of the characteristics of refugees everywhere were to be found here in this crowded inn. One woman I particularly remember, a plump, comely German type with masses of fair hair, who complained that she had left Graslitz in such a hurry that her Sunday coat (her *Sonntagmantel*) had been left behind. I had heard exactly this sort of complaint a few months before in Spain, a few years ago in China: it was the eternal effort of the homeless and persecuted to forget the big disasters in concentration upon the little.

And I was reminded of Spain again as we were going away—sharply, violently, as if a thrill of life had suddenly shot through a corpse. We got into the car to drive off, and gathered speed slowly from the courtyard of the inn, through the groups of men who were standing there. As we passed into the village street a column of young or youngish men caught our attention. There were no more than eight or ten of them, walking by twos toward the inn, but they were walking in unison. One fellow in the lead had immense solemn eyes which he fixed on us. All of them raised their clenched fists to their heads in salute, and all said—not loudly, in fact very quietly; not a cry but a statement of faith—"Freiheit."

Freedom. The clenched fist. We all raised our fists at

them in reply, although I at least had never been much given to that gesture: in the circumstances it was the one movement of hope I had seen in the whole Sudeten area. It made me think of Spain the immortal, the Spain of our day, the pride of our common humanity.

And as the days and weeks passed it was necessary to think of Spain very frequently: otherwise the general level of cowardice, treachery, bad faith and cruelty throughout Europe was too oppressive to be borne. Spain alone had resisted and was still resisting the limitless claims of Fascist imperialism; Spain alone raised its clenched fist against the bombs. Mr Chamberlain's pilgrimage to Berchtesgaden was followed by his expedition to the Führer's Rhineland pleasaunce, Godesberg; and the maneuvers there were followed by a conscienceless order to the Czechoslovaks to mobilize; general war seemed (and only seemed) to be very near for a day or two as the result of the hopeless botch that had been made of every negotiation for weeks; fear, horror and unbelief came down on the darkened cities. In Prague or along the roads of the Sudetenland it was not possible to endure the degrading spectacle of the time without the thought of Spain. The Czechoslovaks, brave, calm and disciplined, were called to arms and disarmed again at the orders of Chamberlain, Daladier and Bonnet; their national independence was used as a ransom for the spineless West. The refugees piled up on the roads by the hundreds of thousands; the wandering Jew resumed his wandering; Nazi and Fascist trumpeted their easy victory. The inn kitchen at Horse's Neck imposed its philosophy upon the world.

But not quite. There was one little detail that did not quite come off according to the plans of the black-browed mistress of the inn. She and her menfolk had said, "The

[233]

frontier is here." But by some extraordinary oversight of the Messrs Chamberlain, Daladier and Bonnet, the frontier was set a good bit further along, and Horse's Neck remained for a season within the confines of the Czechoslovak Republic—a republic in vassalage to Germany, to be sure, but still not openly annexed. On the last few occasions when we stopped at the inn in Horse's Neck the German newspapers and magazines had vanished from the wall of the beer parlor. Some Czech gendarme had found them too much for comfort during a period of martial law. The black-browed Bohemian woman looked more sullen and angry than ever as she slammed our beer down on the blue-and-white checked tablecloth. The triumph of Horse's Neck was very great, but it was not yet—quite—complete.

CHAPTER VI

The Last Volunteer

THE TRAIN that leaves the Gare d'Orsay in Paris at eight-fifteen for Perpignan and Cerbère has carried an immense cargo of cares, fears and resolves during the two and a half years of the war in Spain. On the platform were to be seen the range of possible farewells, signs of enthusiasm or of grief, a variety of emotions drawn tense in the bad light and the noise as the train attendants banged the doors and sang out: "En voiture!" There were passengers from stations between Paris and Perpignan, of course, but every evening the train also carried a large number who were bound for destinations beyond the Pyrenees. Of the passengers on the eight-fifteen for Perpignan, a good many have never returned.

On the night of March 31, 1938, the platform of the Gare d'Orsay was unusually crowded. There was a Spanish delegation of some sort going down, and there was the usual scattering of people belonging to other nationalities who were bound for Spain. We had just become aware of the Aragon disaster, which was then approaching its climax; it seemed that the army of the Republic was broken and in full flight, that the Ebro might prove no barrier, and that the Fascists might be at Barcelona before long. I was going to Spain for the first time since the outbreak of the war—going with Ernest Hemingway, who had been there a number of times since March, 1937, and also, as it turned out, with Jim Lardner.

I did not know Lardner and had no idea he was going to be on the train until half an hour before. Then I was told that he was bound for Barcelona with credentials from the New York *Herald-Tribune*, for which I was also going to write dispatches. He was on his annual holiday from the Paris edition of the paper and was taking it in this way. Beyond this, and that he was the son of the late Ring Lardner, I had no information.

We were all busy with our various farewells until the train moved out of the station. My first and last departures by the eight-fifteen to Perpignan were curiously alike: both on March 31, 1938, and on January 23, 1939, the Republican armies had broken and Barcelona was in imminent danger. The difference to be seen in retrospect was not apparent last March, and of the two it was perhaps the earlier journey that aroused the more intense feeling among the passengers and those who went to say good-by to them. When the train at last began to move past the crowded platform and we turned to find our places in it Hemingway asked, grinning: "Are you *muy emocionado?*" I said no. "It's old age," he said.

At this point I became conscious of the presence of a thin young man in a brown checked tweed coat. Hemingway introduced me to Jim Lardner. "One of you has to decide which is the *chef de bureau*," he said, "since you're both from the *Herald-Tribune*." We adjourned to my compartment, where the three of us settled down to this decision over copious draughts of whisky from Hemingway's flask.

This flask, a battered silver contraption of great cubic capacity, must have had a long career in its owner's service. It had developed a certain flexibility with the passage of years, and when rhythmically pressed between the thumb and forefinger it emitted a tomtom noise like the drums that accompany a Moorish dancing girl. I saw it afterwards under a variety of conditions in Spain, and always with pleasure. The old flask must have been a welcome sight to many besides myself, for it was as inexhaustible as its owner, and as generous.

Lardner seemed in high spirits. He was a pleasant-looking youth, not particularly robust, with brown hair and eyes protected by horn-rimmed glasses; he had the long legs, the slight awkwardness and the ready laugh which belonged to his age and type. He was twenty-three: Andover, Harvard and the *Herald-Tribune* in New York, followed by a stage on the Paris edition of the same paper. He had taken the liveliest interest in Spain for at least a year past, and knew a good deal more about the geography of the war and some of its leading characters than I did. This departure on the eight-fifteen to Perpignan was a tremendous event for him, an embarcation on perilous seas where he had obviously wished to roam for a very long time. His ideas about the struggle in Spain were exact and his opinions decided. He knew what he was doing.

At one point in our long hilarious talk Hemingway turned on me one of the blankest of his blank looks.

"I don't know why you're going to Spain, anyhow," he said. "You can't get a story there. The only story you could get would be to get killed, and that 'll do you no good: I'll write that."

"Not half as good a story as if you get killed," I said, "and I'll write that."

Lardner seemed to think this one of the funniest jokes he had ever heard; he leaned back in the *wagon-lit* and roared.

Eventually even the Moorish dancing-girl flask yielded no more, and we all went to bed. With the regular churning of the wheels I was soon asleep. I suppose Lardner must have lain awake a long time, thinking those involved interminable thoughts that you do have when you are twenty-three and starting out on such a journey.

In the morning we were routed out in time for Perpignan. The morning was rosy (as it seems to be usually in those parts) and the snow-tops of the Pyrenees cooled the air a little; otherwise it would have been downright warm; the sun was hot enough when you got it in a sheltered place. We left our bags and typewriters at the station and went across the way for some coffee. The hilarious mood of the evening before continued. When the shops were open we hung about the street, buying a razor, some soap, some bread. Hemingway went off to the Spanish Consulate to see about getting a car to the frontier and beyond. I had not known enough about conditions in Spain to stock up on food, whisky and cigarettes, and tried to remedy this defect (a little) in the next hour or so. The morning passed before we could get ready to go, and we lunched early. The local newspapers were full of disasters in Spain and refugees who had come over the Pyrenees from Aragon. It was perhaps half-past twelve when we got ourselves and our luggage piled into the car and set forth.

Hemingway had most of the luggage. He was an old hand at the game and knew what to bring in. He had a huge amount of food, a couple of big cans of gasoline, and plenty of whisky and cigarettes. He also had a customs pass to permit it all (and our bags as well) to get into Spain without examination. The car was one belonging to the Spanish Consulate—perhaps to the Carabineros—and all we had to do at the border was to change drivers. When we had climbed to the height of Le Perthus and passed the last French post we met Captain Arizmendi, the Basque who acted as Providence to all travelers during 1938, and he saw us through the rest, passports, customs and all. The thing that struck me most at the passport place was the discovery that Hemingway was only a few months older than I. For a good many years I had assumed that he (or anybody else who had been in the Great War) belonged to a different generation. While I was still a freshman in college he was already driving an ambulance in Italy. That was what might be called an early start.

From La Junquera on to Barcelona we never stopped again, except once at Figueras for two or three minutes to drink some charged and sweetened water—some *gasiosa*. (There was still *gasiosa* in the Catalan provinces for another month or two.) I think we rather expected the road to be bombed at any moment, as people always did in their first few hours in Spain. The alternative attitude—which takes bombings as the exception, not as the rule—was quick to come after a day or so, but I observed afterwards that those first few hours beyond the frontier were always of the same quality, no matter how many times you had been in and out of Spain. The entrance into danger (like the exit from it) has its peculiar effect, and you do not have to have any particular liking for war to admit that it brings a definite exhilaration. It was not an exhilaration that was worth having at the expense of so much general concomitant misery, but it did give some hint of what Fascists, professional soldiers and others found to enjoy in the enterprise.

NOT PEACE BUT A SWORD

It was getting dark when we reached Barcelona. We drove first to the Subsecretariat of Press and Propaganda in the Diagonal, the office presided over by Constancia de la Mora, one of the remarkable women of the war. She gave Lardner and me some sort of slip which would admit us to a hotel (the Bristol, near the Telefónica) until such time as the Majestic had room for us. Constancia was busy and smiling: the disasters in Aragon did not seem to have impaired her spirits. The glass in her office windows was all crisscrossed with strips of paper pasted on to lessen the danger of shattering when the bombs fell. The great bombings of March 19–21 (the worst there have been since airplanes were used in war) were still painfully recent, and the ruins made during those days of horror had not been cleared away.

As it happened, either the outcry that was raised in the world at large, or some lingering remnant of humane feeling, or perhaps even a strong protest from General Franco and his junta, kept the Italians from repeating this exploit, and although all the cities of Republican Spain were repeatedly bombed thereafter, and many villages and small towns destroyed, the foreign aircraft did not actually bomb the crowded center of Barcelona so intensively again. Nobody was to know this in March and April, however, and the population of the city lived in nervous apprehension of the bombs. It was not until much later that the inhabitants of the center of Barcelona grew more assured and learned to look on the air raids as a spectacle. In the spring every call of the sirens summoned up the memory of those ages of terror so short a time before, when the planes came in from the sea and bombed the city every two hours for three days and three nights.

Hemingway had a reservation at the Majestic Hotel, and

went there; Lardner and I, after depositing our belongings at the Bristol, went out to find a restaurant. There were still restaurants in the city then and for a month or two afterwards. We ate passably well somewhere off the Plaza de Cataluna, a meal with meat, vegetables and wine. (All this was to change very swiftly, but the date was April 1.) There was no light anywhere in the streets, and there was little to be learned by stumbling along through an unfamiliar city in the dark; we went back to the Bristol and turned in early. In the morning we both got rooms at the Majestic, which remained our headquarters (as it was that of the entire press, more or less) afterwards.

The Majestic was as much an oddity among hotels as the eight-fifteen to Perpignan among trains. It was semi-governmental, in the sense that the Ministry of State favored it for the use of the press and friends of the government and kept the prices down for their benefit. All the hotels in Barcelona had been collectivized under the Catalan collectivization laws, and were operated by the workers in the "gastronomic" unions (chiefly Anarchists). The Ritz was kept as "Gastronómica No. 1," and cost a good deal more than the Majestic; it also had much better food. But it was frequented by munitions traders, the salesmen from all over Europe who batten on disaster, and also by the lively ladies (then very numerous in Barcelona) who are violently attracted to munitions traders. As a rule the press preferred the Majestic, which, although almost the worst hotel in Europe, did have a friendly atmosphere and was used to the strange hours and stranger behavior of the foreign correspondents. The long lounge there and the big dining room, walled with mirrors crisscrossed in paper strips, were a kind of general press club, and you could wander along there in the dark when the lights were off (as they often were) and wherever you sat down would probably turn out to be a colleague's table. There might be disadvantages to such a system of life in peacetime, but under the conditions in Barcelona it had its points. Some people found it too much for comfort (Malraux said, for instance: "J'aime mieux les putains que les raseurs") but the fraternity or club system has its proper field, it seems to me, in the state of war, and although we all complained bitterly of the Majestic week in and week out, there were few among us who ever tried living anywhere else.

Lardner was given a room without a bath, and thus acquired the habit of coming down the hall to have his bath in my room. His high spirits lasted all through those first ten days in Barcelona, although the situation at the front grew steadily worse. He and I had the same difficulties getting either a pass for the front or a car to get there in, and some days passed before either of us could get out of Barcelona at all. He got his pass, at last, and Richard Mowrer of the Chicago *Daily News* gave him a lift that same day or the day after down to Tortosa. The fight was on above Tortosa at Chert, with Lister's division holding the Italians off in a stiff and continuous engagement. Mowrer, Forrest of the *News-Chronicle*, and Jim Lardner were down there that day, were on the bridge when it was bombed and slightly damaged, and had a talk with Lister up at Chert under shellfire. It was Jim's first experience of the bombs and shells, and I think he was delighted to discover that they did not terrify him unduly. (This response seems to be universal: it is what Stephen Crane wrote about in *The Red Badge of Courage,* and his "Young Soldier" is in fact almost any young man.) He came back very dirty and tired, demanding a bath, and wrote his story.

What happened to that story was, I believe, partly responsible for the turn his ideas took not long afterwards. It was a good story, written at some length, and was Lardner's first attempt in a field which had obviously attracted him (as it does many young reporters). It was printed in the Paris edition of the *Herald-Tribune* in a much reduced version the next day, and as I remember some of the most effective bits of it were the ones that had been omitted. My impression was that the story was, in fact, edited away to nothing. Lardner obviously thought so too, and after he had seen that paper he seemed to lose his zest for the occupation of war correspondent.

Nobody in particular was to blame for it, but in fact a situation had arisen under which Jim had not a very good chance. When he made his plans to come to Spain his paper was without a correspondent there. I had supervened unexpectedly—on a rather vague arrangement with the New York office—to send occasional dispatches. I was much older than Jim and was supposed to be much more experienced. The dispatches I sent were printed in full and were prominently displayed. His one effort in the same vein (a very good effort indeed) was cut to pieces and put on an inside page. He never tried it again.

This may have been only a minor disappointment to him. I do not know, because when I tried to talk to him about it he obviously wanted to avoid the subject. Perhaps he did not care; but knowing, as I do, what young reporters are like, I think he did. Short of leaving Spain or ceasing to send dispatches from there, there was nothing I could do about it. I tried to suggest that we might alternate or share the stories in some way, but he took the firm line that it didn't matter: that he would write another story when he had one, and in the meanwhile I was to go ahead. I was out on the Ebro for about a week, and during that time I think he was probably considering the whole business and making up his mind. From then on he seemed unduly silent and reflective, and we used to accuse him of being "gloomy." I suppose he was simply thinking.

It was sometime along about then—ten days or so after our arrival—that he came into my room and, after various bits of talk about nothing in particular, offered the information that he wanted to join the International Brigades. He did not quite know how it could be done, but he proposed to set about it as soon as possible.

"What's the good of that?" I asked, amazed at the idea. "It's pretty late to do that. The internationals may be sent home at any time. And anyhow, if you want to work for the Republic you ought to do it in some way that's particularly suited to you. From each according to his——"

"I know all that," Lardner said. "I suppose you mean I ought to get a job pounding out something on a typewriter."

"Well, why not, if that's what you can do? It's better than enlisting in the brigades at this late date. Or, in fact, at any date. One more rifle doesn't matter a hell of a lot in the result of the war. You'd probably be more useful doing something else."

"Suppose I don't want to do something else? Suppose I'm tired of pounding a typewriter? And anyhow, even though I want primarily to help the Republic, I ought to have some choice in the matter. My own choice would be the Lincoln Battalion."

The argument went round and round. At times I produced the opinion that he ought to stick to his own profession and continue to send newspaper dispatches as an American correspondent with no ties to the Republic: this was the point of view he repudiated without qualification.

"There are too many newspaper correspondents already," he said. "One more doesn't make any difference." He was a stubborn youth, and underneath his apparent diffidence, it dawned on me that he had had this idea in his head for a long time. He might have been coaxed out of it by some particularly shining success as a newspaper correspondent —for he was a member of this profession, after all, and the professional vanity might have worked upon him—but his experience with his first war story made him think that there was not much chance of it. He was already very fed up with the exercise of the typewriter; he had been fed up for weeks in Paris before he came here; and he was in the state of mind, familiar to all newspaper workers who take any interest in their living material, in which the whole practice of verbigeration about events is regarded as futile and silly. I could not argue with any conviction against this opinion, for I have often shared it; it is a question of mood. The professional alternative had to be ruled out, then, for his mind was set against it. The rest of the argument could only deal with what he might usefully do to fight Fascism.

"The brigades are not going to stay here," I reiterated at various turns of the argument. "They'll be sent home sometime, probably very soon. There are other places where international brigades will be needed more in the near future. There's Czechoslovakia. In a month or two they'll be needing all the help they can get; there will probably be international brigades there, or a foreign legion. Why not wait and try it there?"

But here and now was his answer to everything. The field of discussion narrowed: all he was really interested in (having made up his mind) was how to go about it; what he should enlist in; how much training he would have to have; and when he could go to the front.

Along about here I gave up. So far as I know he had talked to nobody else about this plan yet, but he had reviewed it exhaustively in his own mind. He had even passed a good many hours writing down his reasons for joining the internationals; as I remember, he had a list of nineteen, a primary group dealing with why he wished to do whatever he could to aid the Republic and to fight the Fascist alliance, and a secondary group naming the benefits of such an experience to himself. I think this secondary group was not very important in his mind, but it was put down because he was so honest that he could not leave it out. He had the usual idea of young men (and it may be very sound, at that) that a war experience would make or break him, probably the former. The sheer excitement of such an adventure did not rank high among his nineteen reasons, but he was much too analytical to ignore it.

There was a vein of cynicism in this boy—not cynicism in the sense of disbelief in any disinterested motive, but a healthy reluctance to accept ready-made phrases and gestures without reflection. He was antibunk: that was it. There was too much miscellaneous heroism lying around loose in Barcelona, and we had phrasemakers and fist shakers enough to make such a mind as Jim's question the validity of everything except direct action. He distrusted the emotionalism the Republic had aroused, but shared the emotions; consequently the army seemed to him the only way. When he got his case stated so objectively there wasn't much I could answer. I had to admit that if I had been his age, and thought as he did, and had the nerve, I would have done likewise.

But when I reached this point (a few days after he first

[*246*]

spoke of the idea) I proceeded to a very thorough piece of hand washing.

"I don't approve of this plan at all," I said. "That's neither here nor there. You know what you are doing. But I am not going to help you go through with it, anyhow. You'll probably find that the I.B. people won't take you. They are not accepting enlistments any more, and you would require training and I don't know how they're going to give it to you. But that's your lookout. I go on record as saying that I'm agin it, and you are a stubborn young mule."

I don't know at what point he talked to Hemingway; I think it was at about this time; and Hemingway gave him about the same answers, only, of course, in far fewer words. Thereupon Jim began consulting various I.B. men, and was to be seen engaged in deep secret conferences with them out in the sunny Ramblas or in the corners of the Majestic Hotel. I was going to the front almost every day just then, and had neither time nor inclination to follow the details of the enterprise, but I believe the International Brigade people at first flatly refused to consider an enlistment. They had no facilities for offering training any more; the idea of disbanding was much in the air; and Jim was, in any case, not military material. His eyesight was much too poor. They did not want him, and said so. He persisted—nothing could put that boy off once he had made up his mind. And at some stage of the proceedings somebody (probably a political commissar) had the inevitable brain wave and proposed a solution going, I imagine, something like this: "Let's take him, since he seems so determined, and send him somewhere back of the lines where he won't be in danger. His name is famous in America; nobody can accuse a son of Ring Lardner of being a tool of the Comintern; and we'll have the propaganda value of his enlistment without risking his life." Needless to say no such program was ever put into words before Jim himself, but the nature of the decision was clear from what followed.

One night we were sitting before dinner in somebody's room at the Majestic, a whole crowd of us. When we dispersed to wash and go downstairs to eat, Jim stopped Hemingway and me on the stairs and said he wanted to speak to us. We went up to Hemingway's room, where Jim said: "I just wanted to tell you that I've got it fixed with the I.B. and I'm going to enlist tomorrow." Hemingway was startled (I don't suppose he had ever believed the I.B. would take the boy) and for the moment said nothing. I proceeded with another piece of hand washing: "You know what I think of it," I said. "I've told you in great detail. I don't want to talk about it any more." I left the two of them there to argue it out all over again if they wanted to.

Hemingway, as a matter of fact, did make a last-minute effort to dissuade Jim from enlisting. All this may sound as if we attached an exaggerated value to Lardner's life in a war which had already cost more than a million lives—a war in what we all believed to be a just cause, the only just cause of first importance in our time. But Lardner's enlistment came so late that it seemed sheer waste; and at that time he did not strike any of us as being military material. That is why we (and in a general way all the colleagues of the press) tried to stop him or divert his determination into another channel.

On the next day (April 25) we went to the first showing of the Spanish version of Hemingway's and Ivens' film, *Spanish Earth*. The film was stopped in the middle by an air raid and we sat in the theater for about an hour, waiting until the alarm ended. It was not a very good place to be during an air raid, and the audience might have been forgiven a certain amount of nervousness, but in point of fact there was none apparent. Riego's Hymn and the Catalan song *Els Segadors* were played, and for the rest of the time we sat and talked. I was with Lardner and Marty Hourihan, a brigade man who had been badly wounded at Brunete. Marty also did his best to change Jim's mind at the last minute, but Lardner was in high spirits again by this time and only laughed at him. When the film was over he went off into the town somewhere to complete the acquisition of his outfit, which was khaki trousers and a leather windbreaker and some heavy shoes. He signed up sometime that afternoon.

The I.B. people listed him for the artillery and sent him to Badalona "for training." That was all I knew about it for about a week or maybe ten days. I did well on the transaction, meanwhile, for Lardner had left me all his food and cigarettes, including some canned stuff and a lot of sugar and coffee. He had given me his books, too, and it was easy to see by them that this was no sudden decision. There were books about the Spanish war and war in general; there was the airplane yearbook (*Fighting Planes of the World*); there were some maps; and there were some books of social and political interest, including a volume of Lenin's pamphlets. Lardner was not a Communist, and maintained his quizzical, questioning attitude about political doctrine as much as about everything else; but he was thoroughly aware of the elements in the world struggle and had been reading for months or years with that awareness. And it was not all politics by any means: for he had a lot of Republican songs (words and music) among his belongings, and some stories of the war and a good fat volume of Shakespeare.

One morning early in May I struggled out of sleep in my

[*249*]

bed at the Majestic, vaguely conscious that somebody was talking to me. When I got my eyes open I saw that it was Jim; he was demanding a bath, as usual. This time he looked as if he needed it: he was very dirty and unshaven and looked tired.

"What the hell are you doing here?" I inquired. "I thought you enlisted in the army."

"I did," he said, "but I'm a deserter now. Can I take that bath right away?"

After he had had his bath and a shave he came back into the bedroom and woke me up again. We got some coffee and I made inquiries.

"How come you have deserted so quick?" I asked. "Don't you like the army?"

"Not that army out at Badalona," he said. "I came in to see if I can't be transferred somewhere else. I don't see why I can't join the Lincoln Battalion."

"You have to get some kind of training somewhere," I pointed out. "Do you know how to handle a machine gun?"

"No," he admitted, "but I'll never learn out there at Badalona. All we do is lie around on some dirty straw all day long, and answer a roll call twice a day. I don't know what kind of outfit it is, but it seems to be mostly deserters and soreheads. Or maybe prisoners. It's pretty hard to tell."

His account of the experience at Badalona was not cheerful. He was in a group of something over a hundred men who had served in various units of the International Brigades. They were men of all nationalities and had belonged to all services, but were apparently at present chiefly occupied in complaining and telling stories of their hardships. According to Jim, they had no work at all to do, no drill and no roll calls except a very loose one at morning and evening. His name had never yet been called, and it was his conviction that nobody out at Badalona knew he was there or would notice his absence. He had reported to the Spanish officer in charge when he first arrived, and had since then received no orders of any kind except—for three or four days of the time—a rough-and-ready assignment to kitchen duty, an order delivered by means of the pointed index finger. It was his belief that if he stayed in Badalona a year he would still have no chance of drill, training or other preparation for actual participation in the war. He was beginning to suspect that the I.B. authorities had shunted him off to what they considered a safe place where he would never see any kind of action; and the suspicion aroused all that stubborn determination which had already brought him so far.

I found out afterwards what this mysterious encampment at Badalona was. It was a group of the so-called *inútiles de guerra*, men judged unfit for war by reason of their incorrigible lack of discipline, their bad spirit, their demoralizing influence on others, their cowardice or their doubtful loyalty. It was the worst possible place to send a young man who had just enlisted, if it was hoped to keep his spirit high; but of course the I.B. authorities had had only one idea in their heads: to keep Lardner away from the front so that his life would not be uselessly risked so late in the game. They had reckoned in this without Lardner's will; he was not to be sidetracked so easily.

The experience with the *inútiles de guerra* had not in the least impaired his desire to serve in the Republican army. He told me some of the stories he had heard from the chronic soreheads at Badalona: stories of bad food, discrimination between men, favoritism, highhanded justice or injustice, and general all-around rotten dealing. Some of the men said they had joined the brigades because they expected high pay which they had not received; others that they had been persecuted in the brigades because they were not Communists; others that their officers were arbitrary, dishonest and unjust. Every character of any special renown in the brigades was attacked by these soreheads as they lolled about on their dirty straw: Merriman and Doran did not escape, and even Milt Wolff—who was perhaps the most popular man in the 15th Brigade, certainly among the Americans—was accused of a long list of minor crimes. Jim had listened to all this with a philosophical detachment worthy of a man twice his age. He was even ready to admit that a great deal of what the soreheads said might have been true from their own points of view. A man known for his cowardice or bad spirit might easily be discriminated against by his company commander, and of course that very discrimination would seem to the victim an example of crude injustice. Jim judged his informants without severity, but without mercy either. He found them a pretty disgusting lot on the whole, and the more they cursed and whined the more he wanted to escape from them to the active service of the brigades which had rejected them. So he had walked out of the quarters of the *inútiles de guerra* after the morning roll call on this day, had hitchhiked and tramped his way to the outskirts of Barcelona and had there taken a tram to the center of the city. Now, bathed, shaved and somewhat relieved by conversation, he was going out to see the I.B. authorities and demand a transfer to the Lincoln Battalion. He knew it was no use asking to go into training "for the artillery," the branch to which he had been assigned in the beginning; there was only one American artillery unit now in existence and nobody knew exactly where it was, although the general opinion in I.B. circles (based on no information) was that it was probably down in Cordoba or on the Estremadura front. This was, in such respects, a very informal war.

I think the I.B. authorities must have been as startled as I was to see Lardner turn up again. They probably thought they had settled the Lardner problem for the duration of the war by parking him harmlessly at Badalona. Now they were in rather a difficulty, since he was able to accuse them of attempting to keep him out of the fighting. If they had refused him from beginning to end they would have been in an impregnable position, but having first refused and then pretended to accept his service, only to relegate him to a place where he would be of no use to anyone, they were in no position to withstand his righteous indignation. Johnny Gates, the political commissar of the 15th Brigade, turned up in Barcelona just then (either that day or the next) and, after a talk with Jim, gave it as his opinion that there was no reason why Lardner should not be admitted to the Lincoln Battalion, then resting and reorganizing behind Mora la Nueva on this side of the Ebro; he could get his training out there as well as anywhere—and in fact, as things now stood, he had no chance of getting training anywhere else. The Fascists had cut through to the sea; the internationals' training camp in the south was abandoned; a new recruit (and Lardner was the only one that turned up, the last of the internationals) had to learn at the front or not at all.

So, at last, this singularly stubborn young man had his own way and went out to the battalion. On his departure he gave me not merely his superfluous belongings (this he had done before going to Badalona) but everything he possessed. I pointed out that some of the things he still had —such as a few cigarettes and some sardines—would be welcome in the battalion. "I don't want to go bearing gifts," he remarked, and that was the end of that. He went out to the battalion equipped with the clothes he wore, and nothing else.

After that I did not see him again for some time. I left Barcelona for Paris and returned only for a few days on my way to Madrid. During the next month I heard only that Lardner was doing well and that the boys in the battalion seemed to like him. This was good news, for his appearance of diffidence and caution had not promised well for the company in which he now found himself. There was every kind of human material of the American genus in the battalion, and on the whole it was admirable material. In that line of goods you do not find anything better anywhere than Wolff, Lamb and some others. But there were also some prize roughnecks in the 15th Brigade, some very tough babies indeed. I had wondered just how Jim would get along with them; his experience of life had not been at all the same as theirs; Andover and Harvard were not the best preparation for dealing with them. There was something gentle and quiet about Lardner that didn't seem suited to the social amenities of the brigade. For one thing, I had never heard him use any really bad language, and the current vocabulary of the brigade was lurid to a high degree. It wasn't that he would be unable to give an account of himself in (for instance) a fight, for he was courageous and far stronger than he looked. It was in the ordinary day-by-day life of the battalion that I thought he might be made to feel strange by a language and habits and systems of thought he had never run into before.

I was wrong from the word go. He loved it and the battalion took to him almost from the beginning. He probably kept very quiet for the first weeks until he knew his way about. That was a way he had. But as he grew to know his routine and the men who surrounded him, and they saw that he was ready and anxious to do the job he had come so far to do, liking and respect came along rapidly enough. The battalion was out on those sunny hills behind Mora la Nueva, licking its wounds, filling up with new Spanish levies, training, re-equipping, resting, preparing for another action which would probably—according to report everywhere in the brigades and in Barcelona—be its last. There was a little indecision about what this action might be. At one point the general staff planned an offensive toward Lerida, and the 15th Brigade (the whole 35th Division in fact, with most of the 5th Army) was transferred to the upper part of the Barcelona–Lerida road. I went up there in the first days of June after my return from Madrid to visit the Lincoln Battalion and found them quartered in some stables near the village of Mollerusa. When we arrived (Joe North and I) we discovered that we were just in time, for they had received orders to march that evening. They did not know where they were going, but as it turned out it was back to Mora la Nueva: the idea of a Lerida offensive had been abandoned, and the next weeks were to see a quiet and thorough preparation for the great final attack across the Ebro in July. The Americans were in their usual uproarious spirits, for they had had plenty of time to rest and eat since the disasters of early April. They were tired of inaction and ready for anything that might come; their marching orders might have meant action for all they knew, and they were full of scarcely suppressed excitement. Wolff told me I could find Lardner in Company 3, which was quartered about ten minutes up the side road from the clump of houses which served as Estado Mayor for the battalion. I went along up the road and found the big stables inhabited by Company 3. The sentry there said they would be back any minute to eat; they had been off drilling in a field; there they came down the road now.

I watched them come near, a ragged, dirty, unshaven and cheerful crew, marching in column of fours, at ease. (I am not at all sure that they knew how to march any other way.) They were, as usual, ravenous with hunger. I knew what they were going to have to eat, for Comrade Archer, the huge Negro who was cooking for the battalion then, had given Joe and me a sample of it a while ago: *bacalao* disguised somehow or other so that it almost tasted like crabmeat. I knew a few of the men in the column, and they sang out lustily. These were not at all the desperate lot who had come back across the Ebro six or seven weeks before: the interval had been well spent. I was looking for Lardner and failing to find him. I detected him at last, somewhere near the end of the column, and with a moment or two of hesitation before I was quite sure: he was not easily recognizable. For one thing, he had no glasses, and his eyes were not strong enough to stand such a regime for long; he kept them half closed. But his bristling beard and his rags were what changed him most. I had seen him last in his spanking new outfit: now he wore a very dirty khaki shirt and a pair of colorless trousers that were torn and ragged. His feet were in canvas *alpargatas*, sockless. He was so shortsighted that he did not recognize me either at first; when he did the broad grin and the shout indicated that he had not changed much, after all. Company was dismissed, and he ran down the slope toward the stable. I gave him his new glasses first thing, and he was as glad to get them as a drowning man might be to get a lifeboat. He had been without glasses for several weeks, and the Barcelona oculist who had the prescription had taken an eternity to get them made. How Lardner ever had managed rifle and machine gun without glasses always mystified me, but apparently he had done not too badly. We went into the stable to the corner where he was lodged and sat down on the straw. Rags and beard and so on disregarded, he seemed superbly well and cheerful, and there could be no doubt that he was (as he said by indirection) happier in the battalion than he had ever been out of it. These are mysteries; but I think it was so. I had some letters to deliver to him from his relations in America and from Walter Kerr; he put on his new glasses and read them at once. We had a desultory talk about this and that. I asked him if he wanted anything from Paris; I was going up there in a day or two. He could think of nothing he wanted, and shouted to another fellow who was in his squad: "Hey, Tony"—or perhaps it was Joe or Bill—"is there anything I want?" The other fellow said reflectively: "I think you want some chocolate, don't you?" Jim smiled and said: "Yes, I guess I need some chocolate, whenever you think of it."

I asked him what had become of all his fine clothes from Barcelona. It was impossible that they could have been worn to rags so quickly. He said—rather shamefaced—that he had given them away piecemeal; they were a little too fine. And so on. It was not much of a talk because it was getting late; it was time for the company to eat and for us to return to Barcelona. I went on back to the Estado Mayor, where Milt Wolff gave us a swig of red wine and I sang a rousing duet ("Sweet Adeline," as I remember) with an infantryman by the name of Brandt. After that Joe and I got into the car and drove back to Barcelona.

2

I had never read *The Red Badge of Courage*. Several months later, when I did, Crane's Young Soldier reminded me again and again of Lardner. It was the story of "the untried man," as Conrad said: Crane's young man was a sort of universal, and Lardner was the same universal with local differences. Lardner was intelligent and educated, with a lively interest in a wide range of things outside the orbit of Crane's Young Soldier. He also had, for his age, a considerable knowledge of the world, having worked on a New York newspaper and lived in Paris. But essentially he was the Young Soldier who believed in something enough to fight for it and yet doubted—up to the crucial moment—his own ability to do so; listened with a sinking heart to the talk of those who knew the dangers of war, and tortured himself with speculation over how they would affect him; discovered, in the end, with surprise and delight(perhaps at first with incredulity) that he could stand it as well as the next one or even better. Perhaps his determination was in part due to a feeling that he had to find out now and not later. There was certainly some such element in his stubborn will to fight for the Republic, for objectively (as well he understood in his cool, modern fashion) there was a great deal to be said for our arguments against it. The subjective reasons were those no other person could quite disentangle, but they must have been almost as powerful as his primary desire to strike his own blow against Fascism. What makes him not exceptional, but characteristic of much wider phenomena, was the way in which the objective and subjective were mixed, so that his personal reasons could not be separated from the social purpose to which they thus powerfully contributed. There must have been hundreds of others in the International Brigades who had gone through much the same processes, and in a wider sense—not in active war alone, but in the contemporary struggle as a whole—the creative thrust of youth against reaction is similarly brought into play on a very large scale everywhere. The passion for justice is nothing new; the generosity of youth, spending its life fiercely for what it believes in, has been the chief capital of political movements as of war itself; but the new thing here is the breadth and sweep of the intention, the immense collective will into which the single will is poured, regardless of the barriers of nation states, traditional patriotism and inherited social caste. The struggle in Spain, ranging all the progressive forces from Right Center to Left in a life-and-death battle against the armed force of the Fascist alliance, rapidly engaged the imaginations of such young men as Lardner all over the world, and some thousands of them who had never taken part in a political movement before—who were neither Socialists nor Communists and had no membership in trades unions or other organizations of the working class—found their way into the fight on the side of the Republic. The Communists were, as has often been said in accusing tones, the organizers of the brigades: it is immensely to their credit. But the brigades had a significance which reached beyond the barriers of any political party, as they ignored the barriers of political states: for the mind of youth, thrusting from the individual toward the collective, and afflicted with pain and rage at the sight of Fascist tyranny sweeping over Europe, here found a body which would enlist its body in the struggle which only action can determine. The Spanish revolution had been arrested and turned into war by means of a counterrevolutionary movement so intensely cruel and medieval in essence, so mighty and modern in physical equipment, that the Lardners of the world could not endure inaction at the spectacle; and the brigades stood ready to receive them. They were not in any sense "dupes of the Comintern," for they knew quite well that the Comintern had first called the brigades into being; they merely chose to strike their blow in association with the only militant corps that had understood their need in time.

After early June I was away for some months—in England, Austria, Czechoslovakia, at Paris, at Evian, on the trail of some element of resistance to the system of bluff and blackmail which had hypnotized all Europe outside of Spain. From time to time I heard news of Lardner, and occasionally I passed on a letter or package to him from his relatives in America. He had prospered in the battalion and was now a corporal. That very night after I had last seen him, while the battalion was marching from Mollerusa back to the Ebro, he had composed a marching song to the tune of "Tit-willow." It was ribald and funny enough to make at least Company 3 laugh: it had been pasted up on the wall newspaper when they got into quarters near the Ebro again. It appears from this time on Lardner blossomed out into one of the favorite characters of the battalion. His diffidence was gone, and his natural sense of humor, his good nature and his keen eye for the ridiculous all combined to make him funny without causing anybody undue injury. (I think his release of spirit may have been partly due to the new glasses, but the physical explanation is not always complete.) He was also what is called "a good soldier," which could not invariably be said of all the comrades. When the offensive over the Ebro was ready, and was launched at last in the early morning hours of July 25, Jim already had his value in the battalion, and this action was to make it solid thereafter.

The offensive across the Ebro was well planned and organized. A bridge was flung across the river at Mora during the night (a ready-made bridge in pieces, like the Meccano toys children play with) and the 5th Army swarmed across before the Fascists had any idea of what was happening. The other side of the river was not held in force: the main strength of the Fascist army, its Moors, Navarrese and Italians, had been pounding away to the south for some weeks in an attempt to reach Valencia. The Republican force reached the neighborhood of Gandesa before it could be stopped. There, on the hills that they had been unable to hold last spring, the Republicans dug themselves in and stuck. The whole Fascist army turned to dislodge them, and the Italian and German aviation was increased to numbers hitherto unknown, but they stayed where they were. The action was, so to speak, a "defensive offensive," since its main object was to turn the Fascist attack away from Valencia. In this it succeeded, the push to the south was stopped altogether, and the new front took up all the time, money and effectives of the Fascist junta until the end of the autumn.

Jim seems to have deserved the good opinion of his company during the big drive; it was at this time, after the first week or so of action, that he became a corporal. In August he was wounded and sent back of the Ebro for treatment. The way of it, according to his own account in a letter to Walter Kerr, was this: he had been put in charge of an escort of prisoners from the lines to Mora. They were all going along the road peaceably when Jim saw some edible-looking apples in a tree near by. He called a halt while he climbed the tree to get as many apples as he could. While he was in the tree a detachment of Fascist aviation flew over, bombing the road. One of their fifty-kilogram bombs exploded in the field, and some of the flying shrapnel caught Jim in the thighs. He came down the tree with wounds which ought to have kept him out of action for the rest of the offensive.

It was here, again, that his stubbornness showed itself stronger than ever. He was clamoring to go back to the front after the first few days in hospital. His wounds justified keeping him back, and he was in fact kept back for about thirty days—a time which seemed to him much too long. In a letter he wrote to me on his last day in the hospital he complained of this excessive solicitude with his usual mixture of good humor and acrimony. I think he probably suspected what was true: that his brigade officers and the medical aid people, like the I.B. authorities in Barcelona five months before, were trying to keep him from the zone of danger as long as possible. His bad eyesight alone would have made them anxious to keep him from the front lines; but by this time they all knew the story of his enlistment —how he had come along after no more enlistments were accepted, and got himself into the battalion by sheer stubborn insistence—and they had a somewhat protective attitude toward the last of the internationals. These considerations were, of course, superimposed upon the basic one which was Jim's fortune or misfortune, luck or jinx, from the beginning—that he was a son of Ring Lardner. Ring Lardner was a writer who still held a very special place in the affections of most Americans, and nobody wanted to see his son take more than the necessary risks. Jim probably suspected (or knew) all this without being told, and set his mind upon getting back to the front in spite of them. He had a few days' leave in Barcelona in September, his wounds healed, and the brigade command had no further excuse for keeping him out of the lines; he went back just as the tide was turning strong and the Fascists were pushing the Republican army with all their immensely superior resources. It was also just before the International Brigades were withdrawn from the fronts and mustered to be sent home.

I was in Prague then, and although the thought of Spain was insistent—was almost a necessity of life—in the psychological horror of those weeks, actual news from Spain was scarce. I heard nothing about Lardner until I got back to Paris again in mid-October. My plan was to spend only a few days in Paris and then return to Spain, not for press material or any professional purpose, but for the private aim of reassuring myself as to the existence of men who still had their self-respect. During those few days in Paris I heard, first, that Lardner had been killed on the Ebro; second, that he had been captured by Moors and then murdered; third, that he had been wounded and captured by Fascist troops and was now in a Fascist prison camp. There seemed no very dependable way of selecting which one of these stories to believe. The American Embassy at Saint-Jean-de-Luz had done its best, by means of its acquaintances in Fascist Spain, to check over the lists of prisoners held in the various camps, and had not been able to find Lardner among them. The death or capture was supposed to have taken place about three weeks before, and the embassy people were beginning to think it improbable that Lardner was still alive.

I did not know (and do not yet know) how efficient the Fascist system of identification of prisoners might be. It was possible that Lardner might remain for months in a prison camp without being listed at the Fascist headquarters. On the other hand, I knew he had kept his passport; he also had letters and other means of identification; American prisoners were not so numerous that these would fail to catch the attention of the Fascists, however elastic their system with captured "Reds." If they had not shot him out of hand, as was their custom in many cases (especially among the Moors and Navarrese), there was a good chance that the *señoritos* of Burgos would preserve his life as a demonstration of their civilized status.

The best way to inquire was in Spain. I took the eight-fifteen to Perpignan again some days later, and drove from Barcelona one day with Herbert Matthews to the encampment of the 15th Brigade (that is, of the Americans, British and Canadians who were in it) at Ripoll in upper Catalonia. The International Brigades had all been withdrawn from the front lines by September 26, in accordance with the promise given by the Prime Minister, Dr Negrin, at Geneva on September 23. A League of Nations Commission was now in Barcelona superintending the demobilization and repatriation of these units. The English-speaking battalions had been quartered at Ripoll, the French, Belgians, Czechs and Germans in other places far behind the lines where they had done so well. Their units—the 35th and 45th divisions of the 5th Army Corps; the 15th Brigade, containing the English-speaking battalions, had been in the 35th Division —were now being filled up with Spaniards, but the old names were to remain: the Lincoln Battalion, for instance, would carry that name so long as it existed, although there were no Americans left in it. Only one day before my arrival in Barcelona the city had said its farewell to the brigades in the most moving ceremony of the war. The internationals had paraded through streets hung with flags and paved with flowers; the girls of Barcelona had broken their lines repeatedly to kiss them; the Spanish units in the parade had marched in full war kit, the internationals unarmed as they had come to Spain. Nothing had been lacking: cheers, tears, speeches; even Azaña, the President of the Republic, had taken his place in the reviewing stand to say farewell to the men who had, a year or two before, saved his government. (It was his last public appearance as President, I believe.) The boys had then gone back to their camps and were waiting to be counted by the League of Nations Commission so that they could go home.

Ripoll was a crowded little town of steep vertical streets in the lovely foothills of the Pyrenees. It had an eleventh-century church, so carefully protected by sandbags that one could scarcely see it. We found Malcolm Dunbar and Milton Wolff, among others; Wolff told me exactly what had happened to Lardner.

It was on September 23 at about eleven o'clock at night —the last night the battalion spent in the lines. They were holding Hill 281, at Corbera, and a change had taken place on Hill 376, to the northeast. Lardner was sent with two comrades, one Spanish and one American, to establish contact with the unit that was supposed to be on Hill 376. It was very dark. He started out to the northeast but veered to the north in the darkness. At the foot of a hill which he took to be Hill 376 he stopped to listen and heard the sound of digging. He instructed Tony Novakowsky, the American with him, to stay at the foot of the hill with the Spanish comrade and wait while he went up to see who was occupying the hill. They did so, and Lardner made his way up the slope. As he came near the top there was a shout and Lardner challenged in Spanish. Loud yells broke out, rapidly followed by machine-gun fire and a series of hand grenades. The Fascists on the hill, uncertain in the darkness, threw out enough fire to repel an attack. The Spaniard at the foot of the hill was killed. Tony Novakowsky had some cover and was untouched. He remained under cover for a long time—nearly two hours—but Lardner did not return. He then made his way back to Hill 281 and reported. From the account given that night there seems to have been enough machine-gun fire and hand bombing to kill a company of men on that slope, and Lardner's officers, after questioning Novakowsky, had no doubt that he had been instantly killed.

Milt, who told me all this, did not know how the subsequent stories of capture had been started. There was nothing to indicate it in the story of that night. The Fascists captured both these hills (376 and 281) the next day, and there was no chance to look for the bodies of the dead. On the following evening, September 24, the Lincoln Battalion was withdrawn from the lines and ordered back to Ripoll to prepare to go home. Lardner, the last American to enlist, had been the last to be killed.

3

I asked Milt Wolff what he thought of Barcelona's farewell to the internationals. He said he would never forget it. "We've never been what you call very good at parade marching," he said, "and when we got on those streets with flowers up to our ankles I guess we did a kind of shag." He demonstrated the difficulties of marching through flowers. "I guess it was a pretty good show," he said. "You should have seen it."

I saw a lot of photographs of it afterwards: Capa, Buckley, Matthews and others had kept their cameras busy. You never saw so many weeping people all at once as there were in those photographs. Malraux told me about it a day or so later. "C'était toute la Révolution qui s'en allait," he

said. Perhaps that was why the people wept. These boys—
all these Lardners, their average age about twenty-three—
had come to Spain to help save the Republic, and now it
was clear that the Republic could only be saved by some
greater help from outside, some extremely improbable
assistance from those altruists, the French and British governments. The assistance required was, to be sure, no more
than that which would normally have been given under
international custom to any government: i.e., the right to
buy arms. But it was precisely this modest right which the
French and British under their "nonintervention" policy
were refusing, while Italy and Germany poured in materials
on the Fascist side, and time no longer worked to the benefit
of the Republic. The impulse which had sent all these
Lardners to Spain had been a reflex of the conscience of the
world, but as against unlimited supplies of planes and guns it
was not enough. Since Teruel the Republic had never been
able even to replace its losses in artillery and aviation; after
June 13, when the suicidal mania of the French government
closed the Catalonian frontier for good, even the materials
which had been bought and paid for were not delivered.
Toward the end of the Ebro offensive the disparity between
Republican and Fascist equipment became so great that
the best troops in the world could no longer have remained
in position under attack. I was out there just at this time,
a few days after the trip to Ripoll, and in the positions beyond Mora de Ebro, from which the 5th Army was now
retiring, I heard only two big guns on the Republican side
replying at rare intervals to the incessant cannonade of
the Fascist artillery. I saw no Republican airplanes at all,
and the Fascist planes were free to come down over the
lines for machine-gunning as often as they pleased. Dr
Negrin had withdrawn the internationals and was sending

them home not because they were no longer needed—few as they were in number, they had always been troops of the first line, and among the best—but because there existed one forlorn hope: that France and England might then insist upon "nonintervention" in fact, and demand the withdrawal of the Italian and German effectives on the Fascist side. The inability of France and England to insist upon anything had been demonstrated throughout the year and especially in September; but Spaniards understand pusillanimity least of all the human defects, and although Dr Negrin's speech at Geneva was made within a week of the Munich disaster, he probably had no idea that it was coming. The withdrawal of the internationals was a movement of chivalry, perhaps of bravado, as well as an invitation to the powers to withdraw foreigners from the Fascist side; it was a promise given in a moment of difficulty and fulfilled in a moment of catastrophe. The last contingent of Americans was in fact sent out from Barcelona in January, 1939, on the last train that left the capital before it fell into Fascist hands. Negrin kept his word; but on that day of the parade in November, when Barcelona turned out into the streets to say good-by to the internationals, it was perhaps a presentiment of the end, as well as gratitude for service past, that filled the eyes of the million with tears.

The surviving Americans, British and Canadians went home in December and January. Their wounded had been going out since May, 1938. All told, about half of those who had once taken the eight-fifteen to Perpignan went home again. Singly and in groups they had made their way to Spain from early in 1937 until the spring of 1938. They left their dead on Jarama, at Brunete, at Teruel and on the Ebro, their dust mixed with the Spanish earth, their memory an eternal part of the unconquerable soul of Spain. In an army of half a million men they had been the merest handful; all the internationals together did not come to much more than twelve thousand at the end, and the English-speaking units were less than half the total; but in the long epic of the war they not only did more than their material share, but suffused the total effort with a moral value more precious than their lives, the sense of a world not altogether lost, of peoples not completely stultified by their governments, of a common conscience in which whatever hope there is for any possible future must rise again.

4

Some weeks afterwards I got a letter from Lardner, a cheerful, ordinary sort of letter, the one written on his last day in hospital, full of his determination to return to the front. His papers were sent on to me sometime in December. They were not numerous. Among them I found a lot of tickets to the Berlitz School in Paris, where he had been studying Spanish. His Spanish got very good after a while, they told me in the battalion, and he was speaking it fluently by September.

There is, of course, a possibility that he may have escaped that murderous fusillade on Hill 376 the night of September 23, or have been merely wounded in it. Even now there appears periodically some kind of story that he has been seen in a Fascist prison camp. The chance appears to me remote. I would like very much to see him come through the door demanding a bath, in the pidgin Spanish lingo we had evolved in Barcelona: "*Hay* hot water? *Quiero un baño* pretty damn quick." Or fiddling with the light: "*Hay luz? No hay luz.* What do you do without *luz?*" But there is scarcely an incident in wartime which does not give rise to innumerable unfounded stories, and I think the stories of Lardner's capture by the Fascists are of this kind. In all probability, as his officers believed on September 23, he was instantly killed. At first it may seem that this was intolerable waste: that his gifts might have been more usefully employed in another way, and for a longer time. But he wanted to offer his life—that is clear—and if it was taken, merged into the aggregate of all those lives given for Spain, it was his unanswerable contribution to a cause much greater than any single life. So he would have said himself; he was no Indian giver. All those Lardners did not die for nothing. If the world has a future they have preserved it. They must overcome the Chamberlains in the end, for provinces and nations can be signed away, but youth and honor never.

CHAPTER VII

Seberov 94

AT FIVE O'CLOCK in the evening of Wednesday, September 21, 1938, the loud-speakers in the streets of Prague announced to the people that the government of Czechoslovakia, under pressure from Great Britain and France, had agreed to the readjustment of frontiers accepted by Mr Neville Chamberlain in his meeting with Hitler at Berchtesgaden.

The announcement came at the end of a day of rumors and uncertainties. Thousands of bewildered Czechs roamed the streets that day, waiting for some word of what was to become of them. It was known throughout the city that an ultimatum had been presented to President Beneš by the British and French ministers at two o'clock that morning. The terms of the ultimatum and the manner of its presentation were more or less secret, but all sorts of stories got about and contributed to the general feeling of disillusionment, distrust and unease. Everybody in Prague realized that if Neville Chamberlain was to receive Hitler's approval tomorrow on his visit to Godesberg he would have to have something definite to offer—something in the nature of a surrender by the Czechs, an abdication of the Czechoslovak sovereignty into the hands of the trustworthy British and French governments. The Czechs had faith in Beneš, but in the terrible alignment of forces now united against him—Britain and France joining with Germany to demand partition of the country—it seemed doubtful to most people whether even Beneš could hold out.

Months later I received, from private sources, an account of the matter and manner of this ultimatum at two o'clock in the morning. The British part in the business was brief; Great Britain had no military alliance with Czechoslovakia and had not specifically (except as a fellow member of the League of Nations) guaranteed the Czechoslovak frontiers. The British minister had only to present his government's views and await an answer. The French minister was in a very different position. He came as the representative of a country which had twice (in 1925 and 1935) signed the most solemn guarantees of the Czechoslovak frontiers; which had influenced the whole development of Czechoslovakia since 1918, had designed and built the Czechoslovak fortifications, supervised the creation of the Czechoslovak army, and owned an important share in the Czechoslovak munitions works of Skoda, at Pilsen; a country which had remorselessly used Czechoslovakia's political, economic and military force as a pawn in its own game since 1918, and which on all counts, however you looked at it, stood under the strongest conceivable moral and legal obligation toward the Czechoslovak Republic.

President Beneš rose to receive the verbal communication presented by the representatives of these two worthy powers. The French minister had learned his text by heart and recited it with some shame—as was only natural—but quite clearly. In concluding the statement of the French government's intentions and recommendations, M. de la Croix said that if Czechoslovakia, by disregarding these representations, should find itself in a war with Germany, *"la France ne s'y associera pas."* (Future tense, not conditional.)

This was the clearest form of repudiation of France's pledged word. President Beneš, whose lifework as a Czech nationalist had been based upon the alliance with France, received the blow without protest. He merely asked—after a silence of a minute and a half or so—that this verbal communication be delivered to him in writing.

The French minister was well aware of the momentous nature of the words he had just said. He replied, in some confusion, that he had no instructions for a written note, that he would have to ask the Quai d'Orsay. President Beneš requested him to do so without delay.

The French Foreign Ministry—or rather, to sling the mud where it precisely belongs, the minister himself, Bonnet —produced a written version during the course of the day, which De la Croix sent to Beneš. The phrase *"la France ne s'y associera pas,"* which had been the crux of the verbal note, no longer appeared in the written version, but the sense remained the same. In the written note it was stated that if Czechoslovakia went to war in defense of her frontiers she would do so alone. The word *"seule"* took the place of the lurid repudiation which was contained in the earlier phrase.

Beneš had been in the hands of the French and British since the spring. He had obeyed their directions in all things, had reluctantly conceded plan after plan of concessions to the Sudeten Germans, had accepted British mediation and had put his trust blindly in his allies. With his long past of dependence upon France he could have done little else. He was a single-minded Czech nationalist, and nationalism of any sort is not conducive to clear vision or thought. He was unquestionably blind to the urgency of the Sudeten German question for years, and his culminating blindness was to trust the French as he did. But by September 21, 1938, after everything that had happened for over twenty years, it was no longer possible for Beneš to be other than what he was. He had played France's game without scruple or remorse since 1918. Everybody who went to the League of Nations in the 1920s remembers how Beneš and the Petite Entente—an organism he created —operated as the instrument of French imperialism even when the French delegates themselves were restrained by common decency from showing their hand too plainly. On all questions concerning Germany or the Germans, Danzig, the Saar, reparations, Beneš and the Petite Entente were more French than the French. Even in such remote affairs as the questions of the mandated territories (in particular of Syria) the Quai d'Orsay could count on Beneš before it could count on the French political leaders. In the postwar system France had no more constant servant than Beneš, and he had thus earned the sincere antagonism of all north German political thought. Hitler's language just at this time about Beneš, although crude and violent as usual, did represent an attitude of mind common among German politicians and journalists since 1918, and derived from a genuine hatred based upon experience. The "fence around Germany," although built with the bodies of Czechoslovak peasants and the bayonets provided by France, owed its political structure and duration as much to Beneš as to any man.

Now, in the extremity, France had betrayed not only Beneš but Czechoslovakia and the whole postwar system which had been, from first to last, a French creation. The terms now forced upon Czechoslovakia by ultimatum had been already accepted by France and England, and for three days the British and French foreign offices had been urging Beneš to yield to them without further delay. Beneš had proposed an international conference, a court of arbitration, anything rather than straightforward national suicide for his country. Hitler's Berchtesgaden terms—now called quite shamelessly the "Franco-British Plan"—were less murderous than the ones finally enforced at Munich, but they were bad enough: they called for the cession to Germany of all Czechoslovak territory in which there was a German-speaking population of over fifty per cent. These territories, as outlined on the Hitler map, cut across all the Czech systems of fortifications and communications, destroyed the natural frontier, took over important mines and heavy industries, and made the resulting Czechoslovak state an obvious prey for Nazi domination and an open road to the east. Beneš had never believed that Hitler's aims in the Czechoslovak question were determined by concern for the German-speaking people of the Sudeten areas; he was convinced that the true purpose was the destruction of Czechoslovakia as an independent nation. In that momentous interview at two-fifteen in the morning at the castle on the hill in Prague, he reiterated this conviction to the French and British ministers, who were not prepared to discuss it. They required an answer to their joint ultimatum before the end of the day.

At five on Wednesday afternoon Dr Krofta, the Czechoslovak foreign minister, handed his reply to the French and British ministers. At the same time the news was announced on the loud-speakers in the streets of Prague. The statement of acceptance of the "Franco-British Plan" concluded:

"This case is unique in history: our friends and allies have imposed on us such terms as are usually dictated to a defeated enemy."

2

I had been out in the Sudetenland all day, and returned to Prague just after the loud-speakers had delivered their message. The streets in the center of the city were crowded. I saw women weeping convulsively, men with set, silent faces, boys standing in groups singing. The car with its G.B. plate on it was once openly jeered at by the word "Chamberlain"—a word which, although a term of affection in German areas, had a very different meaning in Prague. I left the car at the Alcron garage and walked around through the Vaclavske Namesti to the Hotel Ambassador, where we now lived. Traffic in the vast square had ceased, for the crowd had suddenly grown so enormous that it filled the whole area from wall to wall. The trams had come to a stop as islands in the crowd, and there were too many people for the police to disperse without violence. There was no sign of any organized demonstration: there were no flags, no marchers, no shouts in unison. All that came later. For the moment it seemed as if the population of Prague had merely turned out into the street, stunned and grief-stricken, for lack of anything better to do. The blow was so crushing that the bewildered people could not realize it all at once. They moved aimlessly, here and there, without direction, most often without speaking. The young ones took to singing patriotic songs, most of them melancholy in cadence, the old songs of the Bohemian people who were now condemned again to serfdom. The loud-speakers in the square occasionally emitted the three or four plangent chords which were the radio station's signal that there was nothing to put on the air. (They were very melancholy chords, too; I thought they came from Smetana's *Libuse*, but am not sure.) I did not know what had happened, but it was easy to guess. Never have I seen an assembly of people so instinctively moved to grief. Hope was to revive again later, and again to be betrayed, but on that Wednesday, September 21, the sure instinct of the people perceived the whole tragedy at once and mourned over the passing of their nation.

At the hotel I learned what had happened. My wife, who is English, was in tears—tears partly of sympathy and partly of shame. Any English or French person who was in Prague on that night must have suffered as she did; it was in fact on that night that General Faucher, the head of the French Military Mission to Czechoslovakia, sent back his war medals to France and enlisted in the Czech army; and on that night most of the English press colleagues, hardened cases as they were, and employed by a corps of newspapers which did yeoman service for Hitler and Chamberlain throughout the crisis, were made violent by shame. Three different English correspondents, at different moments on that evening, congratulated me bitterly on being an American: and although America's record in 1938 is far from clear —the Neutrality Act alone blackens it enough—I knew what they meant. The cowardly, treacherous and unnecessary sacrifice of Czechoslovakia to Hitler's appetite was consummated ten days later, after centuries of anxiety and tension throughout the world, but its full impact fell on us in Prague on the night of September 21.

The demonstration of the people gradually fell into certain semiorganized forms. The young men and women took to marching arm in arm, singing the Bohemian patriotic songs. Workmen from the factories appeared in their over-

alls to march down the Vaclavske Namesti and over to the
Parliament. Men and women of all ages and classes, in every
sort of costume, joined in the marching. Flags began to
appear after an hour or so. Before the Parliament building
the women set up a cry to the government: "We give you
our sons. Give them arms!" For hour after hour the marching, singing, cheering went on; there must have been four
or five hundred thousand people in the streets, half of the
population of the city. Many thousands of these people were
weeping all through the night. I even saw a policeman in
tears. A less belligerent or revolutionary mass demonstration
has never taken place, and yet it was reported in the German
press and wireless that night and the next day as a "Red
riot in Prague." Those who witnessed it, in whole or in
part, know that it was a truly spontaneous expression of the
grief of a people; in years of experience in such matters I
have never seen anything like it. The "spontaneous demonstrations" of Europe are almost always highly organized
affairs, with a technique as elaborate as that of a pipe organ.
The cry of the people of Prague on that night was from
the heart.

All night long the people marched, sang and wept, with
those occasional chords from the 'oud-speaker sounding
over their misery. At three o'clock in the morning, when I
went to bed, there had been some diminution in numbers,
but the demonstration was still going on. It was still going
on the next morning at a quarter to ten, when I got up.
From our balcony on the third floor of the hotel we could
see the whole Vaclavske Namesti. Shops and factories had
been closed; there was a general strike; no trams or taxis
were running. During Thursday morning the trades union
leaders and political parties took a hand in the matter and
the demonstrations began to have a look of organization:

small flags had evidently been distributed in enormous numbers, for most of the marchers now carried them. The workers from the factories marched in some order and in their working clothes. Slogans and banners made their appearance, some of the Communist workers carried the red flag, and there were a few banners with the words "Long Live the Red Army." Even so, the demonstration of Thursday was predominantly pacific, democratic and without exact political intentions. It required the specially trained imaginations of the Nazi press to see in them anything at all like "Red riots" or, in fact, riots of any kind. The opposition of the people to the "Franco-British Plan"— to the dismemberment and annihilation of Czechoslovakia— was expressed in this way because there existed no other way. The Czechoslovak government yielded to the unmistakable will of the people that day when it resigned; and in the new cabinet which Beneš formed, there were two generals, with General Sirovy, the head of the army, acting as prime minister.

3

Meanwhile Chamberlain and Hitler were meeting again, that Thursday, at Godesberg on the Rhine. We had only the most confused reports of their conversations in Prague, and knew Thursday night and Friday morning no more than that the talks "were not going well." Months later, in the British White Paper and other official publications, I could reconstruct the course of those talks at Godesberg: at the time I knew little about them. We knew in Prague that Hitler had presented Chamberlain with a map drawn by himself, and that Chamberlain had not understood it exactly (being unfamiliar with the country) beyond the general fact that it contained new demands. We heard that Hitler proposed a military occupation of the Sudetenland to take place immediately, and that this demand (wholly new) had shocked and startled Chamberlain more than anything else. He had gone to Godesberg, apparently, prepared to give Hitler the substance of everything he asked for, but he was politician enough to realize that it would be dangerous to give Germany a military show and an ostentatious parade of victory as well. Opinion in England and France, although it might approve of the sacrifice of Czechoslovakia, would be revolted by such a sudden and violent seizure by force as Hitler demanded. After conversations at all hours of the day and night on Thursday and Friday, Mr Chamberlain went back to London with a memorandum and a map, both the work of Hitler's own hands—and neither of which could be accepted, even by Mr Chamberlain, on the your-money-or-your-life procedure.

Hitler's language in the Godesberg conversations was not known to us in Prague—all those bloodthirsty phrases about the "Red bandits of Prague," and the boasts of what he would have done to Czechoslovakia if Chamberlain had not flown to Berchtesgaden the week before. This has all been published since. At the time we knew that Chamberlain had received something of an eye opener, and an official who was in constant telephonic communication with London told me Friday morning that the British Prime Minister "was afraid Hitler was insane." The telephone wires from Godesberg to London, London to Paris, and from London and Paris to Prague, were busy throughout Thursday and Friday. The world had not yet started to hold its breath (that did not begin for another three days) but in Prague the tension was already severe. The explosion of grief Wednesday night and Thursday had been followed by about twenty-four hours of unnatural calm, of tense and expectant waiting. The fact that a general headed the new Czechoslovak government seemed to indicate that a resistance might be contemplated, at least in the case of any new demands on the part of Germany. And all who had the slightest acquaintance with Hitler's methods knew that he would certainly make new demands.

Before the war of 1914–18 Jules Cambon, the wily old man, used to have a saying which kept his spirits up in moments of great crisis. When everything seemed lost, and the Germans had apparently won everything they wanted with or without war, Cambon used to say: "J'attends la gaffe allemande [I am waiting for the German blunder]." This was approximately the attitude of the Czechoslovak Foreign Office during the momentous Thursday and Friday of the Godesberg conversations, and it was an expectation that was not disappointed. The German blunder came—a whole series of German blunders; Hitler hardly spoke during those two days without blundering to excess—and yet it was, in the end, of no avail because it was matched by an English blunder of even greater magnitude, the blunder and crime of Munich.

I repeat that we did not know all this in Prague. The newspapers were given only what it was good for them to know, which was not much; and officials were not very communicative. The town was alive with stories, but as they all came from afar, and the center of activity was in a little town on the Rhine, nobody knew what to believe. "Secret diplomacy" had left us with a feeling of tension and unrest, premonitions of disaster, flashes of hope. It is undeniable that for some reason the atmosphere in Prague grew a little better on Thursday night and during the day on Friday, perhaps because rumor persistently asserted that Chamberlain was, to some degree at least, "standing up to

Hitler" at Godesberg. The curve of hope can be felt but scarcely understood. On Friday I was out in the Sudetenland again, unable to sit in Prague and wait; Friday evening I came back with some firsthand information about the disorders of the night before at Graslitz and elsewhere, but what took place on that night made any local riot insignificant indeed.

At six forty-five that Friday evening, September 23, the British and French ministers called at the Czechoslovak Foreign Office. This time they bore a wholly new order: the order for Czechoslovakia to mobilize. It was put with the indirection which characterized all the British and French dealings with Czechoslovakia during the year. Previously Great Britain and France had exacted a promise that Czechoslovakia would not mobilize; the ministers now came to state that this promise was no longer binding, and that Czechoslovakia was free to "take any steps she deemed imperative for her safety." Beneš called the cabinet into session; and at twenty minutes past ten on that night the government radio broadcast the order for general mobilization. The breakdown in negotiations between Chamberlain and Hitler at Godesberg had taken place, although Chamberlain was yet to have his final interview with the Führer; and the Czechoslovak mobilization, like all the other moves Czechoslovakia was obliged to make during the prolonged game, was a new form of argument. Among the conscienceless maneuvers of the whole period this was one of the worst, for the Czechoslovak mobilization took place so early that Hitler might have moved with crushing force at once. Perhaps this—an attack of Germany on Czechoslavakia alone—was not altogether outside the possibilities considered by the confused minds then directing the affairs of France and England. It was known to every

informed person in Europe that the German mobilization
had been chiefly on the Czechoslovak frontier and not on
others; there were thirty divisions of the new German
army down there and only eight on the so-called Siegfried
Line in the west. France's variance of opinion was so considerable that nobody could have counted upon such a
localized war with certainty; many important elements in
the French government, including the Prime Minister,
Daladier, and the general staff of the army, would have
honored France's signature if they could; Bonnet alone,
operating his independent policy in this crisis as he had
done at important moments during the preceding six
months, was to be depended upon for enough sabotage
and double-dealing to ensure the maximum of disaster in the
minimum of time.

Whatever may have been the Franco-British motive in
telling them to do so, the Czechs mobilized that evening.
And for some days after that Prague had no communication
with the outside world. The international telephone and
telegraph ceased at once; all direct wires passed through
Germany and were controlled by Berlin or Vienna. The
roundabout ways (such as through Warsaw or Bucharest)
may have worked occasionally. I believe the government at
Prague was communicating with its embassies abroad by a
line which ran through Bucharest. We of the press, and even
more of the general public, had no such facilities. For two
or three days we were totally blockaded. After that we
could send out telegrams by the government wireless station,
which did actually reach London, Paris and New York after
much delay; but we received no replies. Still later (after
the *Diktat* at Munich) telephone communication across
Germany was restored, but did not return to normal for a
long time. Mail ceased altogether for about ten days.

Under such conditions our notions of what went on in the outside world were not good. We received information from the Czech and German newspapers of Prague and from the Czechoslovak Foreign Office, but it was necessarily brief and heavily censored. We knew when France mobilized and when the British fleet was called up; we could hear speeches on the radio, usually; we got the news bulletins of the B.B.C. at nights. But for any comprehensive and detailed picture of what Europe was like during the crisis we had to wait weeks. I am still hearing, to this day, things which were public knowledge in England and France at that time but never reached our ears in Prague. When I first saw trenches dug in the peaceful gardens of the Champs de Mars quarter in Paris, some weeks later, and heard about the darkened streets and the rations of sand, I thought with some surprise: "Ah, just like Prague." It was even more surprising to be told, in the altered circumstances of November, about the fear that had swept England during those September days, the frenzied digging, the improvised systems of evacuating women and children from cities. While it was going on I suppose we all assumed that only Prague was in grave and immediate danger, that only Prague passed dark nights, waiting for the bombs.

One reason for this, in my case, was that I had never believed France and England would stand firm. From the day when that *Times* editorial appeared (September 6) I always believed the British government would find some way of turning Czechoslovakia over to Hitler without war or real danger of war. This belief was not shaken except on one day (September 28) when Chamberlain spoke of war in the House of Commons, and even then I suspected reservations which were rapidly proved in the invitation to Munich and its acceptance. What I did believe in Prague

between September 23 and September 29 was that somehow or other the French and British might succeed in washing their hands of the whole matter so that Hitler would be
enabled to attack Czechoslovakia alone. In this contingency
Czechoslovakia could not have held out, by the most
optimistic military estimate, longer than six weeks. It was
possible that French public opinion, enraged and humiliated
at the dishonor of their national pledges, might have forced
the Daladier-Bonnet government to intervene before the six
weeks were up, in spite of Bonnet and in spite of Chamberlain; but this was only a possibility; and in any case, even if
France moved, even if Russia moved, Czechoslovakia was
geographically so placed as to be at Germany's mercy. Supposing even a world war with England, France and Russia
aligned together, Czechoslovakia would have been quickly
overrun; the only help could come from Russia, and that by
one single railroad across Rumania. Under these circumstances the danger of Prague was by all odds the gravest in
Europe, and it was not merely because we happened to be
there that we thought so. I doubt if any other city in Europe
actually expected the German bombers night after night as
Prague did from September 23 to September 26 (Friday to
Monday). Nor was there any city, any country, any people, which affronted such frightful possibilities with such
calm.

The Czechs apparently believed, like the Spaniards, that
it was better to die on your feet than to live on your knees.
At any rate the whole atmosphere and feeling of the
population changed from the moment of mobilization on
September 23. The worst was expected, and without reservation; but it was faced with resolute calm, without emotionalism and without flinching. The men and boys went off
to the war with their suitcases in their hands, grinning; the

women were rapidly taking their places in commerce and industry; the mobilization was effected with great rapidity and efficiency. Many of the inhabitants of Prague had possessed gas masks since last spring, and thousands more appeared during these days. I think most people carried them, the sinister gray cylinders slung over their shoulders, from Friday on for several days. Girls used their gas masks as handbags. Boy Scouts and young Sokol people took the place of men in directing traffic, especially around military areas. There were no demonstrations of any kind, no assemblies in the streets, no unusual noises or manifestations of popular disturbance. The country had been thoroughly prepared for such a day as this and knew what it had to do. In the David-and-Goliath metaphor which was familiar to us just then, David at least was fearless, grave and resolute.

I thought there were many serious deficiencies in the general equipment, and above all there were no underground refuges. This is, indeed, true throughout Europe (except perhaps in Germany). Gas masks were all very well, but there remained a possibility that the Germans might not use gas at all. They had never done so in Spain; neither had the Italians. I believed that in the brief, disastrous war which I thought possible (or even probable) for Czechoslovakia, Germany would choose between two courses, either one of which would have made gas masks a pathetic triviality. The first possible course was unrelieved frightfulness, all speed ahead, with the object of finishing the war quickly. In this contingency every weapon would be used, and everybody knows by now that gas is not at all the worst weapon. Incendiary bombs of the new variety, developed in the past two or three years in all countries, can destroy a whole city and all its population with relative ease; I have been assured by experts in England, America and France that no material now known can stand against these bombs and nothing has been developed which can arrest their action. They (the new, small bombs based on thermite—not the older thermite bomb which was known in the World War, and was used by the Germans at Guernica) have never yet been employed anywhere. Their frightfulness is, indeed, totalitarian, and fear of world opinion—German and Italian opinion as well as that in other countries—has prevented their use in either Spain or China.

The second course open to Germany was a war of tempered or adjusted frightfulness, as in Spain. Here again it was unlikely that they would use gas. Gas is a sort of middle weapon: it horrifies everybody, causes great suffering, but does not decisively obliterate whole populations. The ordinary bombs used in Spain kill just as many people without unduly shocking the sentiments of average people outside of Spain. If it was desired to humor public opinion (even German public opinion) the bombings of Prague would be ordinary bombings on a large scale, but not with gas. And against such bombings the only possible defense for civilians is underground refuges. Spain proved that over and over again. Antiaircraft guns are nearly useless; the most they can do is oblige the attacking force to fly high; and the defense by means of aviation is extravagant, deadly and only fractionally effective. As an expert from the British War Office once said to me, "There is no active defense whatever against bombing from the air. The only answer is *retaliation*."

I believe this statement, in all its horror, is no more than the truth. Active defense against aviation cannot protect the cities. Squadrons of chaser planes piloted by boys who are ready and willing to die will do damage to the attacking bombers but will not prevent the bombing. For the civilians of the bombed places there is only one defense, and that a passive one: to burrow into the earth and wait until the vultures have passed over.

Digging was going on in Prague, of course, but it seemed to be mostly shallow trenches. The effectiveness of such shelter is very limited; it can only protect against lateral shrapnel. Proper, tested refuges, such as those developed in Valencia and elsewhere in Spain under the system of *Defensa Pasiva,* did not exist here. A city of a million people would be on the surface of its streets, in its vulnerable houses and office buildings, when the bombs came.

All sorts of notions were in circulation about what constituted a shelter. My wife was taken by Maurice Hindus to see a "bombproof cellar" which was near enough to the Hotel Ambassador to be of use to us in the bombings. It turned out to be a warm and comfortable cellar indeed, but only about ten feet below the surface of the earth; and moreover it contained many water pipes which would have burst, of course, during a serious bombing. The owners of this place considered it a perfectly safe refuge for themselves and their friends. Cellars of a similar kind were much in demand throughout Prague, and nobody seems to have doubted that they would be useful. My own opinion was that they would be more dangerous than an open trench.

Another superstition due to inexperience concerned the darkening of the city. This was complete: no lights were shown anywhere, and dark blue bulbs had been substituted for the ordinary ones in our hotel as in houses throughout the city. Dark blue paper had to be pasted over all lights on motorcars. These were probably wise precautions: at any rate they seem to have been adopted throughout Europe outside of Germany. I am sure an attacking force of bombers would have had no difficulty in knowing where

Prague was; their instruments alone would tell them; and the antiaircraft guns would make the information quite definite. Even so, it is accepted as wise to darken the cities in such cases, and there is probably good reason for the practice. But to carry the thing to such extremes as they did in Prague is mere civilian superstition. I was obliged to drive about a good deal during those nights, and I was in constant hot water with the police and the civilians in the streets, because the lights on my car could not be made dark enough to suit them. My lamps were already so darkened that I could not see where I was going, which constituted a much more immediate danger than the German bombers, but I was held up dozens of times by people who wanted me to make them darker. The theory that any flicker of light, such as a cigarette or a match, can be seen by a busy aviator flying three miles high, is a characteristic notion of people made nervous by unfamiliar danger. In Madrid at the beginning of the war the Anarchist patrols—a jumpy lot— actually used to shoot people for showing a crack of light at a window. It was supposed that such shreds of light could be seen from the air and constituted signals to the enemy. A similar state of mind about lights was developed in Prague from September 23 on, and was the only sign of raw nerves that I was able to detect among the ordinary people.

4

Ah, those blue nights! The bulbs issued for all lamps were so darkened that they permitted only a funereal penumbra in which it was impossible to read or write, difficult to distinguish the most familiar objects. Friday, Saturday and Sunday nights we expected the German bombers: after Hitler had spoken on Monday night, and given Europe four more days to obey him or take its punishment, we expected them no longer—for we knew that four days were more than enough for a Neville Chamberlain. It was the nights thereafter that were the worst. This seems materially impossible, since an actual physical bombardment is clearly more to be feared, in the immediate sense, than any moral disaster. But it is the fact just the same. On the night when we knew about Munich (September 29) I did not sleep at all, but lay looking at those dimmed funereal lights for hour after hour, reluctant to turn them off since they seemed to be the permanent illumination of Europe thereafter. The nights when we had expected the bombers seemed, in retrospect, nights of hope: for no material catastrophe could have destroyed the foundations of hope as Munich did. From that night on I knew that France and England would never fight for anything worth fighting for: that their resistance, when it came, would come for their moneybags or their empires, never for a principle of any consequence to the human race; that no pledged word, no law and no reason could henceforth count in the processes by which governments determined the fate of mankind. And that in the end the material catastrophe would come, that it would be far worse than it might have been this week, and that our incalculable common loss by this surrender was in vain, were certainties cold and deadly in the blue light, irrefutable in every dawn from that to this.

5

Colleagues of experience had said days before that we ought to find a place to sleep at nights outside of the city. The bombings of Prague might be intermittent or continuous, but in any case they could not be long endured without sleep. We would have to go into the city every day for our work, but there was no reason why we should not find a village in the neighborhood where we could take refuge at night—if not every night, at least some nights; enough to keep going. This was the idea (I think it was Geoffrey Cox of the *Daily Express* who first put it into words). As I had a car, and was, except for resident correspondents, the only one of the colleagues so blessed, it was up to me to conduct the necessary exploration.

Geoffrey and Walter Kerr and my wife and I went out on Saturday, the day after the general mobilization, to see what we could find. By this time the general geography of Prague was fairly clear to all of us, and we knew there was not much to be found out in the direction of the old city, the Castle Hill and the road to Carlsbad. We had an interpreter along who was all for exploring in the opposite direction, following the number 19 tram to its terminus by the gas works, and out into the country beyond. We did all this, and stopped at intervals to inspect the possibilities. Everything we saw in the immediate outskirts of Prague was ruled out for one reason or another, and the neighborhood of the gas works did not seem the best possible place to live during bombings. We went on to the *octroi*, where a good-natured Czech guard inspected our papers and the papers for the car. He seemed a friendly soul, and on impulse our interpreter told him what we were looking for. The whole *octroi* (three men) gathered round with interest, and there were many jokes.

"You can have some rooms in my house," the customs guard said. "It's only ten minutes down the road, in a village that will never be bombed. The whole village isn't worth the price of one bomb."

This sounded like what we wanted, and the customs

guard gave us the most exact directions as to how to get there. Just over the crest of the hill and down a side road we came to a typical Czech village, alive with ducks and geese: this was Seberov. The number of the customs guard's house was 94, for some reason (although I feel sure that there were not ninety-four houses in all in that village). Numerous eager women directed us down the single street to the baker's house on the corner, by the schoolhouse; there we turned to the left, down toward the duck pond, between neat, recent houses of brick and stone, and the very last house in the village, next to the pond, was Seberov 94. The customs guard's wife was at home, a plump, smiling woman with the broad cheekbones and slightly flattened face of the Bohemian peasant. She took us in willingly: the house was too big for the two of them, her husband and herself, she explained, and we could have all the part they did not use. It was a new house and very clean.

They apparently only used three rooms: their own big bedroom, the kitchen-dining-room and a hall to the door. There were three cheerful, sunny rooms upstairs, freshly papered in some sort of plain modern stuff (not at all the cabbage roses we might have expected). There was not a stick of furniture in any of them, but the housewife explained that she could probably borrow beds in the village, if we could provide mattresses and linen. For a table and a chair or two, she said, it would be easy enough to arrange.

We took the rooms and paid for two months in advance. Our room (my wife's and mine) looked over the flat glistening duck pond. Walter and Geoffrey were to have the others. When we came downstairs the housewife showed us her own bedroom, filled with feather beds and curtains and overstuffed chairs. Against the wall was a very *surréaliste* picture of two small staring boys, hand in hand.

These were her sons, she said, who had been drowned in the duck pond a few winters ago. They had been playing on the ice, the ice cracked and one fell through. The other was drowned attempting to rescue his brother.

For other colleagues—Knickerbocker and Whittaker were the ones we had particularly to look out for—she suggested the baker's house on the corner. The baker occasionally took in lodgers, and he had the only telephone in the village. We thought it all-important to put somebody in the house with the telephone, so that we might not be altogether out of touch with Prague during our time in Seberov. They said that Seberov was on the regular Prague telephone exchange, so that we were assured of service so long as the telephones worked in the city.

Under the guidance of our customs guard's wife we visited the house of the baker at the corner of the road. It was apparently the social center of Seberov, for an uncountable number of women and children swarmed up and down its narrow stone staircase. The room which was offered for lodgers was clean and sunny with an enormous bed; a Madonna and Child looked down on the elaborate bedspread and the flowered carpet; we took this for Knickerbocker and Whittaker, also for two months. The telephone, the one telephone in the village, was just outside this room, in a hallway redolent with onions. It made us laugh to think of how angry Knick would get when the children of the house and village (the uncountable children) began clattering up and down stairs just when he wanted to sleep. Knick's anger (because of his red hair) had something especially peppery about it.

The whole village seemed a sleepy and forgotten sort of place, even though it had a small garrison of soldiery near by. It was beyond the crest of the hill: to see Prague we would have to walk at least five minutes down the road to the place where the peak was reached and the valley of the Moldau lay out like a map in front of us. Seberov would be bombed only in case of extreme and extravagant carelessness, or of extremely bad marksmanship, on the part of the German aviators. In itself it was not worth wasting a bomb on, as our friend the customs guard had truthfully said.

We returned to Prague, satisfied that we had made the best arrangement possible for a difficult time. We intended to take wing for Seberov whenever circumstances advised it. There was some thought of going out there even this night (Saturday, September 24) but on the whole we thought it not worth the trouble. Hitler's bombers had not come the night before, and there was therefore a good chance that they might not come until Monday night (the night on which, as we had just learned, he was to speak at the Berlin Sportspalast). We had no idea that Seberov 94 would altogether remove us from the dangers of bombing; such a notion would have been absurd under the conditions which so closely threatened Prague. But we did believe that we could get some sleep there at nights, some nights; and I had privately resolved to make my wife stay out there even in the daytime unless she had very sound and unanswerable reasons for going in to Prague. The bombings in Spain were bad enough, but they were nothing in comparison to what we expected here. Even at the most optimistic calculation (that in which the Germans would be anxious to humor popular opinion in Germany and elsewhere by mitigating their horrors) Prague was in for a systematic destruction. The ordinary bombs used in Spain would be quite enough if used in numbers and frequently. The other hypothesis, of unmitigated frightfulness, presented far grimmer possibilities. There were the in-

cendiary bombs, first of all; and there were the unknown
elements of chemical and bacteriological warfare, of which
we knew as yet only rumors. It was possible that cholera or
the bubonic plague might be sown in Prague from the air
on a very large scale; anything of the kind was possible;
our Seberov 94, in such a case, would have been a very
pitiful little expedient, something like the shiny gray gas
masks in which the girls of Prague kept their powder and
combs. But we did not know at all what was coming, and
we did what we could.

For the next two or three days my wife was busy with our
interpreter buying blankets and other articles we thought
needful at Seberov 94. We acquired sardines, coffee, sugar,
ham, cheese and all sorts of aliments and condiments; we
bought candles and dishes; we became the possessors of
thermos bottles and picnic knives. Our interpreter had some
quaint ideas of what might be necessary in case of siege, and
she had the whip hand in the way of language. We piled up
enough materials to sustain us for several weeks, all stowed
away in the back of my car in the place of the confiscated
gasoline.

Preparations were being made at this time (and for three
days thereafter) for the evacuation of the Czechoslovak
government and its employees from Prague. The papers,
files, typewriters and other physical machinery were to be
moved to a place in Slovakia chosen for its supposed in-
accessibility; the government was to go there on Wednesday
or Thursday. I believe that if the invitation to Munich had
not been sent and accepted the government would have
moved on Thursday, even without a bombing of Prague.
The city was obviously untenable in the conditions foreseen—a war between Germany and Czechoslovakia, in
which for at least two or three weeks no ally of Czecho-

slovakia would make any difference. Prague was within an easy half-hour's flight from the nearest German airdrome.

Our friend Milos Safranek, the head of the press bureau in the Foreign Office, arranged for the evacuation of the foreign correspondents with the government. It was planned to make places for all who wished to go, and to take the equipment of the government's radio stations, so that there would be communication from Slovakia to the outside world. A certain number of correspondents wished to remain in Prague for at least a time, to write about the bombings of the city. (Tom Delmer of the *Daily Express* first pressed this necessity upon Safranek and the Foreign Office.) It was my plan also to remain in Prague—or in Seberov 94—for ten days or two weeks, until the process foreseen had been carried through, and then to drive in my own car (if I could get gasoline) to the place appointed in Slovakia. From there I thought we could drive straight through Rumania to Russia and out to the non-swastika world by whatever route seemed advisable, Finland or Siberia as the case might be. For the accommodation of such correspondents as wished to stay for the bombardments, the government agreed to leave one of its six radio stations and a staff to operate it. The details of the evacuation, although worked out in great haste, were as sensible as it was possible to make them in the fever of the time. I believe every eventuality had been foreseen except, perhaps, the one which came to pass.

In Prague during those days we could write nothing for the press: there was no means of communication. But even if we had been able to write and send stories we should have had almost nothing to say. The city was calm. We had said that dozens of times before, and when the radio started to work (I think on Monday) we said it again, day after day; it was true. Under the most terrific stress, facing an ordeal so unprecedented that it was impossible to imagine it with any exactness, the inhabitants of Prague went about their business in disciplined fashion. It was self-discipline, for there were no unusual numbers of police about. The resolute calm with which these things were done deserved that abused and abusable word, heroic. Men went to the war; women took their places at work; that was all. The emotionalism of Wednesday the twenty-first had vanished altogether; there was a solemn kind of contentment in the air that was hard to define, for it had no hint of joy in war or satisfaction at the prospect, but lifted the whole people, so far as one could tell, to the firmness and finality of a crisis resolved, a sacrifice decided upon. These people were ready to do what was asked of them although they knew that it meant death for an enormous number among them. It was worth while noticing and recording these rare (very rare) evidences of a people united in one purpose, partly because they were rare, and partly because the German radio stations at this moment were emitting the wildest lies about the subject. To listen to the Leipzig station one would have believed that the gutters of Prague ran with blood, that not a shopwindow in the city was intact, that the Red flag floated over the Hradschin, and that the triumphant Communists were massacring foreigners and bourgeois twenty-four hours a day. The sober truth of Prague, swept clean and made taut by the moment of crisis, was something so remote from these Nazi inventions that it was impossible to listen to the poisonous lies of the German radio without falling into a rage. The worst thing was that one realized in listening to these inventions that the hapless German people, enslaved in every respect conceivable, had no means of knowing the truth and even no desire to know. In this moment of crisis, when the fate of millions of human beings, of the world itself, was being determined, the mightiest nation in Europe was chloroformed with lies.

6

Hitler's speech at the Berlin Sportspalast was delivered on the night of Monday, September 26. We listened to it after three days and nights of dazed fear and apprehension —cheerful enough we were, and all that, but we were certainly all afraid that he meant war. Apparently it was only *after* this date that western Europe began to fear war and dig up its public parks in a belated and foolish attempt to make refuges. In Prague we knew that the night of September 26 was the crucial night. We expected bombers that night if ever. I thought Hitler might make his speech in very much the usual terms (just as he did make it) and then announce that his bombers were already starting for Prague or had already reached Prague. (This was his system when he remilitarized the Rhineland: word and deed synchronized.) On this occasion he merely announced that if he was not given what he wanted within four days he would go and take it—a very different thing, and one which could have been met by a firm refusal from England, Russia and France if they wished to stand to their guns. Their guns were obviously more numerous than his, and more certain of victory.

We went out to Seberov 94 to hear the speech. We took our luggage with us, or some of it, as we expected the bombers then or not at all. We intended to stay the night at Seberov if the bombers came, and return to Prague the next day to try to collect the pieces of a story and get it out to America by whatever means might be provided. The customs guard and his wife at Seberov 94 had bought a radio during the preceding summer (which must have been quite an expense for them) so that they could hear the prating and jabbering by which this crisis was worked up on all sides for months. The radio was in the kitchen. The man understood German much better than his wife did, and kept translating to her in whispers while the speech was going on. Walter Kerr, Geoffrey Cox, my wife and I sat by the kitchen table and tried to take notes. We had not much German between us: my wife and I knew some, Geoffrey Cox most of us all. "Der Führer spricht!"—and off it went, the rasping voice and inhuman accent, the insane fury and the jagged, raw and gasping nerves of the semi-maniac who controls the fate of Germany. I cannot pretend to have understood very many of the exact words. I had never heard Hitler before and was particularly interested in all sorts of incidental things—the crazy monotone of his voice, rising occasionally to a shriek as of extreme suffering; the queer noises and sound effects produced by the crowds at his bidding; the extraordinary transparency of the whole machinery. For example, when he referred to his "friend," Benito Mussolini, with an obvious attempt at sincerity—an attempt which was in fact the cry of necessity in a moment which must have gripped him with mortal fear—his trained cheerleaders set up a cadenced yell of "Duce, Duce, Duce," mispronouncing the word in German style, and making it sound just about as artificial as the alliance between Italy and Germany in fact is. It was obvious that Benito Mussolini was also listening to this same broadcast at the Palazzo Venezia, or wherever he was just then, and that he was supposed to be gratified by the compliment. It amused me (even in the tension of that evening) to think of how enraged Mussolini must have been at the compliment: as a very clever and shrewd man, which he is, he could hear as we could hear the hollowness of this cheering, the emptiness and sterility of Nazi Germany's "friendship" for anything in the world except Nazi Germany. I was set to musing over this temporary phenomenon (the Fascist alliance) for so much of the time that I missed a good deal of the actual speech. Walter Kerr was taking notes as copiously as he could, since he had to broadcast something to America for the N.B.C. that evening. Geoffrey Cox made no attempt to take notes and was—or so I thought—rather enjoying the performance, as most reporters do, whatever happens. My wife was struggling with the German, which was plain enough at times and obscure enough at other times. And the radio itself faded out and faded in, was interrupted by static, and at times was totally drowned out by some station in Russia or elsewhere, so that the mechanical difficulties of hearing the speech were as great as those of language or intelligence. All we wanted to know, anyhow, was whether it was war or peace, and as soon as we heard about the four days of grace—"if I do not get this territory by Saturday I will go and take it" or words to that effect—we were well aware that the accommodating Mr Neville Chamberlain would find some way of satisfying the orator without undue violence or disarrangement of the London traffic system. Consequently we returned to our car and drove back to Prague without delay. (The police stopped us a number of times because our lights were not dim enough—black though they were—and only the persuasive accents of our Czech interpreter got us through without difficulty.) We left the customs guard and his wife in the kitchen there at Seberov 94, and I have never seen them since. We did not need the rooms we had taken there: the Western democracies took care of that little problem for us. I am glad to report that we did pay in advance for these rooms, and that we sent the key back to the customs guard's wife before we left Prague.

CHAPTER VIII

The Triumph of the Swastika

THE DAYS AND NIGHTS of the world crisis—those usually dated Tuesday and Wednesday, September 27 and 28, although I believe the true moment of crisis had been on the twenty-sixth—passed for us in a sort of nightmare of agitation and gloom. I doubt if anybody with a trace of intelligence in the world hoped for war, and yet the alternative as understood by France and England (i.e., submission to Hitler) seemed so much worse for the whole structure and future of humanity that it was almost impossible to contemplate the results. Apparently the Western world did not see what the results would be—felt nothing at all except the deadly fear of war. Consequently it was possible for Mr Neville Chamberlain to accomplish his flight to Munich, taking the acquiescent Daladier along, and arrange the whole surrender without any important or powerful opposition arising in either France or England at the time. (I am aware that there was oppositit(ion, but it did not become very active until the crisis was well past.)

It was done, anyhow. I doubt if any of it surprised us much in Prague after what we had been through for some days. The Czech army was bewildered, stunned with astonishment and humiliation at their treatment by these far-off friends and allies who were so anxious to deliver them over to their enemy. There was weeping again in the streets, but people were so dispirited that they could not make demonstrations or engage in any of the show of grief that had sprung so spontaneously from the whole city on September 21. The feeling of nervous exhaustion, of an unbearable tension unbearably resolved, was too much for visible expression.

We drove out to the Sudetenland to see the state of the border during its interregnum. The whole procedure of transfer was very curious indeed: I doubt if anything of the kind has happened often. The Czechs kept control of most of the areas out there until half an hour or so before the first of the Germans entered, and all those who might have objected to the German victory (i.e., Jews, intellectuals, Social Democrats and other Germans as well as Czechs) were no longer in the conquered areas when they were occupied. The Germans entered to the unfeigned rejoicing of a whole population—that is, such population as was left.

I saw the entry of the Germans into Carlsbad and noted it step by step. My wife and I, with Walter Kerr, drove out from Prague very early that morning, so as to get to Carlsbad at nine o'clock. There had been a little misfortune two nights before. We three (with Geoffrey Cox and Bill Morrell of the *Daily Express*) had gone to Eger on the night when the Germans had taken possession (October 2).

We had driven into a town bedecked with swastikas, alive with the agitated and happy movement of a people who thought themselves "liberated" by their change of masters from bad to worse. (Eger was, as I have stated before, about a hundred per cent German and never at ease under Czech domination: but the place is probably a good deal worse off in every way now.) At the press headquarters we were told that "the Führer was expected tomorrow." The military headquarters had been less communicative: the officers there said they were "not sure." We walked or drove in the streets of the jubilant town, sat in the hotel and drank beer, and even telephoned stories through Berlin. (That is, Geoffrey and Walter did; mine never reached its destination.) Then on our return journey to Prague, late at night—leaving Geoffrey to await the expected visit of the Führer which we all thought impossible so soon— we ran into all the usual difficulties and apprehensions of a trip on any border in time of war. The men at the bridge at Eger told us we could go no further: that the Czech guards were murdering everybody who moved along the road, that passage was impossible, etc., etc. In the darkness it was not very reassuring. We drove as slowly as we could, with our dimmed lights, expecting a shot to be heard at almost any moment. I drove the car, and when we came up the slope to the place that was supposed to be most dangerous (a crossroads) Bill Morrell got out and walked ahead so as to be able to talk to any Czech sentry there might be. He did exactly that, and the Czech sentries were, as common sense might have told us, poor devils who were just as frightened of us as we were of them. They turned their flashlights on the car and its inhabitants, asked us a few questions, examined our passes, and let us go.

THE TRIUMPH OF THE SWASTIKA

But by returning to Prague on that night we had missed the best story of the week: Hitler's triumphal entrance to Eger and his speech to his new subjects. I did not particularly suffer professionally by this: my idea had been (for some days) to see his entry into Carlsbad and write that one story and no more. But in any case it was all-important for Walter Kerr to get the Carlsbad story, and it was important enough for me, as it would be my last from Czechoslovakia. The North American Newspaper Alliance* had asked me to continue sending dispatches for at least another week, but by this time I was so sick and weary and angry that I was incapable of writing a story fit to be printed in a newspaper. I fixed on Carlsbad as the last occasion on which I could bear to cable, telephone or otherwise communicate anything about the horror of this vivisection while it was still going on.

The drive from Prague was the usual swift and uneventful flight across Czech and German villages. We made our usual stop at Horse's Neck for a quick breakfast and then hurried on along the familiar road to Carlsbad. The first swastika we saw was, I think, on the windows of a farmhouse in a hollow on the right side of the road, just beyond Buchau. Buchau itself was the frontier of the areas surrendered to Hitler by Chamberlain; it was an ordinary Bohemian village with a mixed population, Czechs bearing German names and Germans bearing Czech names, a muddle and confusion of races like most of those villages. I always remembered it because the turn of the road came at a place marked "Freiwillige Spritzenhaus"—i.e., the headquarters of the volunteer fire brigade. Just beyond Buchau,

*I had sent dispatches from Spain and Austria to the New York *Herald-Tribune*, but in Czechoslovakia I was sending them to the North American Newspaper Alliance.

down one of those beautiful fertile slopes which are characteristic of the Bohemian countryside, there was a brick farmhouse which had anticipated the Führer's advent by sticking up a swastika, even though the Czech army was still in possession of all this area for another day. At Buchau we saw one more evidence of preparation for the Führer's visit, although at the time we did not know what it was. This was a sort of maypole with evergreens on it, lying alongside the road, which was later to become a triumphal arch.

The rest of the road seemed to be in better repair than it had been for days past. There had been barricades; there had been dynamited bridges; there had been every sort of improvised difficulty in case this road might have to be defended against the invader. Now efforts had been made to clear it all away so that traffic (if there had been any traffic) might be unimpeded. The approaches to Carlsbad gave us our first notion of what to expect. The Czech army, retreating down the road, dispirited and not in good order, let us pass with only the most cursory glances at our documents. We went through a kind of continuous mob of them of all the different varieties, eating their breakfast and slogging along home. They were an unhappy and beaten lot—beaten without having had the chance even to fight.

On the hill above Carlsbad we encountered our first real signs of the joy of the German population at their annexation to Germany. Swastikas were going up on nearly every house, at the windows, on the roofs and on the doorways. There were ladders against the houses so that the inhabitants could put the swastika as high up on the façade as possible. Men, women and children greeted our car as it passed with the Fascist salute and shouts of "Heil Hitler!" This annoyed us all a good deal, but there was nothing much we could do about it except ignore it.

We went down the winding road to Carlsbad and passed the two great Jewish charitable institutions—one a hospital, the other a home for the aged. The hospital was shut up tight, without a sign of life and without a swastika on it. The home for the aged still seemed to be inhabited (by whom I do not know) and actually had several swastika flags hanging from the windows.

We reached the bridge over the Müllerbrunn at nine o'clock, just as the first carloads of German officers in uniform started to come across it from the other direction. They were cheered by a crowd which was, as yet, very small, but they saluted with broad grins and reached out to take the flowers that were offered them by the girls along the way.

The Müllerbrunn is a small stream through the middle of Carlsbad. If you turn to the left at the bridge, as we did, you come before long to the Schmuckplatz, the square beside the Municipal Theater. Here we were told that Hitler would definitely arrive today (a fact we had been unable to determine by what anybody else told us—the stories were all contradictory). The hotel where press people usually stayed had been taken over by the press and propaganda services of the Nazi party and some officers of the Wehrmacht. All the other hotels in Carlsbad had been closed for about two weeks for lack of either guests or workmen. Some of them were now reopening—at least those on the Schmuckplatz—to afford places and food for the throng of visitors expected either as part of the Hitler show or as spectators at it. We found a place at the Hotel Goldene Schild, which had just reopened that morning and

was in a rare state of dither over the great event. The proprietor and his wife were both agitated, the proprietor, I
think, rather more than his wife: her chief trouble seemed
to be where she would find enough food, dishes, knives,
forks and spoons for so many people. They had a son who
had just returned that day from across the hills in Germany
somewhere: he had been a member of Henlein's "Freikorps", that body of volunteer local Nazis who were never
called upon to do any fighting beyond an occasional murder or assault on a Jew. We got a table by a window and
started to have breakfast. By almost inconceivable bad luck
I was given two rotten eggs, one after the other, and spoiled
breakfast for all of us by jumping so that the bad eggs fell
on the floor. After that I gave up trying to eat anything.
The sight to be seen through the window was, however,
worth any number of such minor misfortunes. A regiment
of men, women and children had suddenly appeared and
started uprooting all the plants, trees, rosebushes and other
growing things in the Schmuckplatz, the Municipal Gardens. What had been a formally planted garden was transformed under our eyes, in due course, into an open square.
At first we wondered if this could be plain looting—whether
the retirement of the Czech soldiery at seven o'clock had
not left the town too unpoliced, so that industrious looters
could not be prevented from taking what they pleased, even
for firewood. But the German officers by this time were
plentiful in the square, and it did not seem reasonable that
they would go placidly about their business while the popu-
lace destroyed the Municipal Gardens. In half an hour or so
it became clear what they were doing: they were simply
making room for a crowd for the Führer to address.

After breakfast we went out and wandered about the
streets of the town. The S.S. had already arrived and estab-

lished its headquarters in one building (the old police station) and there were a good many gray-uniformed men of the regular army, as well as Brownshirts, to be seen here and there. The crowd was getting to be so thick that the problem of where to park my car took me a good long while. I think I was aided in this chiefly by a local Nazi who was influenced by the Great Britain license plate—that G.B. license plate which, cheered in German areas and jeered in Czech districts, showed so clearly who was the author of the present rearrangement of Europe. There were a lot of people in this crowd who were weeping for sheer joy. "This is the happiest day of my life," they told you when you gave them a chance. There were also some who had got mixed up in it by sheer accident, as you could easily notice if you looked. I saw two old ladies walking along the street who had to stop and give the Fascist salute on one occasion (perhaps at the passing of a carload of officers). Both of these saluted perfunctorily, and one of them was obviously too puzzled either to know why she saluted or to do it halfway correctly. She flapped her right hand in the air as if she wished the whole thing—Fascism and Hitler and the rest of it—would go away.

But there could be small doubt of the natural enthusiasm of most in that crowd. They were glad of the annexation of this area to Germany: they were anxious to greet Hitler with as much adulation as they knew how to muster for him. Czechs, Jews, Social Democrats and all other anti-Fascists had gone away at least by seven o'clock this morning; none were left except those who were glad to welcome Hitler as the new master of Europe. My wife and Walter Kerr and I got back to the Goldene Schild only just in time, as the bridge across the Müllerbrunn on that side was closed by a line of S.S. men and the crowds which pressed from all directions by now were being admitted to the Schmuckplatz in small, orderly groups.

We saw the big trucks of the propaganda department arrive and distribute their swastikas. Great swastika banners were hung out over the balconies at the Municipal Theater, where Hitler was to speak. On the Hirschensprung, the high peak of mountain which towers above Carlsbad—the peak from which the legendary hind sprang and created the health-giving springs in the days of Kaiser Karl—the crucifix which always stands there now had a swastika flag planted beside it. On the mountainside (called Friendship Heights) workmen had been busy since early morning making a great white swastika in painted wood and canvas; by noon it was complete, a huge sign spread over the hillside and visible to all who stood in the Schmuckplatz below. Loud-speakers had been installed in the four corners of the Schmuckplatz, and by now (eleven-thirty or so) had been wired so that they worked. All of this equipment, the radio and recording machines, the propaganda leaflets, banners, swastikas and what not, had been brought in to Carlsbad from Germany, of course; truckloads of such material had been pouring in since the last of the Czech soldiery left the town that morning.

The army began to enter in force before ten o'clock, big lorries filled with infantrymen and machine gunners. The bonnets of their cars were festooned with flowers; they had flowers on their rifles and helmets; all the girls in the streets reached out eagerly to touch their hands as the trucks passed. At eleven forty-five there was the trooping of the colors, a drill performed with terrifying precision in goose step. I doubt if any other troops in the world could perform a parade drill like the Germans when they are on their mettle. Shortly after this the tanks began to move in, great and small, and aligned along the street next to the theater —the street named, in Carlsbad fashion, the Old Meadow.

By now the loud-speakers were announcing Hitler's progress from Eger, point by point, interspersing these bits of interesting information with advice and orders to the crowd. The sound trucks and film cameras were busy in all this from eleven o'clock on, and the scene was one they did well to take—it was, in fact, something like a movie to watch, and must have been excellent material for the sound film. It rained intermittently during the morning, and the first crowds in the Schmuckplatz put up their umbrellas. The loud-speaker admonished them about this, saying that the Führer was on his way to them in an open car, un-protected against the elements, and that they should be pre-pared to endure a little rain while they waited for him—especially as it was not raining at that moment. "Umbrellas will be raised the next time it rains," this announcement said. There was a general laugh and the umbrellas went down.

The loud-speakers in the square and all along the streets urged the people, as time passed and the hour for the Führer's arrival grew nearer, to crowd on into the Schmuck-platz. "There is room in the Schmuckplatz for fifteen thou-sand people," the booming voice reiterated many times. I doubted if there were fifteen thousand people in Carlsbad just then, unless all were brought in from all the streets leading to Eger: and in that case who would there be to line the streets and cheer the Führer as he passed?

The Schmuckplatz filled up slowly. I think the officers in charge of moving the crowd wanted to make quite sure that there would be a crowd everywhere along the Führer's line of approach, and it took a little careful management to make the available number of people look like the usual frenzied mob of Berlin or Munich. My wife and Walter and I had obtained a room directly facing the Municipal Theater, in the Golden Shield Hotel, and there was no other place where we could have had a better view of the machinery by which the demonstration was worked up.

At one-forty the loud-speakers began to fill in time by music, but ten minutes later the booming voice of the chief announcer said very solemnly: "The Führer is in Carlsbad."

From then on until the great man appeared in the square, the cheering was continuous. We could hear it starting afar off, out of sight, by the Eger bridge presumably, growing stronger as the cars surrounding the Führer pushed their slow and would-be majestic way through the streets. At one fifty-four exactly, preceded by a sound truck with the movie crank steadily grinding, Hitler entered the square, rigid in his long military coat and cap, his hand at the military salute. The crowd then chanted in unison (started, of course, by the cheerleaders scattered here and there): "Wir danken unserem Führer [We thank our Leader]." This seemed to be the principal slogan of the day, and was chanted again and again both during Hitler's speech and afterwards, alternating with the brief, savage barking noise of "Sieg Heil, Sieg Heil!" At two o'clock exactly the Führer walked out on the balcony of the theater, giving the Nazi salute and receiving it from the massed crowd in the square beneath. The applause—general now, not cadenced or organized, but an outburst of hysterical yells and howls —continued for exactly five minutes, after which Hitler turned it off by signaling with his hand. It stopped as a light goes off when you turn the switch.

H. H. Frank, the local Nazi leader (Henlein's lieutenant, who was from Carlsbad), spoke first, thanking "mein Führer" for the people. "You have taken us home, mein

Führer," he said in a voice raucous with emotion. The people then chanted again, in unison, "Wir danken unserem Führer."

Hitler's own speech, which followed, lasted just ten minutes. (It was broadcast, but the broadcasting arrangements failed and the recording which was taken at the same time, plus some extra crowd noises which we did not hear, was rebroadcast that night.) My wife and I were busy trying to take notes on what he said but it was almost hopeless. I got a word here and a word there, a sentence or two intact, and a general idea of what he was saying, but I could not make a connected account of his speech: I only found out what he said afterwards by reading the newspaper. The speech on the whole was calm (for Hitler) and contained only one moment of the maniacal intensity which we expected. That was when he hit the balcony rail in front of him and said: "Dass ich hier ein Tag stehen würde, das hab'ich gewusst [That I would be standing here one day, that I knew]!" This sentence came after a passage in which he spoke of the seeming impossibility of what the Nazi party and government had achieved in the partitioning of Czechoslovakia. His declaration that he had "always known it" was characteristic of the sort of lunacy which has made Hitler such an unquestioned and unquestionable idol to his own people. He may have always expected or hoped to stand in Carlsbad as conqueror, but he could not possibly have known that it would happen: it reminded me a little of an old German saying to the effect that everybody says he has heard the grass growing once it has grown. Even so, the maniacal intensity was there in the statement, and everybody who heard it felt some kind of electrical shock. There were some women in the crowd who fainted; I saw one carried out of the square and another brought into our hotel.

The speech was short and the whole ceremony ended by half-past two. We went downstairs to the hotel restaurant to eat something, and then ensued a long wrangle over where we should go to telephone our accounts of the proceedings. Walter Kerr was anxious to get to the nearest telephone, and the nearest telephone was probably somewhere in Germany itself. I did not particularly want to cross the border into Germany for fear of not getting back again. We had left all of our belongings in Prague; my vote was for returning to Prague and trying to telephone from there, even though the communication from Prague was still about as erratic as possible. We tried the Carlsbad telephone and found that it would not work (except for official communications) in any direction. The nearest big town in Germany was Bayreuth. It was a rash and almost idiotic idea to go there under such conditions, with a military occupation going on and a world war scare so recent that any foreigner must be subject to pretty severe scrutiny; but the nearest telephone in such cases is the nearest telephone, and go we did.

We took the Bavarian road by Asch—the one, I believe, over which Hitler had made his entry into Czechoslovakia. It was fairly crowded on the Czechoslovak side, or rather on the newly Germanized side, but there was little enough traffic once we got into Bavaria itself. Here we saw our first evidence of the confiscation of Jewish goods in the newly seized areas: a big truck from Carlsbad, belonging to a Jewish department store, was being driven into Bavaria with a lot of German soldiers in it.

At the frontier, which was now a frontier no longer, nobody knew just what to do with us. The Czechoslovak frontier was gone, the posts there deserted and the bars taken down, but the customs and other guards at the German frontier were still on duty. I had the usual international papers for my car, and we all had our passports; there was therefore no reason why we should be detained; but the man who stamped our papers said we would have to go to the Gestapo in Bayreuth to get an *Unbedenklichkeitsbescheinigung* (a certificate of harmlessness or unobjectionability) before we could cross the frontier again back into Czechoslovakia.

We reached Bayreuth in good time to telephone our stories. Walter Kerr got his telephone communication with Paris in about three minutes, read off the story he had written at lunch and in the car on the way, and then went into the restaurant to order a meal for all of us. My telephone communication presented greater difficulties. The North American Newspaper Alliance office in London was closed or did not answer; my only chance was, therefore, to telephone to the New York *Times* in Paris or in Berlin and ask them to pass my message on. But this was what seemed altogether impossible. I called the *Times* both in Paris and Berlin, and the calls never came through. Hour after hour passed. Sometimes I asked the hotel manager to make the call for me and sometimes I went to complain to the operator myself, but the answer always was: "It hasn't come through yet." I was getting so nervous with this delay, and so mystified by it, that I could hardly eat the excellent dinner provided by the Goldener Anker Hotel. There seemed no reason why a call both to Paris and to Berlin should fail to get through when it had been so easy for my colleague. I soon received a delicate little intimation of what was the matter. I went to the telephone booth again to ask for the call and got, not the ordinary operator, but a quite different voice, a new one, saying something like this:

"Ah, so you were in Carlsbad today! You saw our Führer, did you? Now wasn't that fine! I hope you enjoyed that."

I was mystified at this: why should the operator care what I had been doing, and how could she know?

"Yes," I said, "that is all true, but how about my telephone communication?"

"That will be all right," she said. "You are sitting in a nice warm place, aren't you, there in the hotel, with a good meal? You can wait. You will get your communication."

I was so stunned by this way of talking that I went back to the dining room and told my wife and Walter, who did not (of course) believe it. A few minutes later I tried again and got the same general line of mockery from the telephone operator. It was by now half-past ten, three hours and a half since Walter had so easily telephoned his own story of the day. I tried one thing more: went back to the telephone and put my Paris and Berlin calls in again at triple rate, *dringend*, urgent. When I had done this Walter put in a call to his office, the *Herald-Tribune* in Berlin, at the ordinary press rate.* His ordinary press telephone call came through in just under three minutes, and he read my story to his Berlin office with the request to pass it along to the *Times*. I believe all this was done, and in any case it has no great importance: but why was I unable to get a telephone call myself? These are the mysteries of work in Germany under the Nazi regime. I began to believe all the stories I had heard from colleagues, Knickerbocker and Mowrer and others, and the espionage and sabotage and all the rest of it. Even in a sleepy town like Bayreuth, which

*Kerr had been working in Europe less than a year; the Gestapo certainly had no such dossier on him as they had on me.

looked as if it was almost unaware of politics, it was quite possible that the Gestapo was aware of everybody.

We had in any case to pay a call on the Gestapo the next morning, and we did so. That was a little comedy of errors all by itself. Nobody in the Gestapo office knew what to do with us; they said it was unnecessary for us to have an *Unbedenklichkeitsbescheinigung;* that these were only for German citizens. But before we elicited this piece of information we had wandered through half the offices in the police station and talked to several officials who were just as puzzled as we were. At one point I believe one of the officers in charge telephoned to Nürnberg, the local headquarters of the Gestapo, for instructions. The upshot seemed to be that we would have to go all the way to Nürnberg to get the *Unbedenklichkeitsbescheinigung.* We went out and got into the car to think it over; paid a brief visit to the Wagner Festival Theater, just to see what it looked like; and returned to the Gestapo once more. This time I went in alone and found that most of the officials were out to lunch. There was one man on duty, a police officer, very military and heel-clicking in type, who said to me, with a broad grin, "Why don't you just go to the frontier and try to pass through? These are unusual times on the frontier and it might work. It isn't very far, and if they turn you back you can return here and go to Nürnberg."

We took this sensible piece of advice and wished we had been given it sooner. Our trip to and through the frontier was without incident. The same officers who had told us we must go to the Gestapo now said that members of the press were not required to do so: "You should have told me that you belonged to the press." The only incident of note at the frontier was the passage of a *Staffel* (which includes 27, I believe) of airplanes overhead. The army man on duty in the passport place ran out to look at them with glee. "Hermann Goerings Spielzeuge [Hermann Goering's toys]," he said.

Once we left Bavaria and entered the newly occupied territory everything was different. Yesterday had been the day for flowers and jubilation; this was the day of tanks, armored cars, heavy trucks loaded with ammunition, staff cars, and a general movement of the German army to take possession of its prey. The traffic from Franzensbad on to Carlsbad was very heavy. We had expected to be stopped and asked for papers. The frontier guards had warned us that a new motorcycle corps known as the *Feldgendarmerie*, with green arm bands, were patrolling the roads with orders to stop strange cars, and that we should show our papers and ask to be taken to press headquarters when this happened. But, as a matter of fact, although we passed several such patrols of *Feldgendarmerie*, they always saluted us as if we had been members of the general staff and went whizzing on their way. My car was gray, like most of the German staff cars, and I suppose there was no way of telling the difference without stopping us to examine. The G.B. plate on the back may have suggested a diplomatic car; I don't know. In any case among the strange things in those two days of wandering through a sort of no man's land the like of which has seldom existed before, the strangest thing of all was that nobody stopped us or made the slightest attempt to find out what we were doing. If we had had a machine gun, for instance, it would have been fairly easy to kill Hitler and his friends there on the balcony over the Schmuckplatz. Nobody searched us or asked us questions; there might have been lethal weapons in our one suitcase; but in any case we were allowed to circulate without let or hindrance. I began to think that the myth of German efficiency was a mere journalistic approximation, like so many other myths of the age. Certainly the tanks and trucks we saw were no myth, and could have given an excellent account of themselves in any armed conflict; but the rest of the organized occupation of the newly acquired territory— police, press, secret police and all—was nothing very wonderful.

Later on, in Prague, we met one or two of the press colleagues who had witnessed the same spectacle as ourselves, only under official auspices, in the press box and with official guidance. They told us that the press chief from Berlin, who had accompanied Hitler both to Eger and to Carlsbad, had said to a German reporter in the hearing of English and Americans: "We've got them all on the run now; we're not going to stop."

This was certainly the feeling of a great many Germans at that time, just after Munich, when the triumphal occupation of the newly acquired areas was not only taking place, but was rapidly being made known to the whole German people by radio, films and press. At Bayreuth, in the restaurant of the Goldener Anker Hotel, during all that time when I had vainly attempted to get a telephone call put through, the radio was broadcasting records made of the triumph of Hitler at Carlsbad. The same things we had heard that morning were blared forth at us again at dinnertime, and were being blared forth at millions of Germans in their homes, hotels, restaurants, theaters and places of assembly, perhaps at various times during the day and that night. "Wir danken unserem Führer!" and "Sieg Heil, Sieg Heil!"

When we passed through Carlsbad on our way back to Prague we had no notion whether it would be possible to get through the new military lines or even where these lines were. Carlsbad was still bedecked in swastikas and was still in the state of hysteria that had descended on it the day before. The women and children were, if possible, even a little more wrought up than on October 4, and at times the children risked their lives by rushing out into the road and yelling "Heil!" with their hands raised in the Fascist salute. We had to swerve a couple of times to avoid such enthusiastic little idiots who took our car for a German one.

The hysteria died down swiftly after we left Carlsbad. There were still swastikas on the farmhouses, but the traffic of tanks and trucks ceased at the town, and between there and Buchau we saw only German infantrymen, stolid and good-natured, with bayonets fixed but without—apparently —any desire to interfere with our progress. At Buchau we saw yesterday's maypole, which had become a triumphal arch at some point in the proceedings—two great garlanded poles with an arch of evergreen, swastikas and other tasteful bits of Nazi decoration. Beyond Buchau we passed the last of the German soldiery. Here I saw, for one brief flash, a scene which seemed to me to indicate a state of mind. Two officers of the Wehrmacht were standing at the side of the road looking through field glasses at the further hills—the Czech lines and fortifications which had not been surrendered. They were laughing: and there was something about the way they stood, looked, laughed and nodded that suggested a whole set of ideas. "There they are, over there, secure behind some papier-mâché fortifications that we can break through whenever we like," their laugh said. "We have already taken more than anybody believed possible. We have only to wait a little while and we can take it all."

In a few minutes we came upon the first Czechoslovak military post. Here our military passes from Prague were still respected, and we were not even searched (as had been customary at these posts during the previous weeks). We drove on to Prague through columns of weary, dispirited soldiers, sometimes in formation and oftener not—men returning to their homes or to points where they had to report for demobilization. The contrast between the almost pathological excitement on the German side and this deadened, hopeless rout made it clear enough what had happened, even if we had not already known it: that a whole war had been lost here, and that without fighting.

Prague after the crisis was the home of discouragement and pain. There was one Slovak lady at the foreign press office who was in tears every time I saw her during those days. The news grew worse and worse: the Germans were occupying their "fifth zone" and taking more or less what they wanted around the edges, without regard to the details of the map imposed on Europe by Hitler at Munich. The general idea was that every Czechoslovak main line of communication (by telephone, telegraph or railroad) should be interrupted somewhere by German military occupation; that towns of great industrial importance to Czechoslovakia, such as Pilsen and Brunn, should be almost surrounded; and that the union and independence of Czechoslovakia must be so shattered that whatever government remained at Prague would be dependent upon Germany. Eduard Beneš resigned and left Prague, unable to take service under the new master. Slovakia was the center of strange disturbance, Hungarian and anti-Semitic demonstrations, separatist agitation; trouble was reported from Ruthenia. Every trace of historical instinct that I possessed told me that Hitler's victory was greater than those who had given it to him at Berchtesgaden, Godesberg and Munich could have understood. I had no desire to stay and note down the details of the disaster once it had reached this point, and on October 8 my wife and I started out in the car for Brunn, Bratislava and Vienna.

That journey was notable chiefly for the evidences of hopelessness and bewilderment on the part of the unlucky Czechoslovak army. We saw them in trains and on the roads; sometimes we got stuck in roads jammed with artillery; we drove through places where the soldiers were standing, wet, hungry and weary, along roads which led eventually to their homes; but why they were ever mobilized and why they were sent home again they probably never knew. The mystery of Munich, which is difficult enough to understand even with the aid of government documents, learned authorities and the press of the time, must remain a mystery forever to those men who were summoned to defend their country and then dismissed without striking a blow for it.

The frontiers to the south were as confused as those up in the Carlsbad area. We tried to go directly into Austria from the Danube bridge at Bratislava: here we were turned back. The German guard said, looking at the British license plate on my car: "I would like to let you pass, especially since England is now on our side, but I cannot do it. This frontier must be closed: we are occupying a new area to-morrow."

We went back to the Bratislava bridge and then tried the Hungarian frontier, about fifteen minutes away. There was no difficulty here (except from a flat tire) and we drove on through a dark and rainy night to the next frontier, that between Hungary and Austria, arriving in Vienna at five or six the next morning. The last I saw of Czechoslovakia was the glittering lights of Bratislava over the Danube. We could see them for a long time after we had passed into Austrian Germany: they were hidden by intervening hills or towns and reappeared as the road turned. I thought of what one of the Hungarian officers at the frontier had said: "Bratislava is a Hungarian town and should belong to us. It will be Hungarian soon." He was wrong in all three statements, but who knows for how long?

The total impression of defeat given by the sequence of events from September 6 to October 4 was overwhelming. The conversations of Chamberlain and Hitler at Berchtesgaden and Godesberg, and the conference of British, Italian, French and German prime ministers at Munich, taken as a unit of the historical process, constituted a tremendous triumph for the Fascist idea. It is obvious from the accounts of the Godesberg conversations—those in which Hitler lost control of his temper and Mr Chamberlain was most mystified—that the Fascist frame of mind is not only incomprehensible but inconceivable to a man of Mr Chamberlain's years and social and economic condition. Except for the parties of the Left (Socialists and Communists chiefly, but including the English Liberals) no political forces anywhere in France or England appear to have been aware of the superneurotic tension and instability of the Hitler menace. In objective fact Germany could never have won a war against the combined forces of England, France and Russia. In objective fact a war against Czechoslovakia alone, although it might have ruined Czechoslovakia for years to come, would in due course have brought in all the others. In objective fact the Germans themselves were as much afraid of war as anybody else was, and the almost hypnotic power of the Nazi mass meeting, of the Hitler speech, of the general Fascist appeal to race memory and blood consciousness, would have been dispelled by the reality of war.

All that was needed in late August or early September—even, I think, as late as September 26—was one firm, clear statement from England, France and Russia. There would have been no war. Nobody can ever prove this now, but there are two opinions which I offer with conviction: first, that a clear statement from the three powers would have kept Germany in order; second, that if Hitler had attempted to force a war after such a statement he could not have carried Germany with him.

These are hypotheses now. What happened in the surrender at Munich was actually the worst of solutions. Czechoslovakia was dismembered according to a plan drawn by Hitler himself, and even this plan was exceeded. The Chamberlain-Hitler agreement never to resort to war—a promise already made by both England and Germany in the Kellogg-Briand Pact of 1928—was obvious nonsense, since it was immediately followed by the most extensive plan of armament England has ever undertaken. The French postwar system collapsed, and perhaps it was good riddance; perhaps it was a bad system from the beginning. Many parts of it certainly were. But up to the day of the Munich agreement, September 30, 1938, treaties had been made at least *ostensibly* in good faith. From that day onward it was clear that they could be broken whenever violence or the threat of violence could be used. The rule of law in international relations was always insecure, always dependent to a very great degree upon national interest and the clash of rival economic powers. It now became not only insecure but unreal. Reality was transferred to the will of the Fascist powers, immensely strengthened by this triumph, to conquer the democracies, to rule the world. The conquest of Spain, the persecution of the Jews in Germany, the penetration of Nazi ideas in South America, the threat of

Fascism in all parts of the Mediterranean basin, were determined, made inevitable, by the Munich surrender. There have been various stages at which the democratic powers might, by a firm alliance including Soviet Russia, have stopped the Fascist advance, but of all these September, 1938, was the most decisive stage. We who saw it only from Czechoslovakia had no clear idea until long afterwards how these weeks had passed in England, France and elsewhere, but we did realize how much the direction and interaction of the historical forces hereafter depended upon resistance to the Fascist will at this moment of its greatest tension. Then was the moment when it could have been broken with least damage to all the peoples concerned, including the Germans and the Italians. From Munich onward the course of events was determined not by law, promises, treaties or even policies, but by the nicely coordinated and perfectly timed thrusts of the German-Italian-Japanese alliance, aware in the East as in the West that the democratic powers, nervous and uncertain, afraid of Communism even more than of Fascism, could be depended upon to hesitate until it was too late to resist. How long this process must continue before it results in general warfare, or if it will in fact achieve its triumphs and establish a new form of empire over Europe and half Asia without having to fight for them, are guesses we can all make with equal likelihood of being right. My own guess is that the day of general war will come, but that there will be other Munichs of one sort or another, other unnecessary triumphs for the swastika, before the Western democracies resolve that they must defend their own lives.

CHAPTER IX

Last Day on the Ebro

THE GLOOMY AND HOPELESS FEELING left by the disasters of the autumn was not to be exorcised by reading the papers of the time. Both in Paris and in London the press—and with it a great part of the public—seemed busy justifying or excusing, when they could not praise, the course of the Chamberlain-Bonnet policy of surrender. Spain remained, as it had been throughout the year, the only place where resistance to the Fascist conquest gave hope for a turning of the tide in the future. I think most observers expected Spain to go next: it was inevitable that such a triumph as that of Munich would urge the allied dictators on to further efforts there. In Czechoslovakia I saw a map, circulated as Nazi propaganda among the Bohemian Germans, which purported to show what Europe would be like when the Fascist powers had finished with it. Areas of complete Nazi dominion were marked in black, and included the British Isles and northern France as well as the Scandinavian countries, the Baltic States, Czechoslovakia, Poland and Ukrainia.

[*326*]

Areas allotted to Mussolini included the whole Mediterranean basin, the French and Spanish coasts as well as Italy and North Africa. The map seemed ludicrous, considered as a reasonable plan, but it showed the extent of the will and intention that had made it. Spain was doomed at Munich even though it was probably not mentioned there.

And yet there was a genuine national resistance in Spain: there were men who were ready to go on fighting against tremendous odds, hoping against hope: there were women and children who survived bombing raids with anger rather than with discouragement. Horrible as that war and all wars might be, there was hope in a determined resistance and no hope in surrender. My wife had numerous good reasons for going to Barcelona: to collect information for relief work she had been doing and was yet to do for the women and children there; I had no practical reason for going—no newspaper assignment—but after the gloom of the autumn a visit to Spain would be tonic: we went together by the eight-fifteen to Perpignan. The road to Figueras, Gerona and Barcelona seemed familiar now, although we had passed along it only in the spring. There were some fresh bomb holes, and there was a detour made necessary by the heavy rains of a week or so before. The Carabineros bus which took us from the frontier to Barcelona was filled with voluble soldiers and the wives of soldiers; one *carabinero* had some wine in a goatskin and passed it around; we all had bread from Perpignan. The countryside was fresh and brilliant in an autumn sunlight that was like summer anywhere else, and it was good to be in Spain again. This was strange but true: while the war lasted, while there was still the resistance of a people against Fascism native and foreign, it was good to be in Spain again. Perhaps there was bravado in the "Salud!" and the clenched fist, and perhaps the sharing of bread and wine with strangers was a little conscious, too, but when you considered what these people had endured for two years, and how little they had to share, you could not move among them without a spirit somehow quickened and made hopeful for your kind.

2

I went to the front only once during that visit to Spain. As it happened, the day we chose was the last day of the 5th Army on the other side of the Ebro: November 5. Mora de Ebro was occupied that night and the whole Republican army was withdrawn across the river in the next two or three days. It was a strategic retreat, foreseen for a long time, carefully prepared and skillfully executed without heavy losses of men or materials: it was in no respect to be compared to the retreat of the preceding spring over the same river. But even so it was the end of the last offensive: the Republic was no longer in condition to do more than resist, and that not for long.

We started from Barcelona in two cars—Hans, who had commanded the 45th Division for two years until the withdrawal of the internationals, was taking Hemingway and Buckley (of the *Daily Telegraph*) with him; Matthews of the *Times* took Robert Capa, the photographer, and me. The familiar road to the south was no longer crowded with military transport or the sad columns of the refugees: it was almost empty in the cold early morning. We stopped at Tarragona for gasoline and at an officers' training camp near Gambrils for breakfast. Hans, who knew every inch of every road in the district—he had commanded in the Tortosa sector for months—was in charge of this expedition. He elected to approach the river by the old dirt road to Falset, thus avoiding the bombs and shells which, we had heard, were now reaching the main Tarragona-Reus-Mora road.

Herbert's car, an ancient Minerva, shook us up thoroughly before it reached the high old walled town of Falset. Here Hans, Buckley and Hemingway were ahead of us and had already found out that Lister was not at Falset: that the headquarters of the 5th Army Corps were still on the other side of the river. (As I have remarked before, we never knew where the front was until we got there.) We stopped at the cold mountain spring alongside the road and watered ourselves and the cars. The reverberation of the shells, which had been in our ears for some time, was very powerful just then, and, being still at some distance, sounded continuous, uninterrupted. Hans consulted one or two Spanish officers and acquired some information. The bridge at Mora was gone, he learned: partly from the bombs and partly from the risen river, for the Fascists had again opened the floodgates at Comorasa, just as they had the preceding spring. The only bridge over the river was at Garcia, and as it served for the whole traffic of the army, it was possible that it might not be open for us. We might get to Garcia and then have to wait fifteen hours to get across. The best we could do was to make a try at it.

We set off again on the road from Falset to Mora, which lay along the curve of the river and at times approached the bank. We had agreed to meet in Mora la Nueva and consult again before going further, as it might be possible to get across the river by boat. Herbert, Capa and I seem to have misunderstood our instructions, as will appear. We drove along the road (which felt very exposed, somehow, although no shells actually fell on it) and saw nobody but a few soldiers on foot. Even the peasants, who as a rule stuck to their fields until they were actually driven off them by shelling and bombing, were not to be seen here. The dusty road and the bare, deserted country lay desolate under the bright sunlight and the upper noise of the cannonade, intermittent now, and more separable into its elements. We heard the hollow reverberant noise of bombing, the sharper violence of the explosion of shells, and at times the drumming of machine guns across the river. We kept a good lookout for airplanes but saw none. After half an hour of this we came to Mora la Nueva, the wreck of a town, with no house or building in it quite intact. At the point where our road turned into the main Mora-Reus-Tarragona highway we stopped and looked to right and left: no sign of Hans, Hemingway or Buckley. It was just here that we failed to understand our instructions. The shells were coming over here: we could hear the beginning, middle and end of their trajectory, the long whistle in the middle constituting (for me at any rate) a considerable element of suspense. To the left was the ruined village street leading to the ruined bridge: there we could see nobody. To the right was the main road going up the hill, and the road to Garcia must branch off somewhere there. We turned to the right and drove up the road for a few paces until we were stopped by sentries running out from both sides.

"You cannot pass here in any direction," they said. "Where do you want to go?"

We asked after Hans: he had not been seen. We asked for the road to Garcia: it was just there, in front of us to the left, a paved side road leading northward, but the sentries told us we could not take it. The shells were now passing overhead and the sentries in true Spanish fashion warned us, very seriously, against going anywhere at all. "Es muy peligroso." And one of them made the characteristic warning shake of his hand in the air, saying: "Muy fuerte, muy fuerte."

We had to do something. There was a sort of shed just beyond the Garcia crossroads, a barrack which might have been once a stable before the war hit it. Herbert drove his car the few feet beyond that shed and parked it in the lee of the building. It was flimsy enough protection against any possible bombing or shelling, but it satisfied the instinct for shelter: and anyhow we could not leave the car in the road and risk having no means of transport thereafter.

We then retired to the door of the shed to discuss what we might do. We agreed that we had been told to meet Hans, Hemingway and Buckley at the Garcia crossroads. This was wrong, as it happened, but it was what we thought. Under the circumstances all we could do was wait until they appeared.

I do not know how long we waited. It might have been about a quarter of an hour. It certainly was not long. But during that time the shells were passing directly over and landing about fifty yards up the road. Both Capa and Matthews were much more experienced in this kind of business than I was, but I do not think either of them was exactly comfortable. When we heard the whistle of the shell we would hurl ourselves to the ground, inside or outside the shed, and wait until we heard the explosion up the road. One thing made me laugh in the middle of this exercise. I got up from the stable floor and saw Capa brushing bits of straw off his coat.

"This is a bad day for photographers," I said to him.

He smiled disdainfully.

"This is the only kind of day that is any good for photographers," he said, carefully removing another wisp of straw from his brown tweed coat.

That was what Capa was (and is) like. That was why he took pictures which make you wonder, when you see them, how anybody could have photographed them and still be alive.

On this occasion I sustained my only wound. It was a small cut about a millimeter in length on the tip of my middle finger, and it came from one of the bits of broken glass that lay among the straw on that stable floor. I had hurled myself with a little too much enthusiasm, at the whistle of a shell; thus I did leave perhaps one drop of blood in Spain.

Presently we saw the huge bulk of Hemingway stamping up the road, and realized that our relief expedition had arrived. He was in a fine rage.

"I thought by this time you all knew where the bridge at Mora was," he said. "Where the hell have you been?"

He and Hans and Buckley had been waiting all this time down by the river. We left Herbert's care in the dubious shelter of the shed and followed Hemingway down the road to the Ebro. The shells were all passing well beyond this part of the road and the country beyond; a lot of what we heard was no doubt directed to the Garcia road; but even so it constituted the steadiest cannonade I had ever heard. Down by the river, just north of the ruined bridge, Hans and Buckley stood in the mud and sedge with some Spanish soldiers and boatmen. They were taking photographs—an enterprise in which Capa and Matthews soon joined. Of this particular day on the river there must be some hundreds of photographs in existence. I have seen them since, and they recall a dozen details of that bright autumn day, the yellow treacherous river swirling in flood and the spiky wreck of the Mora bridge protruding dangerously above it; the red-brown-yellow bluffs along the river opposite, and the muddy slithery bank on which we stood;

they recall the moan and the explosion of the shells. For some acoustical reason—something to do with the configuration of the land, the hills behind us and the scoop of the river—the swift murderous trajectory was plainer to the ears here than anywhere else. The sound very nearly blew me over each time a shell passed. None were landing in the river or on the banks; all passed safely over us and well beyond; but separately and together they were like the swift beating of the wings of death. All the others were more used to this than I was, and perhaps it made less impression on them; but even so I think it was a fairly active day for the Fascist artillery.

Hans had found a boat for us—a flat-bottomed scow with four men to the oars. Hemingway paid for our transport in cigarettes. We all piled in—a good load for the boat, for at least three of us were exceptionally heavy—and shoved off. The currents in the river were strong and tricky now that the floodgates were opened higher up: it must have been a good deal like this in April when so many of the brigaders had to swim it. The four oarsmen had to pull mightily to keep us from being swung downstream. As we were in the middle of the river we saw the Fascist airplanes in front of us swooping down to machine-gun the lines. We could see and hear this operation distinctly, and could hear no anti-aircraft against (as I remember) seven airplanes. There was also some bombing going on somewhere behind us on the other bank. We pulled up at last at a rickety wooden landing, climbed ashore and started down the riverbank to Mora de Ebro.

Mora de Ebro had now been reduced to something very like Tortosa or Sagunto—a ruin. It had been taken by the Fascists in April and retaken by the Republicans in July; it was now (in fact, that very night) to be retaken by the

Fascists again; it had been subjected to so much shelling and bombing that there was nothing intact in the place. Military traffic had to go through it, as the only road led from there up the riverbank to the single remaining bridge at Garcia; but aside from the military trucks and tanks the place was empty. Those who had cameras (that is, all but Hemingway and I) took pictures here. There was one particularly good example of the kind of destruction often seen in Spain, the house cut in two with some of its furniture left untouched. On the second floor of such a house, half of which had been blown away, a table stood with two chairs set precisely on either side of it.

"That shows just what you've got to do when a bombing starts," Hemingway said. "Just sit down at the table. Easy."

We climbed the hill to the Gandesa crossroads and made our way up the crest to Lister's headquarters. It was hot, walking in the sun here; we all peeled off coats and sweaters. The nearer we got to the artillery the less we seemed to be under it; or else I was (as usual) mixed up in the directions. In an olive grove on the right of the road were the headquarters of the 5th Army: a white house on a rise, commanding an excellent view of the whole river valley and surrounding country. There was a battery of Republican big guns (two, I believe) somewhere here, replying to the intense and interminable cannonade of hundreds on the other side. We heard the rattle of the machine guns quite near, and realized that the actual front lines ("the trenches," whether there were any proper trenches or not) were just beyond. Lister came out to talk to us, jovial and hearty, but with a look of worry in his eyes. Twice while we were sitting there on the bench that ran along the little terrace of the house he had to go inside to talk on the telephone. After a while he asked Hans to get us away; he wanted to get rid of us, and for good reason; as we learned afterwards, he was about to evacuate this place and, in fact, the whole right bank of the Ebro.

From this high place you could see the winding river and the red-brown country on both banks. I tried to determine where we were and, of course, got the whole thing confused; Hemingway with good-natured amazement handed over his Michelin map. The whole area of the great Ebro offensive (Sierra Pandols and the rest of it) was in front of us, and I could, with the help of the map, more or less see what the action had been in the past three months.

Back to Mora we trudged, after a while, and met a line of battered tanks coming up to the front (I suppose to cover the retreat that evening, although we did not know it then). The crews yelled at us and shook their fists in the air: more good photographs for those who had cameras. Even so, Capa complained. "This kind of thing is no good to me," he said in the mixed French, German, Spanish and English which was his usual lingo. "These are not pictures of action. I cannot take good photographs unless I am actually in the front lines." But it was the judgment of our chief, Hans, that we must return across the river at once, and of course he was right: the evacuation was about to begin, and perhaps he knew it then even though we did not.

I wondered why the Fascists were not shelling this road and the Gandesa crossroads. Here was where the tanks were coming up; this was the only road on which reinforcements or material could come; and yet it was apparently immune from shells or bombs. Probably hundreds of thousands of dollars were wasted on that day alone by shelling and bombing the wrong places. The Fascist observation posts and scout planes must have been exceptionally inefficient not to see this; but of course munitions of war were cheap for them, being supplied by Mussolini and Hitler against mortgages for the future; and perhaps they enjoyed throwing away the money. The greater part of their ammunition on that day was, I believe, wasted on empty fields beyond the river, fields from which life had departed some days before.

In the middle of Mora de Ebro, as we passed through, we heard a guitar strumming away busily: a soldier passing the time. As we had come through there earlier we had seen a boy trying to learn to ride a bicycle, round and round the Plaza, between the ruins, with the bombers audibly active not far away. These were the things that always struck the foreigner in Spain: the ordinariness of life in the midst of death.

At the river, when we finally got there through a congestion of military traffic (drivers stolidly lighting cigarettes in a jam of munitions trucks that would have gone up in flames with one bomb), we found a boat but only two boatmen. One of these was a scrawny peasant, probably undernourished for months, who did not look quite equal to the task ahead of him. Nor was he: for halfway across that twisting, treacherous river, with its sudden shallows and swift deep alternating currents, the boat began to veer sharply down toward the spiky wreck of the bridge.

This was a really dangerous business. We all saw it coming but did not quite know what to do about it. Hemingway grabbed the oar in front of him and pulled for dear life: by luck he was on the side where the oar was needed. Buckley, his face strained and intense—a kind of warning in itself—yelled sharply in cadence: a coxswain on the Thames. Herbert Matthews grinned; I don't think he realized how dangerous this was until we were well out of it. Hans began to struggle out of his heavy military boots so as to be able to swim if the boat crashed on the spikes. Capa took photo-raphs. I sat and watched them all, wondering. This was a very strange profession altogether and you sometimes could hardly believe the way things happened; stories, that is, be-came stories almost before they had finished happening; fact arranged itself into legend before your eyes; I think I already knew that I would one day be writing about this on a train thousands of miles from where it happened. I was, to tell the truth, not very alarmed—shells and bombs were my real alarm system—in spite of the definite, instan-taneous danger. I suppose this was because Hemingway was pulling us out of it. I had the kind of confidence in Hemingway that a Southern Negro has in the plantation owner. ("It's all right, the cap'n's here, ain't he?") It even seemed a little funny, the tense and desperate struggle to get across the river without being smashed on those spikes. Like Matthews, I was inclined to grin. For a few moments there the noise of artillery faded into the dimmest distance. We landed on the other side, cursing and swearing pro-fusely. We now had just one more difficulty to get through: the road that was being shelled.

Hans and Hemingway went ahead on foot and left the rest of us to follow in Hans's car. Up at the Garcia cross-roads we left that and took to Herbert's car, which was still intact in the lee of the shed where we had left it. Buckley was with us.

"The only thing to do," he said, "is to get around into the road and drive like hell until we get through it."

Herbert grinned. "Drive like hell" was a very rhetorical expression when used of the ancient Minerva: its maximum speed was perhaps thirty miles an hour, and the road that now lay ahead of us was all uphill. He backed into the road and headed for Reus-Tarragona (the main highway),

giving the old car all the gasoline it could take. We could
see the freshly shelled houses alongside the road, and holes
in the road itself; we had heard shelling there just a few
minutes before, and it had been fairly regular all day;
and yet it so happened that the Fascists ceased firing for a
while just then. We got up the hill and onto the plateau
beyond (somewhere beyond the point where I had first
seen the Ebro the previous spring). Here we judged that
we were beyond the shellfire, and we stopped to wait for
the others. They came up the hill and passed us at top
speed; we fell in after them. A little further down the road
we stopped to eat our belated lunch (it was about four in
the afternoon, I think) in an olive grove. Another carload
of press correspondents, Okin of the Associated Press and
Allan of Reuter's and James of the United Press, came along
just then and joined us. They had driven to the neighborhood of Garcia and had been forbidden to proceed further
on account of the shelling. The whole foreign press, it
seemed, went out toward the river that day—and for the
last time.

I drove back to Barcelona with Hans after lunch. He
still had the privileges of a major general. (He was
a *jefe de division*, although his technical rank was never
more than colonel.) Consequently we could drive through
the cordons established to stop traffic during air raids, one
at Reus and one at Tarragona, without stopping. Hemingway and Matthews got caught in both, I believe, in the
other car. Hans told me stories of the war. He had come
into Madrid in November, 1936, with the first of the internationals, and had just now been retired with the last of the
internationals two years later. He was a German of Germans, and had been an officer in the war of 1914–18. The
anti-Nazi Germans in the Spanish Republican service were

among the internationals for whom little or nothing could be done abroad: most of them had Spanish Republican passports by now, but it was doubtful if France or any other country would grant them visas, and they had been withdrawn from the Spanish army in accordance with Negrin's pledge at Geneva in September. Their status was thus obscure and their future doubtful, but if many of them are like Hans they will be equal to any difficulty.

3

Bola had a party on the night of the sixth of November, the next day. It was a gathering of newspaper people, writers, intellectuals of one kind or another. Bola (Boleslavskaya) was the correspondent of the *Pravda* in Spain and had been there for a year and a half. The party was for a double anniversary: the birthday of the Soviet Union and the beginning of the defense of Madrid. It should have been on November 7, but as there was a scattering of the clans the next day it was advanced to the night of the sixth. Malraux, Hemingway, Eddy and Mary Rolfe, Georges Soria and perhaps twenty other people took possession of Bola's two rooms and sang and danced. Agrippina, who used to go out to the front and sing to the troops in the front line, sang all the songs of the war that night: the "Quinto Regimiento," "Asturias la Roja" and the rest. She was an Asturiana with a fierce, implacable voice. At midnight somebody suggested that speeches should be made. Various of the intellectuals spoke briefly and rather solemnly. They were all a little self-conscious—aware that speechmaking was of no use, especially to each other, and yet equally aware that the defense of Madrid must be commemorated if any anniversary is to be marked. They were of many nationalities and spoke in a number of languages. Perhaps we were all self-conscious and restive. However that may be, Bola's chauffeur, a very tall Madrileño who had been sitting against the wall saying nothing for a long time, suddenly got to his feet and said that we had had enough speechmaking. He suggested that we stand in silence for a few seconds and think of those who had died in the defense of Madrid. We did so. It was the proletarian, I thought, the only real proletarian in the room, who was un-self-conscious enough to declare in so many words what was the occasion we commemorated and to command a silence.

That was a night of soft, bright moonlight which made all Barcelona as distinct as in the light of day. We had had air raids earlier in the evening, including one quite serious one. People went on to the roofs and terraces to watch it by the light of the moon. The red tracer bullets made fireworks in the sky and the antiaircraft guns almost drowned out the noise of the bombs. There would be more corpses in the morgue tomorrow and there would also be people so dispersed and annihilated that even their corpses could not be assembled again. Occasionally the silver body of an Italian plane could be seen flying very high and swift across the shaft of a searchlight in the moon-washed sky.

Early the next morning I took an airplane to Paris, and that was the last I saw of Barcelona.

4

The city and the river live for me in a region of super-reality that will survive their own changes. There were efforts of the human will made here in common that time and failure can never altogether wear to nothingness. The flat roofs of the city in moonlight, the yellow rushing current of the river, the spiky ruined bridge and the high cliff opposite are part of a reality that survives in time so long as any are still alive who shared the perception of their meaning. In an age of such political decay that no words pronounced in legislative assemblies or governmental exchanges carry the weight of an intention behind them, when reality has at last wholly deserted the concepts of international law and order to lodge itself in the power of the Fascist will-to-conquer, these times and places and the people who lived through them resume in the surviving mind that force which they exerted through the last days of the Spanish Republic, the force of light struggling against the turbulent onrush of the engulfing dark.

CHAPTER X

Epilogue

THE MATERIAL OF THIS BOOK is not to be confined within its covers: the processes here described are continuous, not episodic, and involve the existence of all now living, not of one alone. To cut, snip and trim, to hold for a while within a little frame some part of the perceived reality, is the task of the writer, whereas to perceive the reality in its contemporary terms and in the places where it was to be seen plain was the task of the journalist. In this case the one effort intermingled with the other to a degree that made exact completion of the appointed task at the appointed time almost impossible, and just as the newspaper piled up into memory and assumed the neater dimensions of a book, so the book dissolved before completion into the ceaseless proliferate daily notes and mentions of the recording newspaper. Such must be the fate of any book that describes a contemporary rhythm so general, continuous and accelerated: it is closed without coming to an end, and is continued in the pages of the daily press, as its living material continues in the struggles which are thus—with whatever inaccuracies and imperfections—made known approximately to all at once, not to scholars or students or politicians, but to the crowds going home in the subway in New York, to those who read headlines alone as well as to those who can take their pick of the wisdom of the ages. The phenomenon of contemporaneity is one that has never been experienced by the world as a whole until now, and there are still many parts of the inhabited earth where events are not known until long after they have taken place; but in the alert and anxious countries of Europe and the Americas, parts of Africa and Asia, the countries which make up our conscious world and are responsible for its possible courses of historic development, there is only the slightest lapse of time between an occurrence of importance and a general dissemination of the news to the innumerable varieties of minds that are prepared to receive it. The entry of Adolf Hitler as conqueror into Prague on March 15, 1939, was translated into a headline in Boston (for instance) some hours before it had actually taken place, thanks to a conspiracy between the solar system and the Associated Press of America; and the fall of Barcelona was known in New York before we knew it in Catalonia. The day of reflection cannot be forever postponed, and the newspaper headlines themselves no doubt instigate some kind of reflective process among those who read nothing else, but a book which deliberately sets out to describe, narrate and cogitate, to range past events in sequence and suggest the curve of their future extension, must be in both directions a shifty and uncertain affair, too close to life to be severed sharply from it, and too mixed in nature to achieve either the cool serenity of thought or the glaring definition of a newspaper statement. "HITLER IS IN PRAGUE." That was the headline in Boston. What does it matter, then, that he once also went to Carlsbad, and that they tore up the trees in the Municipal Gardens to make room for his audience, or that the swastika flag was raised there beside the crucifix?

It matters just this: that the news alone, however stated, cannot signify much to the mind unprepared to relate it to the recent past. Statements in newsprint are the record, often incorrect or incomplete, but at least approximate, of the rhythms of contemporary history. There is reason and justification for books which attempt to catch some part of those rhythms into words, recording not the whole but the part that can be caught by one writer at one time, translating the general into the particular and back again. But whatever may be the value of such records, they draw upon themselves the penalty of the hybrid and the freak: nobody can tell exactly how or when they begin and end. They come from the press and to the press they must return, their end and their beginning merged into the chronicle of the time.

Here general chronicle and particular chronicler, book and newspaper, time and geography, seemed inextricable. While I was writing this book the processes it deals with reached a series of further climaxes in their logical development. I was in Paris, which is to say, in the place from which almost anywhere in Europe seems conveniently accessible. It was difficult to keep my mind fixed on what had happened in July or September when what was happening in January was also a part of the story. The book was interrupted several times by circumstances which seemed to me so much a part of it that I could not ignore them and keep my study doors closed. One of these circumstances was the passage of the American volunteers returning home from Spain. They were treated with such suspicion and harshness by the French authorities (for whom, in my view, they had been doing a very neat job of fighting in the past eighteen months) that my indignation was uncontrollable, and I quite unnecessarily resolved to stick by Havre, Cherbourg or any other port where they might be sent until I saw them actually leave for New York. Even if the French had thrown them into jail or shipped them back to Spain there was very little I could have done about it, but I was determined to see at least what did happen and report it in due course by any means in my power. In reality the American volunteers were, as I know now, treated shabbily enough, but not half so shabbily as the German and Central European internationals—not even so shabbily as some of the French volunteers themselves, who were jailed on their return from Spain because they had not done their French military service. At the time it seemed to me an outrage that the Americans should be shipped through France in a sealed train and kept as prisoners in a concentration camp (a sort of miniature Ellis Island) at Havre. I had not recovered, and may indeed never recover, from the belief acquired in childhood—taught in the prairie towns somehow, although not in so many words—that American citizenship is a kind of insurance against misfortune.

But of the winter's events, the newspaper breaking into the book, the time invading the study, the geography abetting the interference, none disturbed me so much as the Fascist offensive in Catalonia during the first weeks of January. At first I was content to follow it in the newspapers with no more than the keen but almost impersonal interest of an observer who had once visited these places and known some of the people involved in the struggle. That was while the defense of Catalonia went well, and even after it had begun to go less well. It was only at the end of the third week in January that I began to get restless, to sleep badly, to be unable to work at anything. I dreamed of bombardments and Spanish names ran in my head. I still did not know that the disaster was actually at hand, but on Sunday, January 23, I began to know. All the dispatches on that day—which I got by telephoning to the *Herald-Tribune* office, badgering them unmercifully there—were bad, and each was worse than the one before. The Fascist offensive had broken through the Republican lines at decisive points a week or more before (Borjas Blancas and Artesa de Segre were the worst) but now it was rolling forward almost without opposition, approaching Barcelona on two roads and getting very near. I did not sleep at all that Sunday night, and the next morning I was out and about at a preternaturally early hour, getting my passport and visas in order to go to Spain. These formalities usually took three days, but by shameless agitation and wire-pulling I got them all done in a few hours, even the "nonintervention" visa from the French Prefecture of Police. Then I heard that Alvarez del Vayo was in Paris, at the Spanish Embassy, and I went at once to see him. As the Republic's foreign minister he had just been in Geneva making a last plea at the League of Nations Council. The footman at the embassy took me up to a room on the second floor where Del Vayo and his wife were sitting. They had just been talking to Negrin in Barcelona and seemed—to my astonishment—neither worried nor disturbed. Del Vayo talked with his usual confidence.

"Things are not so bad as the papers say," he said. "Barcelona will resist. You must remember Madrid."

I had come to ask him for a passage on one of the Douglas airplanes which the government ran in a regular service between Paris and Barcelona. He said that these planes were no longer available.

EPILOGUE

"But there is no hurry," he said. "My wife and I are going down on the train tomorrow night. Come with us. Our car is meeting us in Perpignan and we will drive you straight through to Barcelona."

I record this not to impugn Del Vayo's judgment, but to show how even the most intelligent and courageous mind can go astray by cultivating the habit of optimism. Del Vayo had been, as foreign minister, so accustomed to putting the best possible interpretation on events that he had almost lost touch with reality. By every sensible standard the military situation was at this moment as bad as it could be, and the fall of Barcelona seemed almost certain. Yet Del Vayo and—if he was correctly quoted—Negrin, the highest officers of the Spanish government, had not yet brought themselves to the point of admitting it. A state struggling for its life, as the Republic had been for two years, must develop moral defenses inside and out; the habit of confidence and the habit of propaganda were by this time the same thing with Del Vayo, and he was a foreign minister even when he talked to himself. Or so it seemed to me.

Even so, I did wait to take the train with him on Tuesday night, the twenty-fifth. The dispatches from Barcelona grew steadily worse, and throughout that last day in Paris the Italian bombers were almost as terrible to think about as they must have been to listen to in the city down there. The raids were almost incessant, according to the Paris papers; the bombers were coming over Barcelona every fifteen minutes; they had still not bombed the center of the city but might begin at any moment; the antiaircraft had grown steadily weaker for days and was now very nearly silenced for lack of ammunition. But if Del Vayo was right there would be a real resistance in Barcelona, and I proposed to see at least some of it, to write at least two or three more newspaper stories before I locked myself into the book for good. By some hasty telephoning and telegraphing I got myself a commission to write these stories for the North American Newspaper Alliance shortly before it was time to take the train.

By the time the eight-fifteen left for Perpignan the situation had grown so much worse that I doubted whether we could ever get to Barcelona. The last dispatches said, in fact, that the city was being evacuated and that the government was moving to Gerona. Del Vayo remained confident even at the railway station, although he had had a long and no doubt crushing interview with M. Bonnet that very afternoon—an interview in which Bonnet unquestionably washed his hands very thoroughly of the Spanish Republic and its fate. There was a crowd at the Gare d'Orsay, as there usually was for the eight-fifteen. A Basque delegation was going, as well as the Del Vayos, and there was an atmosphere of tension curiously like that which had surrounded my first departure for Spain in the spring of 1938. When I remembered that occasion, and the exaggerated fears we had all had for Barcelona and the Republic, there seemed to be some sense in Del Vayo's optimism after all.

Bob Murphy of the American Embassy and Fred Thompson of the Friends of the Lincoln Battalion were on the train. They were going to the border to meet a contingent of American volunteers who were being sent home (the last or next to last). Even in the pressure and confusion of these final days, Negrin was keeping his word about the volunteers. It must have been difficult enough to find a train and make it run from Barcelona to the border, but somehow it was being done.

I hardly slept at all that night, and when I got up at five in the morning, at Toulouse, I perceived that Del Vayo was in the same case. I met him in the corridor at that dismal hour. He was fully dressed and looked worried.

"I have had bad news from Barcelona," he said.

I gathered from this that we might never get to Barcelona at all. Gerona was more likely; or even Figueras if there was a real retreat.

At Perpignan I sent telegrams to my wife, to reassure her, saying that we could probably not go beyond Figueras. I did not know that this was the baldest unvarnished truth: I still had some hope of getting on further.

The Del Vayos and I went to the Spanish Consulate for breakfast. Henry Buckley was in Perpignan and came to the consulate to talk to us. He had left Barcelona the day before and could tell us about it. He had no hope left for the city at all and said so. He told me the roads would be choked and we could probably not go beyond Gerona at the furthest; that Figueras was more likely. His chief worry was about Fascist reprisals and revenges, which he expected on a savage scale. He said the shells were not reaching Barcelona when he left but that their explosion could be clearly seen on the southern hills.

We got into Del Vayo's car at half-past nine or thereabouts and set forth for the frontier. At Le Perthus, the French frontier town, while our passports were being examined, I fell upon some colleagues coming out of Spain: Peters of the United Press and others. They said firmly that we could not get beyond Figueras and that Barcelona would be in Fascist hands during the day sometime. They had left Barcelona on the evening before.

At La Junquera, the Spanish frontier town a little below the mountain pass, we met with considerable crowding, disorder and excitement. In the midst of all this an official of the Ministry of State divulged the extraordinary fact that he had seen Juanito, the Del Vayos' young son, in Barcelona the day before. Señora del Vayo, who had thought her son safe in Figueras, was overwhelmed at the news and came near, I think, to fainting. She was haunted by the idea of what the Fascists might do to her son if he fell into their hands, and for the next few hours she was almost prostrate. We drove on for the half-hour that separates Figueras from the frontier, and in the Plaza in the middle of the town—now crowded, like the whole place, and filled with an anxious sort of excitement—we drew up before the building used as the local office of the Subsecretariat of Propaganda.

Here numbers of acquaintances appeared, and I began to realize that Barcelona was indeed evacuated. Marthe Huysmans came to comfort Señora del Vayo and explained how Juanito had run away to Barcelona; Okin of the Associated Press suddenly appeared, having driven from Barcelona with great difficulty in twelve or thirteen hours instead of the usual two or three; André Malraux walked across the square to say, very coolly, that he had been going back and forth to Barcelona for the past few days and was going to try it again tonight.

I realized within the first few minutes in Figueras that an evacuation had taken place and was continuing; that the roads would be crowded; that the Del Vayos undoubtedly must stop here. Under the circumstances I had little chance of getting a car or a passage onward, and I seized on Malraux as my one hope. He said he would try to get some kind of pass from the military authorities for me and would take me along to Barcelona that night when he returned to get some remaining equipment for his film. (He had been making a film in Barcelona for the past eight months or so.)

There we were, in the middle of the Plaza, within half an

hour of the French border, and the retreat was already hitting us in the face. The square was busy with a very abnormal amount of traffic; there were soldiers everywhere; the big bomb refuge in the middle of the Plaza brought to mind what might so easily happen in this little town if the Fascists chose to direct their attention to it. After a while Del Vayo heard that Negrin was up at the Citadel on the hill, and we piled into the car again and drove up there.

The Citadel is a stone fortress of medieval aspect with great thick stone walls and a winding approach as for defense. In its big central courtyard there were refugees sitting on the ground with their bundles—scores of them, women with patient eyes and knobbly hands, sitting and waiting. Some of them had moved six or eight times in the course of the war, always with less and less of their own to carry with them. How they had reached Figueras I did not know. The roads from Barcelona by now would be filled with others like them, toiling along on foot or with donkey carts or sometimes loaded on trucks by the soldiers.

Under the colonnade at one side of the courtyard there was a sign roughly chalked up beside a doorway: "Consejo de Ministros." This, then, was where Negrin had landed. Del Vayo went in to talk to him. Presently Negrin came out to reassure Señora del Vayo about her son: the boy had left Barcelona and would soon be here. And indeed, as we all stood there in the middle of the courtyard, Juanito arrived, tall and awkward, very embarrassed. He had just driven in on a military truck from Barcelona.

There are miseries in defeat: you begin to carp and sneer and haggle, to distrust motives and to disbelieve. There was an unmistakable feeling of defeat about everything at Figueras. Even Negrin, so robust, alert and smiling, could not overcome that by confident words. His very presence

[*351*]

here at Figueras was a signal proof of defeat. When I left Paris I had supposed him to be still in Barcelona, organizing the resistance. If he was here there would be no resistance —none at all. It was incomprehensible.

We went back down the hill to the town and took possession of a back room in the office of the Delegación de Propaganda. Here we spread out what we had to eat: our bread from Perpignan and some meat Señora del Vayo had brought. Ruth, one of the girls from the Propaganda Office in Barcelona, seemed to be in charge of this local office, having arrived the day before. There was an aviation alarm while we were eating but no bombs fell.

That back room in the Propaganda Office became exceedingly familiar to me in the short space of two days. When I first saw it we had it to ourselves—the Del Vayos and one or two secretaries, Ruth and I. There were two or three other secretaries in the front rooms on the Plaza. The place —which had been a flat, a dwelling, at some time or other, and had a big kitchen and bathroom—was clean and orderly when we arrived. Two days later it looked as if the whole retreat had passed over it and wrecked it. Wave after wave from Barcelona had washed up the odds and ends of the Ministry of State here, and it was crowded, noisy and dirty at almost every hour of the day and night. Correspondents came and went that first day; they were all on their way to the French border; the Delegación de Propaganda seemed to be the only stopping place for large numbers of people.

We had hardly finished lunch when Capa blew in, his camera over his shoulder. He had just arrived from Barcelona in Herbert Matthews' car. He said Matthews was down in the Plaza.

I went down to the car and saw Herbert there with Willy

Forrest (the *News-Chronicle*) and another correspondent. They all looked dirty and exhausted. They had been in the car since two o'clock the preceding morning and had been actually making their way from Barcelona for about thirteen hours of that time. They said the roads were choked and it was next to impossible to move along them; Herbert, who knew the roads well, had succeeded in getting through by driving along side roads and making numerous detours. All were gloomy enough: the roads had not been a cheerful sight.

I asked Matthews a few questions, enough to discover that none of the correspondents in Barcelona had expected this debacle to come so quickly. It had apparently dawned on them in Barcelona at about the time it was dawning on me in Paris—that is, on Sunday. By Monday they were all making their plans for transport (allotting places in the few available cars) to the border. Matthews, Forrest and Capa had left the Hotel Majestic at two o'clock the night before— two o'clock, that is, on Wednesday morning.

Capa, who was never willing to leave any post or line until bludgeoned out of it, had not wanted to leave Barcelona; he now elected to stay here in Figueras on the chance of taking more photographs or on the chance, even, of returning to Barcelona. The others went on to Perpignan to write and telephone their stories. The telephone service from Catalonia to France had now broken down for all ordinary purposes, although official communications were still going through.

I spent a good part of that day either chasing Malraux —upon whom I counted for a military pass and a means of transport—or appealing to the military authorities themselves. I still wanted to go to Barcelona and had a strong idea that if I succeeded in getting there I could sit on a balcony at the Majestic Hotel and watch the Fascist occupation of the town without let or hindrance. I had heard that two of my acquaintances in the American Consulate had received orders to stay in the city (received their orders at the last moment as they were about to get on the gunboat that took most of the Americans away). If they could stay I could. I did not feel so sure of Capa's safety: he was Hungarian, and Jewish, and was by this time well known to the Spanish Fascists as a friend of the Spanish government. They might shoot him. But Capa was bent on going back if he could, and from the moment he heard that Malraux was going he, too, joined in the chase for that elusive and extraordinary character.

For part of the afternoon I stayed in the back room of the Propaganda Office talking to Del Vayo. It was being borne in upon me that the Minister was a prey to fearful bewilderment and indecision. He walked the floor and returned, ever and again, to the big map of Spain on the wall, peering at it shortsightedly and sighing. I asked him once where Azaña was. He made vague motions over the map with a hand which covered all northern Catalonia, France and part of the Mediterranean. "Somewhere here," he said. I had had it in my head since last spring that Azaña would probably evaporate at the first sign of final disaster, and it looked rather as if the moment of his evaporation had arrived. At times Del Vayo pored over the provinces of central Spain, counting them. "And then there is the navy," he said, poking a finger at Cartagena. "There is the navy. The war will go on in the center."

Figueras was already so crowded that even persons in the most privileged positions could not find sleeping quarters. The Del Vayos themselves did not have a place to go to until six or seven in the evening. I should not be surprised if

EPILOGUE

Negrin was sleeping that night in his office, on a cot or on the floor. The press—what there was left of it—elected to sleep on the floor in the Propaganda Office; the alternative was, so far as I know, the gutter.

Malraux never appeared; I never saw him again, and from all accounts he did not return to Barcelona. He had no doubt forgotten all about me in the pressure and turmoil of his own business, for he had a great deal of film and equipment to get safely out of the country if his last eight months' work was not to be totally lost. Del Vayo could do nothing for me: the control of the road from here to Barcelona was in the hands of the military authorities alone, and they were slow, reluctant, discouraging. That night we had food and talked in the back room of the Propaganda Office. In one air raid alarm we did gravitate slowly toward the refuge in the middle of the Plaza, but it was so crowded that we could not get in; and in any case no bombs fell. Sometime during the evening Boleslavskaya arrived, having had an interminable journey from Barcelona.

"I assure you," she said, "that to be caught tight in a traffic jam in a small village, in a narrow, winding street where you cannot possibly move in any direction, and then to hear the bombs begin to fall, is the worst kind of experience I have had in the war. Nowhere to go and nothing to be done. We just sat there. And a lot of idiots up and down the road started honking their horns, as if that would do any good."

Refugees arrived by twos, threes or in groups; anybody who had ever had anything to do with the Ministry of State, or who possessed a relative who had once worked in it, made straight for the Delegación de Propaganda. The little flat was so crowded that it was difficult to get in or out by about ten o'clock that night. We all chose our par-

[355]

ticular corners of the floor. Toward midnight Manuel Quiroga, who had been head censor in Barcelona, arrived; he had been hitchhiking on military trucks and by such conveyances as he could find for the past twenty-four hours, unwilling to take up a place in a government car. Quiroga, Bola, Kell of the *Basler Nazionalzeitung*, and one or two other refugees of the press contrived a communal bed along one side of the back office, a huge litter made of papers, an abandoned box spring, and a few shawls and coats from Bola's luggage. Capa announced that he had at last found a good use for propaganda, and built himself a bed out of a pile of propaganda leaflets he found in the smaller office alongside.

On the next day the impressions of disorder, demoralization and bewilderment grew even stronger as the real flood of the refugees began to pour in. The Gerona road was choked with them: trucks, wagons, donkey carts, people on foot. The Plaza was more crowded than ever, and the streets of the little town were as busy and noisy as those of a city, and far more depressing. I started the day in encouraging style by losing my passport: it had vanished during the night. Without a passport I had little chance of getting back across the French border or to Barcelona either. The loss of a passport under such conditions is paralysis. I made arrangements through Bob Okin, who was going out to France, to get an emergency passport for me from the American Embassy in Paris—and then later, of course, my own passport turned up again.

I went several times during the day to the headquarters of the general staff to ask for papers and, if possible, transport to Barcelona. They eyed me with considerable curiosity and put me off again and again. Finally I obtained an official paper signed by Cordon, the chief of staff; but it was then six o'clock in the evening and no means of transport was available. Not only that, but with every new arrival from down the road we heard rumors that the Fascist troops had entered Barcelona.

The people in the streets were hungry. There were no bread rations; there was in fact no bread. Capa and I tried to eat in a restaurant reserved for the Medical Service, and after some argument we got the rations allowed there: a plate of rice. There was nothing else. For most of the refugees in the streets—women, children and old men, many of them peasants who had moved half a dozen times already in the course of the war—there was not even that.

We were sitting gloomily in the back room of the Propaganda Office that night at about ten o'clock when one of Del Vayo's secretaries came in and said he had a communiqué for us. He read it out solemnly.

"Gentlemen," he said, "Barcelona has fallen into the hands of the enemy."

That was all. And the accredited foreign press correspondents there present to hear it were only Bola and myself, with Capa.

We slept on the floor again that night, but I slept hardly at all. Bola, Quiroga, Kell and I were on the floor; Capa had chosen the table on this occasion, and perhaps its hardness had an effect on his nasal passages; at any rate I never heard anybody snore as loudly as he did. The whole place was stuffy, smelly, crowded with people sleeping in all the rooms and even down the corridor. Along about half-past three or a quarter to four in the morning I decided that it was hopeless to try to sleep any more; I got up and went into the street.

I shall never forget what I saw there. Refugees had been arriving for the whole of the past twenty-four hours, but each hour brought more than the hour before, and by now there was a refugee population of thousands in the town of Figueras. They were sleeping in the gutter and on the sidewalk, huddled together for warmth around their bundles, which served as pillows. Those bundles contained all their possessions. Often enough they were bundles of rags, but sometimes a pot or a pan would be attached by a string. The sidewalks and gutters around the Plaza were filled with these human figures in the cold, very dark night, many of them sound asleep, others stirring uneasily or talking or sighing. There were children crying up and down the street in the dark, sometimes small babies. In every doorway, courtyard, arch or other opening which afforded any kind of roof or shelter against the bitter weather, the dark figures huddled together or crouched against the walls, black against the surrounding blackness.

I wandered in the streets for a long time, perhaps for three hours or more. It seemed to me that this must be the end. I had seen refugees before—many of them; I had been in defeats and retreats before now; but this accumulation of suffering after two years of war struck me as too much for reason or hope. If the Spanish Republic had been supplied with food and arms at any time in the past six months, or if it stood any chance of obtaining food and arms from abroad, the quality of its determination might have won out over the immense power of the enemy even now. But it was blockaded now; with Catalonia gone—and I felt sure Catalonia would be all gone in ten days or two weeks at the most—there was no frontier left; there was only Madrid nearly surrounded, the eight central provinces with enemies on three sides and the enemy's sea on the other. There was no artillery, no aviation, no food. Scores of thousands, perhaps hundreds of thousands, of the civilian population of Barcelona and of the refugees who had come there from other places would now be swarming up this Gerona–Figueras road in their misery, tramping along hungrily in the bitter cold, getting toward France. The French would have to deal with a refugee problem of the first magnitude on their borders. And I could see no hope for the Republic to survive this blow which left it without outlet or inlet, without a chance to sustain the life of its people while it struggled for their liberty.

The demoralization, too, was much worse than anything the Republic had seen before, I felt sure. A thousand details of the past two days stuck in my head. Nobody had seemed to know whether the official seals or stamps had arrived; the Ministry of State had had only two typewriters at its disposal; Del Vayo had been frankly doubtful whether a letter from him would carry any weight with the military authorities. Some of the important officials of the government appeared to have vanished altogether; nobody knew where they were; others (of lesser rank, to be sure) had elected at the last moment to stay in Barcelona and accept the rule of the Fascists. This was division, bewilderment, the full horror of defeat and confusion and fear. With many officials the main preoccupation seemed to be personal safety, and this among men who had never shown much care for that before. Men who had struggled for years under the military dictatorship and the monarchy for a modern republic, and had continued the struggle when that modern republic was threatened by the blackest reaction of the century, now seemed—to me at least—to have lost their courage. Perhaps it was only that they had lost their hope. Without hope courage has little meaning, becomes the most sterile heroism, attitudinizing, barren and useless suicide; I knew all those arguments and my reason accepted them fully. But it was desperate enough, all this, to darken the reason and obscure the view. Nobody wanted martyrs; martyrs were no good to the Republic; and yet when you heard the children crying up and down the cold dark streets you wondered if these were not, indeed, the martyrs; and you thought that the government belonged not here but in Madrid.

This was Friday morning, and most of the people who lay shivering in these gutters had had nothing whatever to eat since Monday night or Tuesday morning at the latest.

And what was I doing here? I could not help these people in any way; I was eating food which other people could use; and I had nothing of consequence to write for my newspapers. I had intended to reach Barcelona, if possible, to describe the resistance which I expected there. But I had failed to get to Barcelona, and anyhow no resistance had been made. From all indications the city had simply been yielded to the Italians and the Moors, the Navarrese and the generals of the Fascist command. I did not understand how this had happened, and there was no explanation available in the confused stories I was told by those who arrived, wild-eyed and exhausted, from the city. The only thing I could do was to get out at once, finish my book and sail for America as I had planned.

I went back to the Delegación de Propaganda at a little after seven o'clock in the morning. (Actually six: Loyal Spain kept an hour's advance on its clocks in order to save electricity.) Capa had a car which he had mysteriously acquired the preceding evening; he was going to try to go down the road and take photographs in it this morning; I could borrow it to drive me to the French frontier. In half an hour we were at La Junquera where the borrowed car deposited me and returned to Figueras.

EPILOGUE

At the frontier posts the Spanish officials were still carrying out the rules and formalities with perfect gravity. I had the usual inspections for customs, currency and passport stamps. A letter from Del Vayo (the value of which he had also doubted) passed me without difficulty through the police inspection and was treated with as much respect as if the Republic still governed all Spain. In the customs house, the police station and the military post at the frontier there were refugees densely packed. They had been there all night sleeping on their bundles. Many of them were now clamoring to be permitted to cross the border to France, and failing to understand why they could not. I heard the police official explaining patiently, again and again, to the sad-eyed, hungry women: "You have no passport. You cannot cross the frontier without a passport. You must return to Figueras and make out an application for a passport. If I let you pass without a passport the French will turn you back, and you will be no better off."

In a few days, I reflected, there would be so many of these people, such a vast population of refugees, that neither the Spanish nor the French border guards could hold them back with anything less than a machine-gun battalion. And whatever contempt I had acquired for the French during this year of disasters, I still did not believe them capable of mowing down thousands of starving women, children and old men with machine guns.

I walked across the border to Le Perthus, the French village at the top of the pass. There I encountered Herbert Matthews, Willy Forrest and William Hickey of the *Daily Express:* they had been in Perpignan and were now returning to Figueras. Herbert said he was going to try to find the army. I told him that so far as I had been able to discover

[*361*]

nobody in Figueras knew exactly where it was—or at any rate where Sarabia, its commander, was.

I went on to Perpignan, where I made an effort by telephone to get out of writing anything about this disaster. I felt sure that everything I had to report had already been reported in the greatest detail by a large number of colleagues; all had been going out in the past two days and all had sent what they had to say. The N.A.N.A. office in London insisted on at least one story, which I accordingly wrote and telephoned. My spirits were so low that I could not keep a sort of subjective gloom from invading the account I gave. The story was therefore "defeatist" in the extreme: it was a sort of journalistic funeral dirge, and was printed in some newspapers in America (as I afterwards learned) under the headline "It's All Over." I had never been able to trim my sails to any wind, and did not trim them now, although everything I had to report was bitter as swill to write. Unfortunately, there was no word of exaggeration or of misapprehension in it, and everything came to pass punctually as I had foreseen. In two days there were hundreds of thousands of refugees at the French border; in two weeks to the day (the second Friday afterwards) all Catalonia was lost to the Republic; in a month Madrid was openly preparing to surrender. The victory of reaction in Spain was assured.

2

So I sailed for America and saw the further stages of the post-Munich tragedy from a great distance, the inevitable, the foreseen, taking place in accordance with the laws of Fascist rhythm and technique. Hitler entered Prague on March 15, 1939, and on March 17 Mr Neville Chamberlain, speaking at Birmingham, professed himself to be shocked and surprised at the course of events, and unwilling to take Hitler's word for anything in the future. This strange, tardy awakening on the part of the Prime Minister was of no worth in the scales of history, and will do little to blind even his contemporaries to the true value of a man who has consistently put the interests of his own class and type above those of either his own nation or of humanity itself. It is not Mr Neville Chamberlain as an individual who stands responsible for the series of blunders by which the democratic powers surrendered the domination of Europe to Fascism: it is the Tory governing class as a whole, including those elements in it (such as Mr Anthony Eden and his friends) who clearly saw where the policy was leading and yet did nothing decisive against it. Mr Eden resigned the foreign ministry, but too late; at present it seems likely that he will resume it, also too late. During his period out of office, during which the greatest advances of the Fascist alliance in Europe and Asia were made, he spoke against the government at times, but he never voted against it, and he did nothing to organize a real opposition to its fatal program of "appeasement." All along the line, in Central and southeastern Europe, in Spain, in China, the Fascist powers of Europe and their Asiatic ally pursued their advantage without a genuine obstacle being put in their way by either France or England. So immense has been the Fascist success, in a continuous and widening process, that it is seriously to be considered whether Germany and Italy may not in time come to divide the continent of Europe between them, or Japan to assume the conquering power in Asia.

3

To an American journalist who had followed this course of historic development from point to point in Europe for one year, from March, 1938, to March, 1939, there was not much room for doubt that a conflict of ideas and interests so tremendous must one day result in general war. The turning point was reached in September with Mr Neville Chamberlain's successive visits to Hitler in Germany. Up to then it would have been possible at any moment to arrest these processes by a clear statement of policy firmly adhered to—a statement that would have had to come from England, France and Russia all three. The statement was not made and there was no firm policy; the Munich agreement was not a policy but a surrender. From then on it was not possible to arrest the expansion of Fascism by peaceful or diplomatic means. So far from "saving the peace" at Munich, Mr Neville Chamberlain surrendered the peace and condemned Europe and the world to a certainty, as I believe, of general war. Such a war will take place when or if the Fascist powers directly attack the immediate possessions of France and England, and not before: that is to say, it will be an imperialist war, fought for no principle except that of empire. The principles all went by the board in September, 1938. So did the treaties, the promises, the obligations and the frontiers; so did the structure of international law as hitherto known and partially observed. The naked greed and selfishness of all the European imperial states are so hideously exposed by the events of 1936–39 that an American must hesitate before expressing a preference between them. And yet we can hardly doubt that, as I said in the beginning of this book, our interests and our emotions will alike pull us in the same direction, and we shall find

EPILOGUE

ourselves again, as we did in 1918, enrolled in the same
cause as France and England. However often those powers
may have betrayed the democratic forces in all parts of the
world, however bad their record as colonial imperialisms,
the rhythm of our pulses brings us to their side rather than
to the side of the Fascist alliance. Neutrality in a conflict
so profound and wide, a conflict involving a whole world,
can scarcely exist in any country, least of all one which
is the conscious child of western Europe; and we shall find
ourselves in due course involved in that catastrophe from
which a little firmness and decision in time might have
preserved us all.

To Spain, the unhappy victim of an earlier phase of this
conflict, I have returned in this book again and again, as I
did in life during those months of the mounting disaster. In
my view Spain was the only place in Europe where Fascism
encountered a genuine resistance. Upon the precedent of the
Napoleonic Era Spain might have stemmed the Fascist advance. But in a much more closely knit world, with a vastly
increased importance for machines and materials over the
human spirit, the side which had most in these physical
respects was bound to win, and all the valor and obstinacy
of the Spanish resistance were of no account against them.
In this case, as in Central and southeastern Europe, the
British and French governments were fatally weak, legalistic
without being honest, and undecided without being fair.
It is difficult to find a good word to say for the conduct of
any French or British government since 1936. The French
embargo on shipments to Spain was in fact imposed in
August, 1936, by a government of the Popular Front, and
the nonintervention policy under which the Spanish Republic was sacrificed to reaction was sponsored by the
cabinet of M. Léon Blum. The dreadful responsibility of

all these men in London and Paris weighs upon Right and Left alike, and is not to be altogether shouldered off by the men in Washington. At least in one respect, the embargo on supplies to the Spanish Republic, the United States of America played directly into the hands of the Fascist alliance and did its best to ensure the victory of General Franco, of Hitler and of Mussolini in Spain.

But valor and obstinacy are still worth more than pusillanimity in a conflict of this significance; and by its terrible sacrifice—the death of more than a million men, the mutilation of perhaps another million, the starvation and half starvation of millions of noncombatants—Spain has delayed the Fascist process immeasurably. The reason why Mussolini's advance in the Mediterranean has not been able to keep pace with Hitler's advance in Central and southeastern Europe is that the Spanish Republic fought on to the last ditch. The end of the Spanish war was confidently expected by the Italian Fascist authorities in March, 1937, and in March, 1939, it was still not quite ended. The two years during which Spain was tortured and lacerated may have saved all Europe, may have provided just that delay which was essential to the awakening of the democracies. Thus, although Spain itself is sacrificed, the world at large may have benefited by that sacrifice more than by any single movement or event in the course of recent history.

So the book returns to the newspaper from which it came, and its conclusions are to be found in the events which will be recorded after its last word is written. The acceleration of the rhythm of Fascist movement is so great that those events may have reached a very advanced point on the road to war before this final page is printed. But whatever devious turns and twists occur in the course of its development, the Fascist will-to-conquer is clearly the dominant reality in

EPILOGUE

Europe, and the pursuit of an equal will-to-resist was the motive power of all the busy journeys and divagations which are narrated here. The general failure of that pursuit, the disaster of Spain, the blunders and deceptions of September, 1938, do not uproot hope from the resilient nature of this very personal historian; I know the world and most of the human beings in it can survive the most stupendous catastrophes, as they have in the past. But if the dark and dangerous future can be read at all, it warns us of worse to come. And if the recent past contains (as Lord Acton says) the "key to the present time," we can at least learn from reflection upon that recent past to distrust diplomatists and prime ministers, dignitaries and dictators of all kinds and to put our faith in those who pay the cost of all past and future wars, in money and in blood, the common people of the world. The peasants and workers of Spain, of Germany, of Czechoslovakia, deceived and overwhelmed; the submerged classes in England which vote for a choice of candidates imposed from above; the hard-working and frugal people who are forever being betrayed in France, voting for parliaments which do not remain loyal to their electoral instructions; all these must determine what settlement is to be obtained in the end from the clashing appetites and ambitions of the opposing forces. Upon the will and instinct of the proletariat reposes such hope as we are justified in retaining for the future progress of humanity through and beyond the conflict which now divides the world.

Pittsburgh,
March 20, 1939